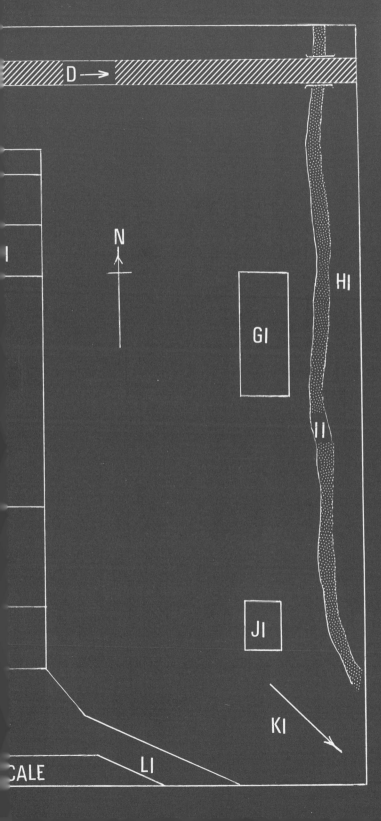

D. To Stafford Road
E. Pendeford Mill Pond
F. Pendeford Mill
G. Cycle Sheds
H. Works Entrance
I. Gate House
J. Canteen
K. Garage
L. Receiving and Despatch,
    Drawbench and Chemical
    Laboratory
M. Wind Tunnel
N. Boiler House
O. Open Coal Store
P. Pilot's Office
Q. Cover and Dope Shop
R. Wood Shop
S. Managing Director's Office
T. Boardroom above Entrance
U. Single Storey Front Office
V. Main Entrance
W. General Office
X. Raw Materials
Y. Office Entrance
Z. Drawing Offices
A1. Works Offices
B1. Research
C1. Machine Shop
D1. Aircraft Assembly Bay
E1. Main Flight Shed
F1. Apron
G1. Sewerage Treatment Plant
H1. High Ground
I1. Stream
J1. Gun Firing Butts
K1. Wolverhampton approx. 4 miles
L1. Runway to Airfield

BOULTON & PAUL
AIRCRAFT

BOULTON & PAUL
AIRCRAFT

The history of the companies at Norwich
and Wolverhampton

by

GORDON KINSEY

Foreword by
DAVID CHENERY
Chief Executive, Boulton and Paul plc

TERENCE DALTON LIMITED
LAVENHAM . SUFFOLK
1992

Published by
TERENCE DALTON LIMITED

ISBN 0 86138 085 1

Text photoset in 11/12pt Baskerville

Printed in Great Britain at
The Lavenham Press Limited, Lavenham, Suffolk

Contents

Acknowledgements vi

Foreword viii

Chapter One   At the Beginning 1

Chapter Two   War Plans and Planes 11

Chapter Three   Home-Spun 24

Chapter Four   Metallisation 36

Chapter Five   Fighters and Others 51

Chapter Six   Pastures New... 71

Chapter Seven   Turret Fighters 78

Chapter Eight   'Diffy' in Service 96

Chapter Nine   War Work 110

Chapter Ten   In from the Cold 122

Chapter Eleven   First Again 136

Chapter Twelve   Deltas, Jets and Odd-Balls... 152

Appendix One   Additional Technical Details 172

Appendix Two   Aircraft Manufactured at Norwich and Wolverhampton 183

Appendix Three   Boulton-Paul Aircraft and Dowty Boulton Paul Directors 186

Appendix Four   Details of Work on Canberra Aircraft under Contract 187

Appendix Five   Modern Aircraft with Dowty Boulton Paul Fittings ... 188

General Index 190

Index of Aircraft and Engines 196

Acknowledgements

THIS BOOK has been made possible by very many people, the majority of whom I have known only through correspondence and on the telephone, and organisations who have greatly assisted my research by their precious gifts of valuable and often irreplaceable documents and information. All are worthy of individual thanks and notes, were space available, but within these limits I must record my thanks to the individuals and groups listed alphabetically.

Mr Gordon Aldridge, Wolverhampton; Mr A.R. Andrews, St Anne's-on-Sea; Mr C.V. Appleby, Penn; Mrs B.E. Badger, Wombourne; Mr J.H. Baker, Wolverhampton; Mr William E. Bean, Washingborough; Mr G. Bruton, Bilbrook; Mr A. Charlton, Wolverhampton; Mr M.D.N. Chelerton, Oxley; Squadron Leader D.H. Clarke, Woolverstone; Mr R.D. Cox, Bilston; Wing Commander Christopher Deanesley, DFC, Edgbaston; Mrs Ruby Dickerson, Pendeford; Mr G.J. Dobson, Tettenhall; Mr S.E. Dyoss, Ch.Eng., MIProd.E, Great Barr; Mr J. Endean and Miss J. Endean, Fordhouses; Mr A.E. 'Ben' Gunn, Shoreham; Mr A.W. Haynes, Wednesfield; Mr F.A. Jackson, Shifnal; Mr B.B. James, Fordhouses; Mr L.H. Jones, Sedgley; Mr R.O. Jones, Franche; Mr C. Kenmir, The Wergs; Mr Stephan King, Wolverhampton; Mr J. Knowles, Bushbury; Flight Lieutenant F.C.A. Lanning, DFC, Darlington; Mr William O. Lee, Escondido, California; Mr R. Lees, BEM, Bushbury; Mr Harry Lewis, Wombourne; Mr M.V. Ling, Beeston Regis; Mr G.L. Marston, Penkridge; Mrs R. Middleton, Minorca; Mrs Phyllis Perry, Wolverhampton; Mr and Mrs D. Potts, Ipswich; Professor S.C. Redshaw, DSc., Ph.D, FICE, FRAe.S, Struct.E, Brewood; Mr John Reid, Coventry; Mr T.E. Rowley, Wednesfield; Mr Alan Smith, Penn; Mr L. Smith, Codsall; Mrs Beryl Sadler, Aldersley; Mr V.M. Smith, Wednesfield; Mr W.J. Taylor, Aldersley; Mrs Helen Tomkinson, Pedmore; Mr Cameron Wilson, Easington; Squadron Leader R.G. Woodman, DSO, DFC, Westbury.

Organisations which contributed material and photographs included: *Aeroplane Monthly*; *Aeroplane Spotter*; Boulton and Paul plc, Norwich and Lowestoft; Boulton-Paul Aircraft Limited, Wolverhampton; British Aerospace, London, Hatfield and Manchester; Dowty Aerospace, Wolverhampton; *East Anglian Daily Times* and its associated newspapers, Ipswich; *Eastern Daily Press*, Norwich; *Flight International*; Imperial War Museum, London (Mr B. King); Martlesham Heath Aviation Society; Ministry of Defence (Air); Norfolk and Suffolk

Aviation Museum, Flixton (Mr Alan Hague, Mr Bob Collis and Mr H. Fairhead); Pottergate Training Services, Norwich; Royal Aeronautical Society, London; Royal Aeronautical Society, Birmingham and Wolverhampton Branch (Mr D. Hammond); Royal Air Force Museum, Hendon (Mr A.E. Cormack, Mr P.J.V. Elliot and Mr P.G. Murton); *Wolverhampton Express and Star* Newspapers, Wolverhampton (Editor).

My very special thanks to Mr David Chenery, Chief Executive of Boulton and Paul plc, Norwich, who not only provided me with the Foreword but also made available all the treasures in his company's archives, and to Mr Colin Manning, the Boulton and Paul Archivist, who laid his hands on all manner of 'things Norwich'. Both these gentlemen left no stone unturned in order that their end of this history would be as complete as possible. A tremendous amount of material came from 'my friend in Wolverhampton', Mr John Chambers, a true enthusiast and complete historian. After a lifetime with the Wolverhampton works, his pride in their achievements showed in the valuable assistance he has given me over the period it took to produce this book. His weekly communiques always brought fresh information which he had gleaned from the most unlikely sources. His love of the Defiant prompted him to write a fine document vindicating this much maligned aircraft.

Mr Ian James of Aldridge made available the contents of his extensive aviation library, and the smallest request always brought forth the desired information. Mr C.E. 'Holly' Hall produced yet another eye-catching jacket for this book, and doubtless enjoyed portraying 'real aeroplanes'!

Reading, checking, checking again and again, and advising with unstinting patience on this somewhat long-distance research was my wife, Margaret, to whom I give my greatest gratitude and heartfelt thanks. A source of measureless counsel, especially when the numerous items for indexing seemed most complex, her co-operation so often sorted out the problem. Finally, many thanks to the publishers and their staff for their co-operation and guidance.

Gordon Kinsey,
Roundwood Road,
Ipswich,
Suffolk, 1992.

Foreword

AS THE leading supplier of joinery to housebuilders in the United
Kingdom for the last thirty years, it is somewhat frustrating to find
that my company, BOULTON & PAUL, is still remembered as a
manufacturer of aircraft, and in particular, of the Defiant. Although the
Defiant originated in Norwich, BOULTON & PAUL's aircraft interests
had been taken over in June, 1934 by a newly formed public company,
Boulton-Paul Aircraft Limited. Production, and some of the employees,
transferred to Wolverhampton two years later and our links with it were
then finally broken.

In my company's history that spans almost two hundred years we
marketed our own aircraft designs for only seventeen of them, from
1917 to 1934. Nevertheless, it was one of the most memorable and
exciting periods, not just for us, but for British aviation. Surprisingly,
perhaps, very little has been written about it other than a few articles in
the specialist magazines.

Gordon Kinsey has produced a remarkable book, not just about our
seventeen years, but also the years that followed, bringing with them the
Defiant, Balliol and the P.111 and P.120 delta-wing jets. But the book is
really about some of the unsung heroes of British aviation and the
principal driving force in Boulton & Paul's Aircraft Division, J.D. North.

Most people can recall the Defiant and its short-lived success over
Dunkirk and in the Battle of Britain, leading to its becoming one of the
RAF's most significant night fighters, but the development work on
power operated gun turrets was carried out years earlier on the
Overstrand. BOULTON & PAUL developed a reputation for pioneering
construction and design work right from the start. The first all metal
aircraft, the P.10, appeared in 1919 with plastics used to cover the
fuselage. The Bittern, with its Townend ring cowlings, had side mounted
machine guns, remotely controlled by the pilot seated ahead of the
shoulder-high wing. Looping-the-loop in the twin-engined Bourges
Mark IA 'military bombing aeroplane' was no mean feat for 1919 and not
many companies were successfully marketing military 'planes in the years
immediately after the First World War. Gordon Kinsey saw and heard
many of the aircraft described in these pages as a youngster living near

Martlesham Heath. His recollections and those of the men and women who worked at Norwich and then at Wolverhampton bring BOULTON & PAUL's craftsmanship, design skill and manufacturing originality vividly to life. It is my duty to make sure that these important traditions linger on in the design and construction of the products we market today.

David Chenery
Chief Executive, Boulton and Paul plc

Mr John Dudley North, CBE, DSc., FRAe.S, MIMech.E.

CHAPTER ONE

At the Beginning

OVER THE years many aircraft manufacturers' names and their designs have become household words: the Spitfire, Hurricane, Lancaster and Mosquito are capable of almost instant recall by the man in the street. A few of the less large companies can also boast that distinction, and to many Boulton and Paul are synonymous with the Defiant. The true enthusiast will also include the Bobolink, Bittern, Sidestrand, Overstrand and Balliol, but few will be able to catalogue the firm's diversified products: steel-framed buildings, wooden buildings, ornamental ironwork, racing car bodies, galvanised wire netting, high speed motor-boats as well as aircraft.

Whilst this book is devoted to the aircraft designs of Boulton and Paul Limited, Norwich, and later Boulton-Paul Aircraft Limited, Wolverhampton, it is of interest to trace the origins of these two companies in order to appreciate later events.

Boulton and Paul Limited dates back to a business founded in the City of Norwich during 1797 by Mr William Moore, a farmer's son from the north Norfolk coastal village of Warham, near Wells-next-the-Sea. This was during the Napoleonic Wars when the Royal Navy press-gangs scoured the coastal villages looking for likely lads to serve on the high seas. At the age of twenty-three young William forsook the farm and journeyed to Norwich, as so many others had before, to seek his fortune. Eventually he set up as an ironmonger in what was then Cockey Lane, now Little London Street. The business prospered and William Moore's efforts were recognised by the community when he became Sheriff in 1824, an Alderman during 1833 and in 1835 the city's first citizen Mayor of Norwich. He was the last mayor to be elected under the city's venerated and ancient charter and his term of office is recorded on a memorial tablet in Norwich's St Andrew's Church. He died four years later during 1839 and was buried at his native village of Warham.

Some years previously he had taken a local man, John Hilling Barnard, into partnership, and the ironmonger's shop, as well as the newly established stove and grate manufacturing business, traded under the style of Moore and Barnard. Barnard for his part became a Justice of the Peace, a leading Conservative and later director of several local companies.

1

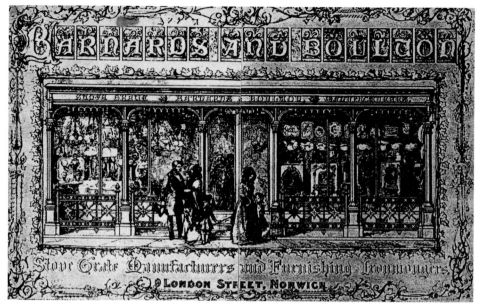

Etching of the original Barnards and Boulton store in Cockey Lane, later Little London Street.

B&P

On Moore's death the business passed to John Barnard who then introduced a twenty-three year old man, William Staples Boulton, as his new partner. The firm's name changed accordingly to Barnard and Boulton, and as the business expanded several new branches were opened in the Norwich district.

During 1853 another young man from the south Norfolk village of Thorpe Abbotts came to Norwich to make a career and the twelve year old Joseph John Dawson Paul was bound apprentice to the company. He served his masters diligently and at an early age was promoted to the post of Manager in the Works Department at the rear of the shop.

William Boulton became the sole proprietor upon the death of John Barnard, and from that time the young, ambitious Dawson Paul played a greater part in the day to day running of the company. He was able to assess market trends and persuaded Boulton that high quality manufactured goods were the products of the future. At this time increasing amounts of cheaper grain were flooding onto the British corn markets from the developing New World and causing redundancy among farm workers. Moving into the towns the ex-farm workers were a cheap source of labour, able to adapt to the new skills.

During his journeys around the Norwich district, Dawson Paul had noticed that a small foundry and works situated in Rose Lane was available for leasing. He informed Boulton and proposed that a lease be taken on the premises. His advice was accepted and on 14th November 1864 Dawson Paul was made manager of the new premises at a salary of £100 per annum. During 1869 Boulton sold the retail business to Messrs Piper and Theobold and concentrated all his energies on the Rose Lane Works.

Paul had settled down well to his new responsibilities and at the age of 27 married twenty-one year old Elizabeth Duffield. For reasons of economy and to be close to his workplace, Paul and his new wife lived in a small apartment in the Rose Lane Works. It is recorded that a large brass bell was attached to a hanging bracket outside his bedroom window and early each morning just before six o'clock he raised the window and rang the bell to summon his employees to work.

Dawson Paul summons his workers to their place of employment at 6 o'clock, by ringing a bell hanging from a bracket beside his bedroom window at the house in Rose Lane Works. *B&P*

The business prospered and during 1869 a Deed of Partnership was drawn up between William Boulton and Dawson Paul to run for five years. The company was now re-styled W.S. Boulton and Company, the capital being recorded as £6,000—£5,500 from Boulton and £500 from Paul.

3

The order book continued to swell as the company's reputation increased so that another deed was drawn up during 1874 and the capital increased to £16,000, Boulton contributing £11,000 and Dawson Paul the remainder. The trading name changed again and for the first time became the now familiar Boulton and Paul. This involved yet another deed, including a stipulation that the partnership was for the period of their joint lives and the survivor would be entitled to buy the deceased partner's shares, payment being made by a fixed annual sum.

Disaster struck during 1876 when much of the thriving Rose Lane Works was damaged in a serious fire which destroyed the carpenter's shop with its plant. Fortunately the premises were fully insured by the Norwich Union Society, and were soon back in full production.

The worry of the past few years took their toll on William Boulton and he died during 1879. Dawson Paul took over the reins but the new premises, now much larger than before, had yet to be paid for and in addition there were the annual repayments of £2,500 to his late partner's widow.

Dawson Paul recorded his difficulties:

> During this year I was much troubled by business matters and it worried me very much to know that I had a large and increasing business on hand, and that I had to find the money for that as well as having to pay out to the executors of Mr Boulton, and also to live myself. I went round to the bank and Mr Henry Birkbeck treated me well; he said, 'Young man, you have as you and your late partner had'—which was an overdraft of £3,500. He wished me every success and I thanked him for his confidence in me, and said I felt sure of being able to pull through all right.

Dawson Paul's business activities had not gone unobserved by the City Fathers and he was made a Conservative Council Member during 1883 and two years later Sheriff of the City of Norwich.

A new manager was appointed during 1893, Mr Henry Fiske, not a new man to the firm as he had been apprenticed during 1868 and had worked his way up. Fiske was an East Anglian hailing from Walpole, near Halesworth, where his father was one of the largest farmers in north Suffolk. He had been educated at Ongar, in Essex, and was also one of the first students of Framlingham College. This released Dawson Paul from some of the more arduous duties and gradually allowed him more time for politics, a subject dear to his heart.

Paul did not promote Fiske right away and it was not until 1893, at a party celebrating Paul's silver wedding anniversary, that Fiske's partnership was announced. He put £1,000 into the company whilst Paul's holding stood at £26,777.

The Rose Lane Works, Norwich—in the foreground—c1868, situated in a mainly residential area.
Alan Hague

Four years later Boulton and Paul became a limited liability company with a capital of £168,000. All the shares were kept in the family. Dawson Paul gradually withdrew from the day to day activities of the company and on 9th November 1900, in recognition of his public service, he was made Mayor of Norwich, the second of the company's directors to hold this office.

At this time Australia was emerging as an agricultural community but it was almost crippled by a plague of recently imported rabbits. Great demands were made on the Norwich factory for hundreds of miles of wire netting to fence in the properties in the hope of containing the pest.

Work now started with another material, wood, and a new department was set up to produce huts and bungalows, garden houses, wheel-barrows and dog kennels. Allied to the new horticultural products division the smith's shop was producing artistic wrought ironware, much in vogue at the time, and this emerged in the form of greenhouses, aviaries, conservatories and many other applications.

The Boer War brought Government contracts for wooden bungalows for use as officers' quarters. This put the work force on full production. Valuable contracts were also made in Argentina for wooden buildings.

5

On the 14th February 1903 the journal *Daylight* wrote,

Boulton and Paul Limited has again the satisfaction of establishing a record, for within three months, 150 large bungalows—to be used as married officers' residences attached to the army of occupation in South Africa—had been completed. The bungalows in question were 80ft long, by 22ft wide and each contained a drawing room, dining room, four bedrooms and a bathroom, with a verandah all round. It should be stated that three large steamers were specially chartered to convey the buildings to South Africa, and each vessel took some 6,000 tons of material manufactured by Boulton and Paul Limited at their Norwich works.

The buildings were manufactured in what is known as the Thorpe branch which is situated on the opposite side of the river from the wharf and is under the management of Mr T.H. Yelf. This gentleman superintended the erection of the handsome Pavilion built by Boulton and Paul on the Britannia Pier at Great Yarmouth.

Extensions were put in hand at the Rose Lane Works, which now covered an area twenty times larger than the original site. There were departments for manufacturing wire netting, woodwork and the artistic ironwork, as well as the foundry products. Space was now at a premium and a forge in King Street was acquired for the production of wrought iron railings and gates for domestic and farm use.

Another acquisition which was to play a large part in speeding up the despatch of the company's products was the purchase of quay frontage on the River Wensum, where a new wharf was constructed.

Fresh ground was broken during 1905 when a department was opened to develop constructional engineering. This was a far-sighted decision on the part of the directors as at that time steel-framed buildings were gradually taking over from the more traditional timber-framed and brick structures. This department was a works within a works, as it was here that structural steelwork was designed, manufactured and prepared for erection worldwide. It was fully equipped with hydraulic and pneumatic riveters and press tools, shearing, punching, drilling, cropping, notching and straightening machinery. This new venture did not replace the woodworking department but supplemented it.

As the structural steel department expanded, more staff were engaged and eventually a large number of designers and draughtsmen were employed in this section. These products became world renowned and were a byword for accuracy of manufacture and ease of erection, sometimes many thousands of miles from their place of origin.

A further diversification occurred when during 1906 a small section was inaugurated to design and build motor-boats and their engines. This department was the brain child of Dawson Paul's son and Geoffrey ffiske.*

*The Fiske family had changed their surname by deed poll back to the old spelling ffiske.

The Norwich built motor boat *Dollydo*, which was twice as fast as any other boat at this period.

B&P

One of this department's best remembered products was a racing motor-boat named *Dollydo* which was capable of the then almost unheard of speed of 21 knots. Two more motor-boats were built, twenty-one foot craft, the *Fuji-Yama* and the *Vicuna*. The latter was sold to an industrialist and the former ffiske took to Monte Carlo where he won £350 in prizes.

Loosely linked to the boat and boat engine activities was another new department formed during 1906 named the Engineering Department. This section designed and manufactured electric lighting sets, engines and pumps for use on country estates, and once again these products made a name for themselves throughout the world.

The building departments, both wooden and steel, were making considerable progress and although both types were advertised as portable buildings, some very large structures were designed and erected. Complete houses comprising several bedrooms, clubhouses, aeroplane sheds and even an hotel were put up in Japan.

Work in the foundry, which used up-to-the-minute techniques, was also at full pressure and quality castings for the farm products were turned out. When eventually surplus capacity was available, sub-contracting work was carried out for other companies.

A swelling order book resulted in increased profits which now realised over £20,000 per annum, and accordingly, during 1906 the general public were given for the first time the chance to acquire shares in the company.

Dark clouds were gathering over Europe and the outbreak of the First World War resulted in the wholesale cancellation of orders, and several teams of erectors who were abroad had to be hastily recalled. Four such teams were in France and chartered a fishing boat to cross the Channel, the leader, Mr J.H. Humphrey, persuading the reluctant skipper to finish the journey by means of a recently purchased revolver.

7

Women metal workers at their benches—the large bench vices are worthy of note.   *B&P*

The early days of the war brought large numbers of troops into Norwich, where the 1st Army Corps was mobilised and outfitted. The factory work-force was badly depleted when Territorials and Reserve men joined their regiments. An order from the new Ministry of Munitions prohibiting further recruitment in the works was issued when there were only just enough staff left to carry out the work in hand. The younger members of the firm's leadership, young Dawson Paul and Geoffrey ffiske, were also among those who joined their regiments.

After the initial lull at the outbreak of hostilities the orders flooded in again, and during early 1915 construction commenced on the new Riverside Works. A considerable amount of site preparation work was necessary but the buildings were erected in three months, and the machinery and stores transferred during Easter Week 1916. Some work was still being carried out in the Rose Lane Works but this gradually tapered off as the main production gained impetus at the new site. The old premises remained in the firm's possession until 1920 when they were purchased by the Co-operative Wholesale Society.

The new site area comprised fourteen acres and this was eventually covered by new buildings and layouts. With its own railway sidings, many running right into the works, connected to the main line and the riverside frontage, the intake and despatch of materials and finished goods by rail and water was speeded up considerably.

Eleven separate tenders were taken for camps to be built simultaneously in East Anglia; these called for huts and stables for six thousand men and as many horses. In four months camps were erected to the value of £100,000. The Allied Expeditionary Force went to France and took with it Norwich-produced wire products which were used for trench revetments, roadways and trellis for camouflage screens. In fact 5,373 miles of wire were used for these purposes, equal to a fence stretching from Norwich to London forty-seven times. It is interesting to note that the 1914 price of wire was £9 per ton, delivered to the works, but by 1918 this had soared to £42 12s 6d per ton.

The motor department was called upon by the Admiralty to increase production as large orders for engines had been placed by them. Electric lighting engines were required for mounting on Leyland lorries used as workshops in France, as well as portable motor pumps for use in the trenches. A number of engines were also ordered for use in launches and tugs, many to replace existing power units. Motors coupled to dynamos were also being produced to provide power for coastal searchlights. When the aircraft work came to Norwich it had a detrimental effect on this department as there were not enough skilled craftsmen to staff both sections, and reluctantly the department had to be closed down.

It was into this scene of frenzied and full production that a move was made to take up a new challenge in the country's hour of need. The directors unanimously agreed that their products did not truly reflect the firm's capabilities. Consequently, on their behalf, one of the local Members of Parliament, Mr George Roberts, wrote to Mr Lloyd George, the Munitions Minister, and offered to place part or all of the works at the Government's disposal.

Another Norwich company, the coach building concern of Howes and Son, also volunteered their services and as a result an official from London inspected both premises. He was not left with any doubts as to the woodworking capabilities of the two Norwich firms nor as to whether they could readily be converted to produce the new product—aircraft. The company was offered a small trial order on a cost and profit basis for the F.E.2b, and they were promised the run of the Royal Aircraft Factory at Farnborough in order to glean information which drawings and specifications might not reveal.

The first Boulton and Paul built machine, F.E.2b 5201, which was delivered to the Royal Flying Corps on 2nd October 1915. After evaluation at Farnborough, 5201 served with No 12 Squadron, RFC, in France.   *B&P*

Other engineering concerns in East Anglia which had previously been engaged in making agricultural machinery, lawn mowers, steam engines and fairground rides were also to join in the aircraft production scheme and all these firms worked in co-operation with each other to sort out their problems.

As part of this programme, overnight, factories were re-designated 'Munition Factories' and their personnel placed under the direction of the War Office. This new work was totally foreign to their previous experience, but like the craftsmen they were they soon adapted to the new tasks and techniques involved with aircraft and aircraft parts.

CHAPTER TWO

War Plans and Planes

WHEN THE aeroplane became part of the now considerable range of products manufactured by Boulton and Paul Limited, the new Riverside Works was still incomplete, so operations commenced at the Rose Lane Works. This called for more space so several of the wire weaving looms were replaced by machinery and benches. The firm's skilled men were joined almost daily by recruits from near and far, the workforce soon topping two thousand men. One such new recruit was Mr John Freeman who during December 1963 was the longest serving employee of Boulton-Paul Aircraft Limited, Wolverhampton, the successors to Boulton-Paul Limited, and throughout his days at both factories was always known as 'Young Jack'. He was probably the last of the old type of premium apprentices.

There was a shortage of skilled labour and the War Office instigated a scheme whereby skilled fitters and tool-makers now serving in the Forces would be semi-released to work in munition factories. They wore their uniforms but received civilian pay in addition to allowances. These men were known as Returned Colour or RC men and at one time over two hundred were employed at Norwich. Two gentlemen worked side by side in the Fitters' Shop who were totally strange to their new occupation but showed all the skills of apprenticed men—a Church of England parson and a Free Church minister!

After a visit from a Colonel Campbell, the company was instructed to employ more women in the light metal fitting section. One lady employee, Miss Lewis, had for many years been interested in engineering as a hobby and she was put in charge of the girls in the metal workshop. So successful was this section that the Ministry of Munitions sent parties of workers from all over the country to Norwich to see how the job should be carried out.

Close co-operation was necessary between the Rose Lane Works and the Chapel Field Works of Howes to ensure that a smooth flow programme was maintained. In this joint venture, Mr William ffiske supervised the woodwork and commercial aspects whilst the erection and final assembly was under the watchful eye of Stanley Howes and Mr Geoffrey ffiske, recently released from the Merchant Service, who also looked after the Engineering Section. Foremen, supervisors and charge-hands were given a crash course in their new duties and when all was set the new work began.

The contract was for the F.E.2b, a single engined, two-seat pusher biplane which had been designed by the Royal Aircraft Factory at Farnborough. Its pre-war conception was reflected in its designation, Farman Experimental No 2, modified to 'B' standard and now classified as a Fighting Scout Mk 1. A batch of fifty were ordered and alloted serial numbers 5201–5250.

Realising that a delay at any time for small components could put the production lines in jeopardy, the company manufactured their own bolts, screws, nuts and washers until they were confident they had sufficient stocks to see them through any break in supply. In the same vein the company produced its own oxygen, a large amount of which was used. When the British Oxygen's Company works were blown up at Silvertown, London, Boulton and Paul were one of the few aircraft makers who were not affected.

In a very few weeks the workforce had grown to over three thousand men and women, the latter largely employed in the fabric and dope shops. Used as they were to precision work, the personnel took to the aircraft work and the first machine was ready for trials during October 1915. One big problem was the lack of space in the Rose Lane Works. This prevented erection of the machines there, so the fuselages were moved to Howes' premises at Chapel Field for the engines to be installed. Once the systems had been fitted, the semi-assembled airframe was taken by road to Mousehold Heath for final assembly and flight testing.

Mousehold Heath—or to give it its local name, Four Mile Square—comprised some 263 acres and had been used as a cavalry training ground. Mr William ffiske had made several visits to London to have this site designated as a flight testing ground for Norwich-built machines and the company had already put up a large shed for the War Department on the site. The officials in London, however, still preferred a Thetford site as an aerodrome and acceptance park for Norfolk-made aircraft. Buildings and other facilities were already being erected there.

After some time the War Department sent two officials to inspect Mousehold Heath whilst the Boulton and Paul management explained that this was the better proposition. The officials were under the impression that Mousehold Heath was too small for an aerodrome, as the ordnance maps they possessed showed small-holdings around its perimeter. The maps were well out of date: the surrounding areas had all been laid down to grass and only required minimal levelling. Indeed, the area for which the War Department were already paying rent to Norwich Corporation included those very perimeter lands. On their return to

Aircraft hangar at Mousehold Heath, one of several that were erected for housing assembled aircraft. *B&P*

London notification was received that Mousehold Heath was to be the flying field for locally built aircraft and Boulton and Paul were given a contract to construct and erect the necessary buildings on the Thorpe side of the Salhouse Road.

On this now busy site, about three miles up the hill from the city of Norwich, sheds were erected for the assembly of the F.E.2bs, and Boulton and Paul's first aircraft was about to make its appearance. The War Department had pressed for delivery, and against the firm's better judgement they had named a date one week earlier than their calculations. Accordingly on Friday 1st October 1915, the 5201 was assembled at Mousehold, Mr Jim Law and his men working through the night to finish the job. Air Inspection Directorate inspectors carried out their examination of the airframe on the Saturday morning.

This was to be an occasion with the Government Director present as well as Mr J.J. Dawson Paul and his fellow directors, together with nobles and notables and as many of the workforce as could be spared. The well-known pre-war Schneider Trophy racing pilot, Captain C. Howard Pixton, had been engaged to take the first Norwich-built aircraft on its maiden flight. A marquee had been erected to house the refreshments, and two cases of champagne were held in readiness. The day dawned fair and bright, and F.E.2b 5201 stood ready to embark on its first venture.

The famous pilot staged his entrance, clad in thick flying leathers, and played to the crowd as they watched his every move with bated breath. He climbed into the cockpit and readied himself, set the ignition switches and the airscrew swung. Despite increasingly desperate efforts the Beardmore engine stubbornly refused to come to life. Everything was

13

tried to no avail; the pilot descended from the aircraft and after stating that he wanted the machine thoroughly examined before he would attempt to fly it again, walked away.

The crowds began to disperse, somewhat dejected, and an official inquest was hastily convened in the shed to pinpoint the cause of the engine's failure to start. Mr William ffiske wrote of the incident,

> Our poor old F.E.2b was wheeled around for general inspection, the pilot and guests partaking of tea and light refreshments in a marquee provided for the purpose. Mr Paul kindly brought up some magnums of 'jump' wherein to christen our offspring; and be assured we could not be held responsible for what we call in Norfolk a 'feeasso', allowed the bottles to be broached.

Unheralded and almost unseen, the next day 5201 took to the skies effortlessly; a wrongly connected engine lead had been the cause of the previous day's non-event. The engines were all supposed to have been tested before being received at Norwich but this one had escaped the requisite inspection and testing at its maker's.

A few days later, when 5201 was to be delivered to Farnborough in Hampshire, Mr Stanley Howes, who had been deeply involved with its construction, volunteered to fly with Captain Pixton. He became the first civilian passenger and on arrival at their destination sent a telegram to Norwich, 'ARRIVED ON SCHEDULE TIME, NEVER WANT TO TRAVEL MOTOR CAR OR TRAIN AGAIN, AEROPLANE EVERY TIME.' After further trials 5201 went to France during February 1916 to serve with No 12 Squadron RFC.

Looking extremely cumbersome by today's standards the F.E. series of pusher biplanes were developed from the onset as first-line combat aircraft. They made their appearance over the Western Front during the winter of 1915–16 and were an effective opponent of the then supposedly insurmountable Fokker monoplane with its synchronised machine-gun firing through the airscrew disc. Two legendary German aces fell to the 'Fee' as it was known: Karl Schefer, who had downed thirty Allied aircraft, and Max Immelmann, who was put in the Victory Book of No 25 Squadron after being shot down in a Norwich-built machine.

Gunners assigned for duty on 'Fee' squadrons were, it was rumoured, hand picked for their agility and total disregard for personal safety. Located in an open cockpit in the nacelle, ahead of the pilot, the gunner was armed with a Lewis gun which could be aimed in a forward, upward and downward direction.

Behind him and in front of the pilot another Lewis gun was mounted on a tubular structure and this could be fired upward and rearward over the upper mainplane. To aim and fire the second machine-gun, the gunner was forced to stand on his seat and great concentration was required in the heat of the battle, when following the enemy in the gunsight, not to shoot away large portions of his own aircraft.

Two hundred and forty-nine more F.E.2bs followed 5201 into Royal Flying Corps service where they gave creditable service. The War Office was apparently impressed with the Norwich product and contracts were placed for a further three hundred improved versions of the 2b, the F.E.2d. One of the modifications was the replacement of the Beardmore engine with a Rolls-Royce design, the 250 hp Eagle Mark 1.

The first aircraft of this type was serialled A.6351 and one of this batch, A.6460, gained fame when it was shipped to the United States for evaluation by the United States Air Corps. Yet another, A.6545, was modified to the later F.E.2h standard and was the prototype for this 200 hp engined version.

At Mousehold the tempo increased as the headquarters of No 7 Wing was formed there on 1st May 1916 as part of the Eastern Group Command. Mousehold Heath had now taken on the role of a full-time RFC station and Boulton and Paul's activities from the airfield had, of necessity, now to fit in with military commitments.

Norwich built F.E.2d A.6355, which carried out trials at the RFC Armament Experimental Station, Orfordness, Suffolk.   *Stuart Leslie*

Success with the 'pushers' landed Riverside Works with an even larger contract when they were asked to produce in batches 1,725 Sopwith 1F1 Camel single seat scouts—the term 'fighter' had not yet come into vogue. This was a vastly different aircraft from the 'Fee', smaller and lending itself to easier and more rapid production. Later during 1918, when Camel production reached its climax at Norwich, the weekly average was forty-three aircraft, with a best week of forty-seven machines completed.

A small, single bay biplane with an 80 hp Le Rhone rotary, air-cooled engine, the Camel derived its unusual name as the result of a nickname becoming official. A raised cover over the twin machine guns on the upper fuselage forward of the cockpit gave the short fuselage a distinctive hump, hence the name, Camel. Clever design by the parent company, Sopwith, had concentrated all the heavy items such as engine, guns, ammunition, fuel and pilot almost around the aircraft's centre of gravity and this combined with the rotary engine's flywheel torque effect made the Camel one of the most manoeuvrable aircraft ever designed. Some 1,294 victories in just sixteen months was proof enough of its abilities, and on 26th April 1918 the German ace, Baron Manfred von Richthofen, fell to the guns of a No 209 Squadron Camel.

A section of a long photograph that showed Boulton and Paul's output in one week of 1917, 45 Sopwith Camel aircraft—an astonishing feat.   *B&P*

Opposite: Employees, both male and female, arrive at Riverside Aircraft Works. Some of the uniformed 'Released Men' can be detected among the crowd.

Norwich-built Camels were to serve in all the major theatres of hostilities with the Canadian, Belgian, Greek and United States Air Forces as well as the Royal Flying Corps and the Royal Naval Air Service. Some were even engaged in operations against the Bolsheviks. Various engines were fitted and ranged from the 80 hp Le Rhone to the 110 hp Le Rhone, the 110 hp Clerget Long Stroke and the 150 hp Gnome Monosoupape, the latter twice as powerful as the original engine. This latter engine differed considerably from the Clerget and the Le Rhone, but the United States Air Service had purchased 143 and wanted them installed in the Camels which they had purchased and gave Boulton and Paul the contract for this work.

One Boulton and Paul Camel was unique in that it was used during June 1918 in air-launching experiments with the airship HMA No 23 from Pulham in Norfolk. Trials to see if an aeroplane could be launched by an airship continued for some time, at first the aircraft being released without a pilot and then later manned. The stability of the Camel was proved when during the un-manned launch programme the aircraft was released and glided down to land almost undamaged in one of the large fields in the Pulham district.

Important to the functioning of Boulton and Paul was a unit, No 3 Aeroplane Acceptance Park, formed at Mousehold Heath on 12th October 1917, its purpose being to accept aircraft from local constructors and to examine them, modify if necessary, flight test and then despatch them to squadrons. A Mr Peter Wilson was engaged to carry out the test flying.

A 150 hp Gnôme Monosoupape-engined Sopwith Camel, purchased by the United States Air Service, carrying out tests at the RFC Testing Station, Martlesham Heath, during October 1917. Note the United States style of marking at this period.   *Stuart Leslie*

An impressive assembly of Sopwith Snipe 7.F.1 single-seat Scouts undergoing final assembly at Mousehold Works.   *Alan Hague*

Camels and later Snipes were received from Norwich, F.E.2s and De Havilland 6s from Ransome, Sims and Jefferies Limited, Ipswich, and Garretts of Leiston, whilst De Havilland 9s came from another Norwich builder, Mann Egerton Limited. This unit further swelled the already over-crowded facilities at Mousehold and by the end of the First World War fifteen hangars and twenty-one sheds had been erected on the north-west side of the airfield near the Salhouse Road. Space was now at a premium and Sir Eustace Gurney was approached regarding the sale of his land on the west side of Salhouse Road. Agreement was reached and the erection of buildings began forthwith.

Apart from aircraft, Boulton and Paul were also engaged on munitions work and produced large numbers of artillery shells. Although extremely busy, Boulton and Paul pledged themselves to participate in this new work. The product called for was the eighteen-pound artillery shell, and production of this item was put under the control of Mr Bosworth and later Mr Mason. Many women and Belgian refugees were trained in this work but after a period word was received that the eighteen-pound shell was no longer required. On Ministry instruction the plant was sold to the Ministry of Munitions and it was transported to Galway, in Ireland, to establish a 'national factory' in that province.

19

For the production of fuses for these shells a new company, Norwich Components Limited, was set up by Mr W. ffiske and Mr H.P. Gould and the premises, known as Foundry Bridge Mills, were acquired from Colman Limited. Female labour was used almost exclusively. Disaster struck during the night of Sunday, 17th September 1917, when the works were burned down due to an electrical fault. About two hundred girls were working at the time but no-one was hurt. Next day arrangements were made to take over the city's skating rink and within three months the company was in full production again. A few days after the Armistice the factory was ordered to close down and all the hands were paid off.

In order to ease the transport of goods and aircraft components between Riverside Works and Mousehold, an ingenious system was devised, known as the Mousehold Light Railway. This was an end-on connection with the city's tramway system which terminated in Gurney Road, about halfway to Mousehold. Suitable electric traction vehicles were modified and old tram chassis converted to goods trucks; these worked up and down the hill from the riverside to the heath.

Success with Camel production led to further work, and the Norwich builders were awarded their largest single contract, No 35A/436/C303 for four hundred Sopwith 7.F.1 Snipe single-seat fighters, serialled E.6137–E.6536. A later contract for another one hundred Snipes was received, but this was only partially completed at the cessation of hostilities; only fifteen aircraft, J.451–465 being delivered. Production ceased on 29th January 1919.

A development of its famous forebear, the Camel, the Snipe was larger and heavier and took advantage of a newly developed power plant, the 230 hp Bentley BR1. Only three squadrons were equipped with the Snipe before the Armistice, but by then a distinguished action against fifteen Fokker D.VIIs had taken place which resulted in the award of a Victoria Cross to Major W.G. Barker. The Snipe had the distinction of being the post-war RAF's first standard single-seat fighter.

Not only were complete aircraft being produced at the Rose Lane and Riverside Works, but their woodworking expertise was also being put to other aeronautical use. Wooden hulls for flying boats, masterpieces of the 'chippy's' craft, were made for the Felixstowe designed F.3 and F.5 flying boats in what became known as the Hull Shop.

The re-design of the original American Curtiss hulls had been undertaken by Commander John Porte. The initial H.12 large America flying boats of Curtiss design serving at Felixstowe and other RNAS stations had a hull profile of a flattish nature and this created a tendency to porpoise, causing take-off and alighting difficulties. Porte reviewed these problems and produced fresh designs which incorporated a V-shaped planing surface to the bottom of the hull, curving from stem to stern, to carry the tail unit well clear of the water, enabling the flying boats to operate in rougher water.

The facilities available at the Norwich factories were inspected by Lieutenant-Commander Linton Hope, the celebrated pre-war yacht designer, and at the conclusion of his visit he gave them his approval. The initial order was for five hulls, but Norwich turned this down as it would mean too much disruption in the works for little gain and so it was increased to thirty. The first ten were delivered to Felixstowe in record time, and Norwich made the boast that they had completed ten hulls before the other contractors had delivered two. Seventy hulls were completed and delivered, a magnificent achievement when one takes into account the problems of construction, not the least of which was the planking of the hull with its complex lines.

Other complex shapes involved laminated woodwork; the Norwich works produced 7,835 aircraft propellers of all shapes and sizes. This work came about as the result of a visit from General MacInnis who was the Controller of Supplies. He mentioned to Mr ffiske that he was having difficulty with the production of propellers. There were only two or three companies manufacturing these items, and the General doubted the ability of any firm, not in the business, to make them. Mr ffiske suggested that Boulton and Paul's woodworking department would have that capability and bet the General a level sovereign that they would be successful. General MacInnis accepted the wager. Later he paid over his sovereign, remarking that he was delighted to have lost the bet.

Opposite: Mainplane assembly shop showing the somewhat fragile nature of these wooden, wire-braced structures.   *Alan Hague*

For modification trials and experimental work, a full-time test pilot was posted to Mousehold, Captain Frank Courtney RFC. He never became a Boulton and Paul staff member but later flew several of their designs on their maiden flights. Post-war, when he became a freelance test pilot, it is interesting to record that his standard fee for three hours' test flying was £50.

Hand finishing propellers, an intricate process.   *Alan Hague*

The administration was reorganised during 1917, younger men taking actual control of the company, although Dawson Paul and Henry ffiske were still Governing and Managing Directors by name. A committee of management now ran the company and comprised Captain Paul, just out of the Army, William ffiske, Stanley Howes and Geoffrey ffiske. With these men at the helm, the company faced a brave new world, with wartime contracts almost completed and a large workforce to be reduced to the needs of what the post-war market would require.

Opposite: Felixstowe F series twin-engined flying-boat hulls under construction at Norwich. This work required a very high degree of skill.   *Colin Manning*

23

CHAPTER THREE

Home-Spun

DURING the autumn of 1917 a young man joined the Norwich firm who would have a unique reputation, in that he would hold the position of Designer and Chief Designer for both the Norwich and the Wolverhampton companies for the entire period that they produced aircraft. This was no mean feat for a lad who had set out on a career of a totally different nature.

John Dudley North was born on 2nd January 1893 in London and was brought up by his widowed mother and grandparents, his father having died while he was an infant. His grandparents, wishing their grandchild to have a classical education in both Latin and Greek, sent young John to Bedford School. It was there that he also learned the rudiments of mathematics, which in original and advanced forms were to be so very much a tool of his trade in later years. There too he showed the first signs of his ability to abstract fact, later scientific fact, in a most amazing manner, and applied this talent to design new concepts with unerring logic.

When school days were over Mrs North decided that a life in the Merchant Navy would be ideally suitable for her son; his grandfather had been a captain in that service. Accordingly John Dudley was despatched to Belfast to take up a marine engineering apprenticeship with the renowned ship building establishment of Harland and Wolff. The apprentice diligently pursued his studies but during his infrequent periods of spare time he was increasingly interested in the then new flying machines. Reading all that was currently written on this subject, he entered a competition sponsored by *The Aeroplane* magazine. He won the first two competitions. Thereafter he was politely asked not to participate further in order to give the other entrants a chance! These achievements did not however go unnoticed as that distinguished aeronautical journalist and editor, Mr C.G. Gray, wrote to him suggesting that he should transfer his energies to the growing aviation industry. On this recommendation North's apprenticeship was transferred to Horatio Barber's Aeronautical Syndicate which was based at Hendon Aerodrome. Unfortunately its activities were short-lived and it soon went out of business. However the young apprentice was able to move along the road to Mr Graham White's establishment.

Such was his grasp of the new techniques of aircraft design and construction that by the time he was twenty years of age he had been appointed Chief Engineer. By this time he had designed the main components for the first British passenger-carrying aeroplane, the Graham White Charabanc. This aircraft was a large biplane with a long nacelle mounted on the lower wing and jutting forward. At the rear end of this nacelle was mounted a 120 hp Austro-Daimler six-cylinder water-cooled engine and this turned a 9 foot 3 inch diameter pusher propeller. Forward of the power plant, in the nacelle, was accommodated the pilot and four passengers, in pairs, seated in wicker cane chairs.

Grahame-White Charabanc about to take eight passengers aloft, one of whom is the aircraft's designer, John Dudley North.

The Charabanc proved to be a solid design and gained two world records for Great Britain. After its first flight on 22nd August 1913, the Chief Pilot, Mr Louis Noel, took off from Hendon with seven passengers who weighed in at 1,134 pounds and flew them around Hendon district for 17 minutes and 25 seconds. This established a record for passenger-carrying aircraft. On 2nd October the same pilot loaded the Charabanc to 'standing passenger' capacity when nine passengers, weighing 1,373 pounds, were airborne for 19 minutes and 47 seconds, which broke the previous record. Later, with Mr Graham White at the controls and five passengers, one of whom was John North, the Charabanc flew from Hendon to Brooklands at an average speed of 76 mph.

The first parachute descent made from an aeroplane in Great Britain was performed on 9th May 1914 by Mr W. Newell, when he jumped from the Charabanc flown by Mr R.H. Carr. Stepping out at two thousand feet over Hendon Aerodrome, the intrepid parachutist drifted down to the ground under his twenty-eight foot diameter canopy in 2 minutes and 22 seconds.

North had made a fine start and at this early age had full grasp of the fundamentals of aerodynamics and aircraft design. Graham White Aviation was making tremendous efforts during early 1914 to enter the military aircraft field; their boyish-looking Chief Designer, tall and bespectacled, was John North. He was designing a biplane, the G.W. Scout Pusher—Type II, to carry a gun, a design in direct competition with the Royal Aircraft Factory's F.E.2 and the Vickers Gunbus. After initial tests the design was discontinued and later, during 1915, North left Graham White Aviation and joined the Austin Motor Company as Superintendent at their new aeroplane factory in the Midlands.

During the autumn of 1917 he left Austin and moving to the East of England joined Boulton and Paul at Norwich. After a short familiarisation period he was put in charge of the Design Department, formed to develop aircraft of that company's own concept.

A Research and Experimental Section was set up dealing with chemical, metallurgical and photographic problems. Another innovation was the construction of a wind tunnel for aerodynamically testing aircraft or component part models. The wind tunnel, or channel as it was known then, had a chamber width of four feet and allowed a scale model of a new machine or component to be placed within the chamber, suspended and connected by various complicated and very exact instruments for measuring wind resistance, balance and so on.

At the age of twenty-four John North was indeed a young man to be in charge of these facilities, but he had a record of achievement and Boulton and Paul were indeed fortunate to obtain the services of such a Chief Designer. Design and research went on apace and it was the company's policy to concentrate on military aircraft types. First to come off the drawing board was the Boulton and Paul Experimental Scout, and a contract was received for six aircraft to be serialled C.8652–8757. Unfortunately much of the detail of this contract has been mislaid, but it is thought that the machines were to be named Hawk. There is some evidence though that the contract was for three machines, each of a different type. It is known however that one example was built, originally named Boblink, and then officially designated Bobolink (an American song bird) and serialled C.8655.

Boulton & Paul P.3 Bobolink C.8655, at Mousehold. The 'N' strutted, double-bay wing structure is well portrayed, as is the Bentley rotary engine. *B&P*

Evaluated against the Sopwith Snipe, the Bobolink measured up well and there was little to choose between the two types as far as performance was concerned. It was however on the ground where the differences showed up. The Norwich-built machine was considered more difficult to handle and pilots reported loss of vision when taxiing. The Bobolink was considered simple to service with easy access to any parts needing attention, but in the end the Snipe was recommended for production and received the contract.

After the Armistice fewer aircraft were required. There were tremendous stocks of machines and spares in Aircraft Parks up and down the country as well as overseas. Established design types which had been contracted out would now be manufactured by their parent firms. Accordingly the order for 150 Vickers Vimy twin-engined bombers and 500 Martinsyde F.4 Buzzard single-seat fighters placed with Boulton and Paul was cancelled.

After the formation of the Royal Air Force on 1st April 1918, a new Government department, the Air Ministry, was established and as a sub-division, the Technical Department. A section in this latter department dealt with the testing of new aircraft types on an official basis, as opposed to the sometimes haphazard procedures which had previously been the case. Although the Bobolink had failed to be accepted, Boulton and Paul received an official contract to design and supply three twin-engined bombers of their own design. Mainly experimental, these machines incorporated a number of unusual features; they were to have varied upper mainplane mountings and to be powered by alternative engine types. The name Bourges was allotted to these machines, Boulton and

Paul Type P.7, and they were to prove to be the fore-runners of a remarkable series of 'fighting bombers' which were to earn for themselves a reputation of extreme manoeuvrability. The design of these machines came as a life-line at a time when the company was making a decision concerning the future of their Aircraft Division.

The new Bourges was categorised and advertised as a fighter-bomber and its later performance fully bore out this classification. It carried a three man crew consisting of a pilot and two gunners, one of whom was positioned in the nose with a .303 Lewis gun on a modified Scarff gun mounting, the other in the dorsal position with a similar armament. Slightly raised behind the front gunner's cockpit was the pilot's position and this gave good frontal and sideways vision, whilst protection against the airflow was provided by a large windscreen. A bomb load of nine hundred pounds was carried in the fuselage between the lower wing spars with transverse doors enclosing the three bomb cells. The engines temporarily installed in order to carry out initial flight testing were two 230 hp Bentley BR2 rotaries that had been used in the Bobolink. The design power units were to have been two 320 hp ABC Dragonfly radials, but this engine had yet to complete its tests by the time that the airframe was ready. In this form the Bourges Mark IIA, as it was designated, was prepared for flight trials. The reader might wonder why the prototype aircraft should be Mark IIA; this was due to the Dragonfly prototype still being designated Mark I.

During the spring of 1918 Captain Frank Courtney was serving in the RAF at London Colney, in Hertfordshire, when the Air Ministry transferred him from the monotony of restricted service flying to a position as Test Pilot for Boulton and Paul in Norwich. He remained a

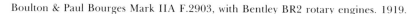

Boulton & Paul Bourges Mark IIA F.2903, with Bentley BR2 rotary engines. 1919.   *B&P*

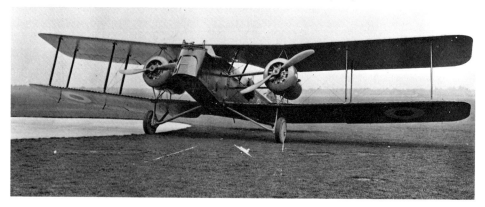

serving officer of the RAF but was removed from the discipline and tedium of the now 'more bull than flying' Air Force. His decision to take up the appointment proved to be right, for it led to a varied and interesting test flying career which was to stretch over many years.

His first job was to continue test flying the single-seat Bobolink, more important however was the new twin-engined bomber which would soon be ready for its maiden flight. Courtney became fully involved with the new aircraft and made strenuous efforts to see that it was ready for its debut. The first flight was uneventful and trials continued at Mousehold; they were very promising and the aircraft showed from the outset its manoeuvrability. After several weeks of successful flight trials with the rotary engines, the ABC Dragonfly radials became available and F.2903 went into the Flight Shed at Mousehold to have the new power units fitted. Emerging some time later, the Bourges was then designated the Mark IA. The Test Pilot's report for the Bourges stated that its performance was excellent and its handling qualities were outstanding due to its general design. Courtney reported in his log, 'Starting off with a few loops, I soon found that I could make the Bourges perform like an over-sized Camel. The Bourges could be thrown around in loops, spins, rolls or any other freak manoeuvre one could think up without any special effort at all'.

A previous project which had been taken on by Boulton and Paul gave Frank Courtney interest, fun and excitement. The American Army Air Corps was in the throes of re-equipping and had acquired a consignment of French-designed Gnôme Monosoupape 150 hp rotary engines. These were to be fitted into a batch of Sopwith Camels they had also acquired. As a building order for Camels was going through the Norwich works at this time, Boulton and Paul were given the task of revising the design and fitting this engine to them. The Mono engine was far more powerful than previous Camel powerplants and also much more temperamental.

The Norwich-built Camels were some of the best made to that design, but the merger of the larger engine to the established airframe was another problem. Eventually all was resolved and the order completed. Courtney recalled, 'One of the strange features of the Mono was that there was not an orthodox throttle as such, this function being carried out by a selector switch which progressively isolated one cylinder after another, until only one cylinder was firing with all the sonic effects of a machine gun.' He used this peculiarity to what he thought was good effect one day. Having been invited over to lunch at the local Harling Road aerodrome, he arrived by diving over the airfield with the Mono engine banging out its tattoo on one cylinder. As can be imagined there was a mad rush for shelter by all the station personnel, and when Courtney landed he was not met with the expected hearty laughter but rather by a lynching party. Rapidly assessing the situation, he decided that discretion was the better part of valour and hastily took off again, beating a retreat to Norwich to make his explanation before the official complaint arrived on North's desk.

One of Courtney's other jobs was that of 'joy-riding pilot' and many such flights were made from the aerodrome at Hounslow, North London, after the war. One family, named Lanning, made such a flight with Courtney during 1919. This was a sedate family flight enjoyed by all, especially the elder son, Francis, aged twelve. Twenty-two years later Flight Lieutenant F.C.A. Lanning was to be an air gunner flying in Boulton-Paul Defiants with No 141 Squadron, a night fighter unit. During operations with this unit he was awarded the Distinguished Flying Cross for the destruction of two enemy aircraft at night.

Captain Frank Courtney poses in front of the Bourges Mark IA after it had been modified. The steps to gain access to the pilot's cockpit are clearly visible. 1919. *Alan Hague*

The Bourges carried out further trials, but the bomb load of nine hundred pounds was considered insufficient for a bomber, and the fuel capacity was not enough for a bomber's operational range. Despite these shortcomings the Norwich-built machine convinced the Ministry that here really was a different aircraft and one capable of development into an outstanding design. A second prototype emerged with the Dragonfly engine, F.2904, designated Mark IB. Once again the performance was exciting and received a good report from evaluation trials at Martlesham Heath. The Norwich Design Office continued the breed and projected another variant, this one to be powered by two 290 hp Siddeley Puma water-cooled engines, but this project was abandoned.

Prototype No 3 was built, F.2905, and designated Mark IIIA. The main difference was that the power units were two 450 hp Napier Lion water-cooled engines, mounted directly on the lower mainplane and turning four-bladed airscrews. It was reported that the Bourges Mark 111A was the fastest twin-engined aircraft in the world at this time. Because of Ministry financial restrictions the Bourges failed to reach production status, but all three prototypes had played their part in developing this type of aircraft.

F.2904 was rebuilt at Norwich in preparation for an attempt to be the first aircraft to fly the Atlantic non-stop. Re-designated P.8 and sometimes referred to as the 'Atlantic', this machine was intended as a contender for the *Daily Mail* Trans-Atlantic Prize. A new fuselage allowed more room for larger fuel tanks to be installed. These comprised six tanks, each fitted with a jettison valve which could be operated from the cockpit and when opened would enable the entire fuel load to be discharged in one and a quarter minutes. When empty the tanks enabled the aircraft to remain buoyant and float the right way up if forced down onto the sea. Additional equipment for the overwater flight were two wireless sets, one for sending and receiving messages and the other to assist with directional navigation. A balloon which could be quickly inflated by a small hydrogen cylinder enabled an aerial to be carried aloft to transmit SOS messages from the surface of the ocean. An aeronautical journal wrote of the P.8,

One of the most important features of the Boulton and Paul machine is that after a short time in the air the machine is able to keep aloft on one engine only. It is further to be noted that the cruising speed of the machine is as high as 116 mph. This is probably the highest cruising speed of any machine entered for the race. When flying at this cruising speed the range of the Boulton and Paul machine has been calculated to be about 3,850 miles, so that there is an ample margin in hand for the transatlantic journey.

31

Bourges P.7, F.2904, rebuilt as the P.8 Atlantic G-EAPE contender for the *Daily Mail* Trans-Atlantic Prize.   *B&P*

The anticipation of its first flight at Mousehold created quite a stir at the Norwich factory. The good-looking biplane with its twin Napier Lion engines was advanced for its time and many of the onlookers were intrigued by the glazed canopy with its sliding hatches for the pilot. Among the official spectators were the Managing Director and a 'Very Important Person' who had been invited as his guest. He was extremely anxious that his guest should see the P.8 fly before catching his train. He explained to Captain Courtney the importance of the flight and, even when told that the engines had not passed full test runs, passed it off as not essential for such a short test flight. So Courtney and his flight observer climbed aboard the P.8, the Napier Lions were opened up and the aircraft rose from the grass-surfaced field. When only a few feet off the ground, the port engine stopped dead, the biplane cartwheeled and the front fuselage complete with the cockpit broke from the main

The demise of the P.8 Atlantic at Mousehold. The photograph shows the wrecked cockpit from which Courtney and his flight observer escaped.   *Alan Hague*

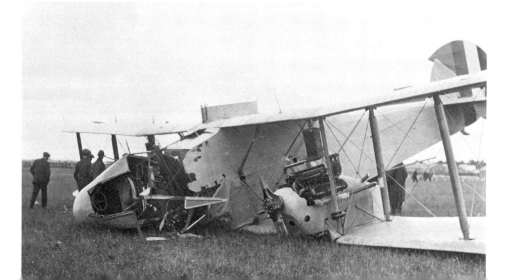

wreckage. The pilot was pulled out suffering only a few cuts, whilst his observer was slightly more.damaged with a large lump on his head and several gaps in his teeth. Examination of the wreckage revealed that the engine had stopped because of an elementary fuel line blockage. Had the engines been put through their complete full-throttle test runs, this would have been detected.

A second P.8 was in an advanced state of construction as a back-up aircraft but before it was ready to participate the first non-stop heavier-than-air Atlantic crossing had been made by John Alcock and Arthur Whitten Brown in the Vickers Vimy. The Boulton and Paul project was cancelled and the aircraft was used at Mousehold in aerodynamic research.

Whilst much time at Riverside Works during the 1918–20 period had been spent on the trio of Bourges bomber-fighters, another interesting aircraft was gradually taking shape in a different part of the works. It was a diminutive single bay biplane intended for full scale research into a number of problems which had been plaguing designers for several years. Designated P.6 and carrying experimental serial X.25, the all-wooden aircraft was powered by a 90 hp RAF 1A engine driving a four-bladed airscrew. A programme of experiments which had been prepared for this machine was successfully concluded and as a result formulated many design characteristics of Boulton and Paul's future aircraft. With the inscription 'Boulton and Paul Ltd., Sales Department' painted prominently beneath the lower mainplanes and along the fuselage, it became a real advertisement for the company.

The experimental Boulton & Paul P.6 X.25 after it had been allocated to the Norwich Sales Department. It carried the firm's name on fuselage and mainplanes.   *B&P*

A small two-seat touring biplane, the P.9 was intended for the post-war flying enthusiast.   *B&P*

Another wooden aircraft which came from the Norwich stable was the P.9. This aircraft was designed for a Lieutenant A.L. Lang to patrol sheep stations in Tasmania. When completed and air tested, it was shipped out to the Antipodes, where it was also used for mail and newspaper deliveries. In this capacity it made the first north-bound air crossing of the Bass Strait on 15th December 1919 when inaugurating the Hobart–Melbourne airmail service. Lang's P.9 was built in six weeks; this was achieved by using a tail unit and centre section from the previous P.6. A production batch of seven machines was put in hand with a quoted price of £800.

Export orders followed for the light biplane and the next three were shipped out to Australia during June 1921. In July 1920 Mr F. Briggs made a record flight of 550 miles from Mildura to Sydney in six hours ten minutes and then three days later, Sydney to Melbourne in six hours thirty minutes. Another Australian owner, Mr H.O. Jolley, entered G-ABCP in the *Herald* Cup Race held at Essendon, Melbourne, on 12th June 1923, and piloted by Mr E.W. Percival (later of Percival Aircraft fame) it won in spite of high winds. G-EASJ flown by Mr C.T. Holmes and G-EAWS by Mr J.E. Tennent entered for the 1922 Round Britain King's Cup Air Race but were unplaced. On 9th February 1929, G-EBAQ broke through the ice when taking off from a frozen lake at St Moritz. It was salvaged and rebuilt locally. G-EAWS, which Boulton and Paul then used as a company aircraft, was damaged beyond repair on 12th June 1929 at Cramlington when it ran away whilst being started.

The P.9 was the last wooden aircraft to emerge from the Norwich design office and also the last single-engined type from Boulton and Paul until the Partridge fighter in 1928. Directed at the sporting flyer the P.9 unfortunately arrived at a time when money was in short supply and it was to be a few more years before the light plane, in the shape of the De Havilland Moth, was to break into this market. Records regarding the production of the P.9 are vague, but it is believed that about twenty aircraft were built to this design.

At this time, after the First World War, the directors recognised that aviation had been of great importance during the war and would continue to be so in the future. To this end they paid very close attention to the quality of the company's products and no aircraft were better or more carefully built than those at Boulton and Paul Limited.

Courtney loops the Bourges F.2903 during one of his spectacular aerobatic displays. On-lookers were astonished to see such a large aircraft performing fighter-like manoeuvres. *B&P*

CHAPTER FOUR

Metallisation

UNLIKE the present time, when an aircraft is a vast complex of mechanical, hydraulic and electronic devices, the designs of the post First World War years were comparatively simple in structure. No computers plotted out involved calculations of stresses and loadings, and there were very few reference books to use for guidance. At the same time the requirements of the day were limited and the only calculations called for were elementary load factors and pressure distributions over a given wing or tailplane. The greatest asset was experience, as it was a time of learning by trial and error, but because loadings were comparatively low, failures were not always disastrous. A failed component was often still available after an incident for detailed examination and subsequent re-design. The number of designers, draughtsmen and stressmen involved in a new design was minimal by today's standards and a small number of Design Office staff could usually produce working drawings in a matter of weeks. Up to this time wood and fabric had been the main materials for aircraft construction, but J.D. North, with visionary insight, anticipated the increasing difficulty of obtaining first-class Sitka spruce. The substantial use of this wood in aircraft production during the war had greatly depleted the stock available. This made North's approach to a new form of construction all the more urgent.

Construction in metal involved totally different types of machinery and completely new methods and techniques of production, but it was this dramatic change that was responsible for the company overcoming the post-war depression during the time of a severe slump in aviation. This new type of construction was to be identified with Boulton and Paul for many years to come and management commitment and enthusiasm in the Design Office were to pay dividends during those dark days.

At the request of the new Air Ministry, Boulton and Paul Limited had turned their attention to the use of metal: not light alloys which were comparatively simple to work and form, but the more exacting and complicated problems of working high tensile steel. After North's proposals had been submitted to the Government, limited support was given for him to set up a design study for construction in high grade, thin gauge steel. Detailed work had been carried out by the Design Team under North's leadership, and these studies applied to all areas including workshop machinery and tools to manufacture the new components.

Up to this time steel strip was received from the supplier's mills, hardened and tempered as it had been drawn out whilst hot. This made a very hard material to work. The Design Office came up with the answer; the steel strip was now to be delivered to Norwich in its soft, unworked state and went through a process which the company patented. Electrically heated furnaces were mounted on the draw-benches and the formed sections in their soft state were then drawn through them at a speed slow enough for the metal to heat up to the required temperature. Hardening was achieved by rapid quenching in water-cooled dies at the furnace exit. This enabled the strip, however long, to be held straight throughout the heat treatment process, which in itself was able to be controlled to precise limits.

The first all-metal structured design from the Norwich Design Office was a development of the wooden P.9, designated P.10. It was assembled for the Salon de l'Aéronautique in Paris during 1919 and was exhibited in an uncovered state so that the airframe could be fully inspected. Many advanced design features caused the aviation journalists to report in full on this exhibit and in particular on the monocoque rear fuselage that was covered with Bakelite Dilecto sheets, which were an early form of plastic. Another eye-catching innovation was the hinged engine mounting which allowed maintenance to be carried out on the back of the three-cylinder Bristol Lucifer radial engine by undoing a few bolts and swinging the complete mounting out to one side. This was to be a feature of later Boulton and Paul designs.

Opposite: The P.10 exhibited at the Salon de l'Aéronautique, Paris. *B&P*

The august aeronautical journal, *The Aeroplane*, described the P.10 as 'the most advanced example of constructional thought in the whole show'. Another contemporary magazine reported,

> The Boulton and Paul all-metal P.10 is the machine of the Show from a constructional point of view. For instance, the weight of the P.10 actually comes out lighter than the same machine, built in wood in the usual way, whilst its strength is, if anything, superior to that of the wooden machine. This, however, is not the chief point of the design, although it incidentally proves to what state of perfection Boulton and Paul have carried metal construction. The chief advantage will probably be found in the longer life of the steel structure.

The P.10 was brought home, but for reasons completely unknown was never covered and therefore never flew, yet it had undoubtedly made its mark at the Paris Show.

At the same time as the P.10 design was being evolved, investigation was made into the process of rendering metal parts rust-proof. As the result of tests on some forty methods of treatment, plant was laid down for metal part anti-rust treatment in accordance with whichever method gave the best results. Work also went ahead on putting the work onto a production basis instead of the individually built machine.

It was realised that if the job was to be done properly, new machinery would be required to work the sheet steel into more complicated sections required for wing spar and other structural members. Help with the financing came from the Air Ministry in the form of a succession of orders for prototype twin-engined aircraft.

To house the new machinery Riverside Works had expanded considerably and the old Rose Lane Works were sold off. Post-war depression was manifest and for the first time a loss was recorded during 1921.

During 1922 the Air Ministry issued a specification for what was designated a 'Postal Aircraft' and several aircraft companies such as Parnells, Westland and Boulton and Paul tendered for this contract. Westland decided on a large monoplane design which later crashed on its maiden flight, whilst Parnells and Boulton and Paul offered large biplanes. The designation 'Postal' implied that the aircraft would be used on mail carrying duties, and although initially carrying RAF markings, it was assumed to become a civil aircraft eventually. To Specification A.M.11/20, the P.12, Bodmin as it was to be named, was of all-metal airframe construction and of the now familiar equal span, unstaggered biplane layout. One stipulation demanded by the Design Office was complete reliability. To provide this, a very novel engine installation was devised; a central 'engine-room' in the fuselage which required power drive to the propellers by shafts mounted between the mainplanes.

When the P.12 emerged it was evident that Boulton and Paul had successfully produced a unique machine with the aid of their high tensile steel constructional methods, and the first flight was eagerly anticipated. This was the largest aircraft to emerge from the Riverside Works to date, and it had to be transported up to Mousehold in large sections, a problem in itself. One of the firm's solid-tyred lorries was used to haul the trailers between the works and the assembly shed. The cobbled streets, some with railway and tram tracks, increased the problems of the large over-hanging load. Several members of the works staff, armed with long pieces of wood, walked alongside and assisted in keeping it steady. A rugger-goal post-like structure was erected behind the lorry cab and by means of this obstacles encountered en route could be assessed for clearance.

Centre fuselage, with engine room and transmission shafts to the outboard propeller mountings, is moved through the streets of Norwich on its way to Mousehold Works. Men are supporting the structure with long poles to stabilise it, and the goal-post structure on the lorry was used to gauge the height of bridges, lamp standards and other obstacles along the route.   *B&P*

After assembly and all final checks the Bodmin was brought out onto the tarmac. At the appointed time Captain Courtney and the engineer climbed aboard and the two Napier Lion engines were started. It was an unusual feature that the motors could run whilst the propellers were standing idle, for it was not until the clutches were engaged that the front and rear propellers began to turn. Courtney thoroughly tested the engines and after full throttle run-ups the chocks were signalled away and the Bodmin taxied over the grass to the downwind end of the airfield. Testing the engines once again, although not to full throttle because the machine was not fitted with brakes, he turned the Bodmin into the wind and, as the engines were opened up, the aircraft gathered momentum. The tail lifted and the Bodmin gently climbed away in a shallow turn in order to avoid the sheds.

After all the tests scheduled for the flight had been carried out, Courtney brought in the large biplane towards the airfield and put it down smoothly before running up to the tarmac and switching off the engines. The machine was soon surrounded by a large crowd and Courtney received the praises of the firm's top men. Mr Martin, the engineer on the flight, was delighted with all his 'bells and whistles', which had functioned as per the book. The newspaper-men were also pleased with Courtney's performance and took him out to lunch in Norwich where later, as he was leaving the restaurant, he was knocked over by a messenger boy on a bicycle. Not all the hazards are in the air!

Built as a Postal Aircraft, the P.12 Bodmin, J.6910, was unorthodox in many ways, particularly the centre fuselage engine-room.   *B&P*

The Bodmin was described in the 1925 Royal Air Force Open List as a three-seat, medium postal aircraft. Another was built and the two aircraft, J.6910 and J.6911, carried out considerable test flying and experiments on their unusual power arrangements. Visits to Martlesham Heath were part of their evaluation programme. Extended air tests proved that the Bodmin was capable of flying level on the power of only one engine and in this respect it scored over conventional twin-engined aircraft. The Bodmin's thrust was always central, irrespective of whether one or two engines were running, as the tractor and pusher propellers were handed, that is they both turned inwards, which solved any torque problems. The first prototype was unfortunately written off towards the end of its official trials when the undercarriage failed, but the second machine was modified and carried on the test programme, which was successfully completed. It had never been envisaged as a production type but many valuable lessons were learned from the design before the second prototype was eventually broken up.

Designed and developed alongside the Bodmin was another twin-engined biplane, but one with military trimmings. Evolved from the Bourges, the new design, Boulton and Paul Type P.15, built to Air Ministry Specification 30/22, was designated Bolton and given the RAF serial number J.6584. The makers were so proud of their new creation that the airframe was photographed uncovered for the press so that all could see the intricate tracery of metal which would have been hidden once the fabric covering had been applied. Successful test flights were carried out at Mousehold and then in October 1923 it was moved to Martlesham Heath for evaluation.

No production orders were received for the Bolton, which was not officially designated as a bomber but as a 'three-seat long-range reconnaissance biplane'. It could nevertheless have easily been converted to the former should the need have arisen. To assist in its 'spying missions', which would have necessitated a stealthy approach to its target, the Bolton was fitted with special water-cooled exhaust silencers to reduce engine noise. Of Boulton and Paul design, the silencers were aluminium manifolds which joined up with steel pipes that incorporated shrouded outlets for the exhaust. After a prolonged period of tests and trials and modifications, the Bolton was broken up. Once again very valuable experience had been gained in the production and maintenance of metal aircraft and many of the lessons learned were incorporated in future designs.

The next design from the Norwich office also had similarities to the Bourges and could have been mistaken for the earlier machine. Bearing the name Bugle and designated P.25, it was another all-metal structured biplane to the now established design format. Crew positions in the fuselage were orthodox with the front gunner's position forward of the cockpit, whilst the other gunner was positioned aft of the mainplanes atop the fuselage. Behind this gun position the upper fuselage became triangulated again giving the gunner a much improved arc of fire. The Scarff gun ring mounting in the front cockpit was canted forward to give the gun an almost vertical field of fire downwards as well as upwards and sideways. Both gunners were equipped with single drum-fed Lewis guns.

Cockpit and front gun position on the Bolton were formed from light pierced steel sections, making a stiff, light structure.   *B&P*

As the Specification 30/22 for the P.25 had been amended from that of bomber-fighter to medium range bomber, a bomb bay was incorporated in the floor of the centre fuselage thus allowing the bomb load to be be stowed internally. The bombs were aimed from a compartment in the forward fuselage and sighting was made through an opening in the fuselage floor. An early form of remote control was fitted to allow the bomb-aimer, who was also the front gunner, to guide the aircraft onto its desired target course.

All metal structured, the P.15 Bolton J.6584 continued the theme of the twin-engined, highly manoeuvrable biplane.   *B&P*

A new power unit appeared on the Bugle prototypes J.6984 and J.6985, the new Bristol Jupiter II air-cooled 400 hp radial engine. These engines were gaining in popularity with aircraft designers due to to their reliability and improved power-to-weight ratio. In the Bugle they were mounted on hinged bearers so they could be swung to one side for maintenance to be carried out on the back of the engine. They turned large two-bladed wooden propellers, and fuel was stored in big streamlined tanks located under the top mainplane between the fuselage and the engines. Although offering an easier fuel flow down to the engines, re-fuelling was a problem and modifications were made in later aircraft.

Designated Mark I, Bugle J.6984 went to Martlesham Heath for evaluation trials during September 1923, and although it received a good report for manoeuvrability and service reliability, it suffered from heavy controls. Stability was good and the Test Report stated that the aircraft could be flown for long periods with hands and feet off the controls.

A third Bugle, J.7235, took shape during 1924 but differed in several respects from the two previous machines. This one was built as a four seater which meant that the full-time bomb aimer did not have to

43

double up as the front gunner. Powered by upgraded Bristol Jupiter IVs, the Bugle Mark I (Modified) carried out trials at Martlesham Heath. J.7235 was sent to carry out Service Trials at No 58 Squadron and was evaluated against their Vickers Virginia bombers. Whilst with them it was shown to the public at the 1925 Royal Air Force Air Pageant at Hendon. During 1925 two more Bugles appeared, J.7266 and J.7267, but these were designated Mark II and powered by 450 hp Napier Lion water-cooled engines mounted on the lower mainplane, Bourges style.

Things now looked brighter at Norwich, but despite its performance the Bugle did not go into production for the Royal Air Force. It would appear that the bomber aircraft contracts were being placed with the established firms such as Vickers and Handley-Page. Undaunted, Boulton and Paul decided to continue the development of their designs and offered the Air Ministry a new sophisticated, high-performance, twin-engined medium day bomber to Specification 9/24.

Bugle P.25A Mark II J.7266 powered by 450 hp Napier Lion water-cooled engines mounted on the lower mainplanes. Fuel tanks were relocated in the centre fuselage.   *B&P*

It was also felt that Boulton and Paul should have a full-time test pilot on the books and in July 1926 Squadron Leader C.A. Rea, who had been stationed at the Marine Aircraft Experimental Establishment at Felixstowe, Suffolk, was chosen for the post. As well as being an experienced pilot capable of test flying, he would also assist the technical staff concerning service procedures.

During the mid-1920s the Norwich workforce had grown considerably and additional buildings had been erected to cope with the increasing workload. The facilities at Mousehold had also grown and as the successive new designs grew in wingspan so new hangars were needed for assembly and pre-flight trials. The Drawing Office designs were produced in high tensile stainless steel and there seemed no limit to the intricate bending and folding techniques now possible. In the main, high tensile steel was used for main structural members such as spars and longerons; light alloy was utilised for secondary structural members.

The 9/24 prototype, when it did appear, was in the Bourges and Bugle mould. The new aircraft was given the name of a small north Norfolk coastal village, Sidestrand, Mark I and was serialled J.7938 and built to a revised Specification, B.30/22. The Secretary of State for Air at the time, Sir Samuel John Gurney Hoare, later Viscount Templewood, lived at Sidestrand Hall and the name may have been chosen in recognition of the order placed. Fabric covered except for the forward fuselage and various detachable panels, the all-silver Sidestrand was a fine sight with the slim profile of the front fuselage emphasised by the dark green anti-dazzle top decking. The aircraft's nose had a pronounced downward sweep which gave the pilot an extremely good angle of vision forward. It carried two Scarff ring mountings for drum-fed Lewis guns, one forward and one in the dorsal position. In addition there was a prone gun position in the lower fuselage with an arc of fire rearward under the aircraft. As only two guns were carried, the rear gun could be mounted above or below the fuselage in accordance with the aircraft's position in the formation. All three gun positions were provided with ammunition storage for six 97-round Lewis magazine drums. One feature of the forward gun position was that, as the front fuselage was narrow at this point, the Scarff ring was slightly overlapping the sides, but this enabled the gunner to bring his weapon to bear on targets almost vertically below the aircraft.

Present day road sign for the north Norfolk village of Sidestrand, the name adopted for the Boulton & Paul P.29 bomber. *Author*

Four bomb carriers, one under each centre section and two in a bomb bay, could accommodate one 550 pound bomb, two of 250 pounds or four of 112 pounds. Release of the bombs was by means of duplicated control release gear, either pilot or bomb aimer being able to perform this function. Fusing of the bombs was actuated by two levers located on the cockpit floor, and an extension from these ran to the front position in order that the bomb aimer could also operate them. It should be pointed out that the bomb bay was not designed like that of a Second World War bomber with doors able to open and close. On the Sidestrand the bomb bay remained open at all times. The bomb aimer lay in the prone position on the floor of the front gun position to perform his duties and through a window was able to see dead ahead as well as vertically downwards.

The first flight test provided a problem for Squadron Leader Rea when, in order to prevent stalling, he found it necessary to land at the unusually high speed of 90 mph. The landing took the entire length of the aerodrome and he finished only a few yards from the boundary fence. An investigation later revealed that a mathematical error in the design had reduced the upward travel of the elevator controls by over thirty per cent.

When stationed at Felixstowe he had become a frequent visitor to Martlesham Heath, and his knowledge of their procedures helped to overcome any problems when he took the Sidestrand to the Aircraft and Armament Experimental Establishment for evaluation trials. They in turn were pleased to receive J.7938 during March 1926 as this was a rather different aircraft. A sister machine, J.7939, had been built alongside the first prototype and this too was presented to the A&AEE during June 1926 for them to carry out a full programme of performance and armament trials whilst flown by Service pilots. With the occasional trip back to Mousehold for minor modifications, the two aircraft were a familiar sight in the skies around Ipswich. At the 1927 Royal Air Force Pageant at Hendon the crowds were delighted with the new bomber and the manner in which it was able to out-fly the attacking fighters.

In spite of the excellent performance recorded during the trials at the A&AEE, a few modifications were required; an aerodynamically balanced aileron which had differential action from Bristol's Chief Designer, Mr Leslie Frise; Handley-Page automatic slats on the upper outer mainplanes, and an aerodynamic balance known as the Flettner servo-rudder. With these modifications completed the Sidestrand returned to Suffolk where the pilots put it through a series of loops, rolls and spins. The second prototype, on completion of trials, returned to Mousehold and became the firm's test aircraft.

Boulton & Paul P.29 Sidestrand Mark I J.7938 climbs out over the Mousehold Heath hangars and shows the somewhat exposed positions for the crew members. Square cut wing tips, wide track undercarriage and high aspect ratio mainplanes were all features of this Norwich designed machine.
B&P

Whitehall was impressed with the aircraft and although at this time only limited funds were available, they placed an order for six more Sidestrands; these were of improved layout, to carry the manufacturer's designation P.29A. The specification was amended to 25/27 to cover

47

Prototype Sidestrand Mark II J.9176, the first of a batch of six built for RAF service and based at Bicester, Oxfordshire, with No 101 (B) Squadron.   *B&P*

some small modifications although the Sidestrand II, as it became known, still utilised the Bristol Jupiter VI engines in their ungeared form. This batch was serialled J.9176-J.9181. It became the RAF's first medium bomber and also the first twin-engined bomber since the wartime De Havilland 10 Amiens.

J.7938 had been delivered to No 101 Squadron during April 1928 for field evaluation and the Mark IIs when completed duly joined that squadron at Bicester. New levels of accuracy were achieved by the bomb aimers over the Catfoss bombing ranges and all previous records broken. During the Annual Air Exercises the six Sidestrands proved that they could carry the load of a night bomber but at the speed of a single-engined day bomber.

Later the Air Ministry issued another medium bomber specification, B.10/29, and this evolved as the Sidestrand Mark III. J.7939, the company test machine, had been re-engined with more powerful Bristol Jupiter VIIF engines and these improved the performance considerably. When trials of this machine had been concluded successfully, the Mark IIs were recalled from No 101 Squadron and after extensive modification appeared as Sidestrand Mark IIIs, one of which was displayed at Olympia during 1929. More powerful 460 hp geared Jupiter VIIIF

Demise of Sidestrand Mark II J.9178 after a landing accident. This illustration shows the ventral gun
position. *Alan Hague*

engines had been fitted and these gave a top speed of 140 mph at ten
thousand feet. Climb was also improved with a respectable nineteen
minutes to fifteen thousand feet and a service ceiling of twenty-four
thousand feet.

J.9176 was returned to Martlesham Heath where, after full Service
Trials, the Air Ministry ordered a modest production run of fourteen
Mark IIIs. This order was less than it appeared, for six were Mark IIs
already built and now converted. The A&AEE were satisfied with the
new version but in their report were concerned that the engines could
not be mechanically turned over by hand, but only by means of the RAE
Mark II Gas Starter. Another feature that the A&AEE mentioned was
the oleo-pneumatic undercarriage, which stood up well to the rough
heather-covered surface of Martlesham Heath, as also did the sturdy,
swivelling, self-tracking tailskid attached to the rear fuselage. After their
experience with the Mark IIs it was not surprising that No 101 Squadron,
now stationed at Bircham Newton in Norfolk, received the new aircraft.

Sidestrands of No 101 (B) Squadron fly in formation. The gunners appear to be taking cover within the confines of their positions.   *B&P*

The second prototype Sidestrand I, J.7939, constantly under review by Mr North, was once again re-engined with Bristol air-cooled radials, this time the geared and supercharged Jupiter XFB. With these power units it embarked on another programme of research and evaluation. The Jupiters now looked unfamiliar as they were surrounded by circular cowlings which closely shrouded the cylinder heads of the radial engines.

Sidestrand Mark III was used to evaluate the new cowling rings both at Mousehold and Martlesham Heath. When the trials were completed, it returned to Norwich where a further new set of engines was fitted, this time the nine-cylinder air-cooled 555 hp Bristol Pegasus IM 3 radials. In total twenty Sidestrands of various versions were built, some of their number seeing service life whilst others remained as trials aircraft.

CHAPTER FIVE

Fighters and Others

NORWICH had now completed a production run of aircraft for the Royal Air Force, albeit only a small one, but the product was approved by both air and ground crews alike. Mr North, with uncanny foresight, was in 1927 already working on a totally new concept for single-seat fighters. His new aircraft, the P.31 Bittern, incorporated armament installations which were accepted on fighter aircraft only during the Second World War, and then solely by the enemy for its Messerschmitt 210 twin-engined fighter.

The Bittern was unusual in that it was a twin-engined, single-seat fighter, completely new to recognised military thinking. A shoulder-wing monoplane of forty-one foot span, it embodied extremely simple lines. On the leading edge of the mainplane were mounted two 214 hp Armstrong Siddeley Lynx seven cylinder air-cooled radial engines. Beneath each engine was attached the main oleo-pneumatic under-carriage leg giving the usual Norwich wide-track, divided undercarriage. The whole airframe was of typical Boulton and Paul metal construction, fabric covered. The cockpit was high set and the pilot was protected from the air-stream by a small windscreen.

Initial flight trials showed that as a cantilever monoplane the mainplane was too flexible. Major modifications involved wing struts from fuselage to mainplane, but this created additional drag and reduced the performance. Two versions were built: J.7936, in which the engines

The Boulton & Paul P.31 Bittern twin-engined fighter monoplane. This is the first prototype, J.7936, with un-cowled engines mounted on the mainplane leading edge. *B&P*

were mounted as described previously, and J.7937, on which the engines were suspended below the mainplane on the wing bracing struts. Both were classified as Anti-Bomber Formation Fighters and were finished in dark green with blue and red roundels. The under surfaces were night-black with large white serial numbers.

If the concept of this aircraft was unusual, the armament was even more so. Twin Vickers machine guns were mounted on the fuselage sides and were sighted through a ring and bead sight forward of the cockpit. On the second aircraft the guns were changed from Vickers to Lewis machine guns and these were mounted on swivelling babettes on the fuselage sides. In this latter configuration they could be remotely controlled by the pilot and were capable of firing upwards as well as forward. The first prototype arrived at Martlesham Heath during March 1927 and carried out full performance and armament trials, and was followed during April of the next year by its sister aircraft to go through the same procedures. Reports from the A&AEE were favourable although it was considered that the top speed of 145 mph was rather on the slow side. After further trials both Bitterns returned to Mousehold where their flight-log entries gradually became fewer and eventually they were broken up. It is difficult to conceive why such low powered engines were used for this project. A higher top speed would undoubtedly have provided a greater opportunity for landing a Service contract.

During the summer of 1924 Mr Ramsey MacDonald's Labour Government had put out tentative feelers regarding the design and construction of two large experimental rigid airships. The specification laid down the design, dimensions and capability to hold approximately five million cubic feet of hydrogen lifting gas. Tenders for this project were placed with both private and State sponsored organisations. Several of Britain's foremost airship men had been killed in the tragic break-up of the R.38 over the River Humber during 1921 and this left the Government-based party with a less experienced team. Vickers had been the prime design source for several other large rigid airships and were therefore the obvious choice for the private company.

The contracts were placed during November 1924 and the State team took up residence at the Royal Airship Works at Cardington. Because the existing Cardington shed was not large enough, one of the sheds at the Pulham Airship Station in Norfolk was dismantled and transported to the Bedfordshire site where it was re-erected in modified and lengthened form. Vickers were based at Howden in Yorkshire and their team included such famous names as Neville Barnes Wallis and his Chief Calculator, Neville Norway Shute, who is perhaps better known as Neville Shute the novelist.

The tracery of girders in position during the assembly of the R.101 at Cardington. This illustration shows the gigantic dimensions of the machine. *B&P*

Since the R.38 disaster light alloy construction in duralumin had come under critical scrutiny, and it was decided that stainless steel should be specified for the two new ships, now designated R.100 for the private one, and R.101 for the State ship. Owing to their pioneering work in this form of construction Boulton and Paul were approached by the Cardington team. Their Technical Director, Mr North, was asked to design and submit experimental girders of the type that would form the main airframe of the R.101. These were extensively tested by the research staff of the Royal Airship Works who gave their approval on the test pieces. The next phase was the construction of an experimental section of the airship and this in its turn was also subjected to extensive testing. As a result of these successful trials, they were awarded a contract to fabricate the main structure as well as the fins, rudders and elevators—no small project, for the streamlined hull was 731 feet long and the largest circular ring in the hull was 131 feet in diameter. A major difficulty with which they had to contend was the layout of the R.101's hull, the cross-section of which consisted of fifteen sides. Mr North had an extremely able assistant in Mr A.D. Adkin and the two men worked in close co-operation in resolving the many problems as they occurred. Others amongst their staff included Alfred Charlton, who had joined them from Ransome and Rapier of Ipswich as a tool maker, and Mr V.J. Johnston, the Stress Engineer. It is interesting to note that in these early days of aviation research the Boulton and Paul design costs for the R.101 amounted to a mere £7,000.

The Cardington Design Team, headed by Colonel Richmond, produced a design which called for triangular frame longitudinal girders in thin gauge stainless steel up to forty-five feet in length. In all over six miles of tubing of this nature was manufactured for these girders. Many of the massive girders were of complex configuration due to the streamlined form of the hull, and nearly all incorporated compound curvature, but such was the accuracy of the finished product that the airframe components were assembled at Cardington, many miles away, without any difficulty.

The R.101 came to a flaming, fearful end at 02.09 hours on 5th October 1930 when it struck the ground near Beauvais, in Northern France, on its first overseas flight, forty-eight of its complement of fifty-four passengers dying on that wet, windy night. The R.101's demise was not caused by structural failure or fault, and at the subsequent Court of Inquiry Boulton and Paul Limited were completely exonerated from all blame in connection with the tragedy. Captain Paul, because of his firm's involvement, had wished to be aboard for this voyage to India; it was fortunate that no place was available for him.

Mr Alfred Charlton, BEM, with a draw bench, a machine he developed so that it could produce the most intricate metal sections in stainless steel.

B&P

The R.101 comprised over eleven miles of girderwork, had a disposable lift of 61 tons and was powered by diesel engines; the R.100 employed petrol engines. It was estimated that the R.101 would have used diesel fuel for the Indian voyage at a cost of £110, compared to £690 for petrol for the R.100 over same distance. Of the contemplated seven airships only two prototypes were constructed; the remainder were cancelled after the R.101 disaster. One of the few pieces of this tragic craft still in existence, a ten-foot section of a massive girder, is housed in the company museum of Boulton and Paul at Norwich.

Mr Dawson Paul retired in 1927 at the age of 87. He moved to a smaller residence in Bracondale where he lived until his death in 1932. His companion, Henry Fiske, had died the previous year, and Captain Dawson Paul was then in command with William and Geoffrey ffiske as his principal directors. Stanley Howes and John North were the other two members of the Board.

An unusual project was the design and manufacture at the Riverside Works of a suitable body for Malcolm Campbell's Sunbeam racing car. This particular vehicle, a 1922 V12 18 litre monster, already held the World Land Speed Record at the hands of Kenelm Lee Guinness. Campbell purchased the car, and Boulton and Paul by use of their wind tunnel produced a more aerodynamic shape that enabled him to increase the speed substantially to 150.86 mph, along the Pendine Sands in South Wales on 21st July 1926. The car is now at the National Motor Museum, Beaulieu, in Hampshire.

A contract was also received from the Wolseley Car Company to construct and fit bodywork onto one of their chassis. This model was known as the 'Doctor's Landaulette'; apparently they were much favoured by medical gentlemen with country practices.

At this period several aircraft companies had designed and built, at their own expense, fighter aircraft to compete in Air Ministry design competitions. These aircraft were known as Private Venture or PV designs, and although their builders had great hopes, seldom were they fulfilled. Many of these designs ended up as flying test-beds for various power units or ancillary equipment, sometimes even as runabouts for the company test pilots. One such PV design was Boulton and Paul's Partridge. It was hoped to be a leading contender for the next generation of fighting biplanes for the Royal Air Force. Air Ministry Specification F.9/26 called for a single-seat, general purpose fighter, to be powered by either a Bristol Jupiter or Armstrong-Siddeley Jaguar air-cooled radial engine.

The Partridge in its original form was a sleek looking biplane, apart from the location of the undercarriage; this was later modified. When the Partridge was ready for evaluation at Martlesham Heath, a revised specification was received requiring re-positioning of the armament; it was to be located lower in the fuselage than originally specified. To achieve this the sleek fuselage profile had to be altered and bulges were added to house the guns. This spoiled the aircraft's appearance and reduced its performance. Although not apparent, extensive use was made of stock standard sections already in production at Norwich so that the machine could have been built both rapidly and economically.

The P.33 Partridge was Boulton & Paul's second venture into the single engined, single-seat fighter market. *Ian James*

For its day the Partridge embodied the latest technology, and arrived at a time when the Air Ministry had decided that all new designs were to be of metal construction. Only the plywood fairings and fabric covering of the Partridge remained of the old style. The P.33's dead square cut wingtips and tail surfaces prompted wags of the day to remark that the Partridge surfaces could be made by the mile and cut off by the yard! Two prototypes, differing only marginally, were constructed; the first, J.8459, was used for Service Trials, whilst the second was not registered and remained without insignia or serial numbers.

For the Air Ministry competition several interesting designs had emerged: in addition to the Partridge, Hawkers had submitted their Hawfinch, Armstrong-Whitworth, the AW.14 Starling, Glosters, the SS Type 18 (which later entered the RAF as the Gauntlett) and the Bristol Type 105, the Bulldog. The usual military requirements included guns, weighing 550 pounds, ammunition, navigation and night-flying lights, radio and oxygen cylinders. In June 1928 all the contestants gathered at the A&AEE and were put through their trials: performance, armament and ground maintenance. A characteristic which perturbed the Martlesham Heath pilots was the Partridge's touch-down speed of 81 mph, which they considered rather high by the standards of the day. Lack of wheel brakes also lengthened the landing run and added to their concern. Performance was well up to the specification requirements with a top speed of 164 mph at 20,000 feet for an all-up weight of 3,160 pounds. As a fighter, altitude capability was excellent, the ceiling attained being 28,950 feet—2,000 feet better than the nearest contender, the Bulldog. After the initial trials at Martlesham Heath, two of the contestants, the Hawker Hawfinch and the Bristol Bulldog, were selected for further exhaustive testing with service squadrons. Eventually the Bulldog was declared the winner and awarded the production contract. After the results had been announced, J.8459 flew home to Norwich where it languished for some time until it was eventually broken up.

It was a disappointment for the Norwich Design Office because a production run, if only a small one, for the Partridge would have helped the fortunes of the East Anglian company considerably. With the shortfall in military orders other projects were needed to keep the workforce busy. The growing interest in civil flying and the formation of new aero-clubs offered them a new challenge, the design of a light two-seat aircraft for club and training purposes. Carrying the design number P.41, the new aircraft was also called the Phoenix, a name it was hoped would have the desired effect on the company's future.

The P.41 broke with contemporary construction methods for light aircraft, using spot-welding at joints instead of the normal riveting. This resulted in a cheap, quick and very efficient structure. A high parasol wing layout was chosen for the Phoenix as this gave inherent stability and also allowed easy access to the two cockpits. Power was supplied by a 40 hp ABC Scorpion air-cooled engine driving a small wooden propeller, but this was only intended to be a temporary power unit for its initial trials. Squadron Leader Rea who tested the aircraft in July 1929 reported that with pilot, parachute and full tanks the take-off run appeared to be about one hundred yards, the best climbing speed 50 to 52 mph, the top speed level about 70 mph and the best gliding speed 60 mph. The view was good, particularly on the glide, but there was a blind spot upward and forward because the pilot had been raised above the normal position by his parachute.

When the flight trials were almost completed the Phoenix was exhibited at the 1929 Aero Show at Olympia where it gained many an interested inspection. Back in Norwich it underwent modifications and then began a further series of proving trials. When these were finished the aircraft returned to the works where a 40 hp Salmson air-cooled radial engine was installed. On emerging from the Flight Shed again, G-AAIT was re-designated Phoenix Mark II. In this form the P.41 arrived at Martlesham Heath for its certificate of airworthiness during the summer of 1930. Unfortunately the aircraft did not live up to its name, and after a period of hack flying at Mousehold the Phoenix was abandoned and forgotten. It was removed from the Civil Register during 1935 and scrapped.

The two-seat P.41 Phoenix G-AAIT in flight showing the original configuration of undercarriage and wing strutting. *Alan Hague*

In 1929 the Air Ministry Specification B.22/27 called for a three-engined heavy bomber, and there were two contenders, Boulton and Paul with the P.32, J.9950, and De Havilland with their DH.72 Canberra, J.9184. Both aircraft bore a marked resemblance to each other as both were three bay biplanes with twin-finned tailplanes and double undercarriages. What was more remarkable was that both were powered by Bristol Jupiter radial engines fitted in the same positions, one on each lower mainplane, and the third mounted in the centre of the upper mainplane.

Side view of the P.32 shows its large proportions, heavy wing aerofoil section and the elaborate undercarriage strutting.   *B&P*

The P.32 was of large proportions and conventional lines, except for the disposition of the engines. The crew numbered five, but provision was made for a sixth member should the occasion arise. The pilot was to be accommodated in the main cockpit on the port side, whilst seated down within the front fuselage the navigator, who was also the bomb aimer, was equipped with a course-setting bombsight. His navigational equipment comprised a chart table, navigation instruments and a swivelling chair. Further aft, in the centre section, the wireless operator was situated in the noisiest part of the aircraft, directly under the centre engine! Front, dorsal and rear gunners were equipped with Scarff ring mounted Lewis guns. A walking tunnel which ran the length of the fuselage allowed communication between all the gun positions. Last but not least a toilet of a rather primitive nature was provided. Bomber by designation, the P.32 was capable of lifting four 500 pound and six 250 pound bombs under the fuselage and a further six 120 pound bombs, three under each lower mainplane.

Both the P.32 and the DH.72 suffered delays due to non-delivery of the engines from Bristols whose Mercury V engines were to be installed. As this type was still at development stage the Bristol Jupiter XF was used until the Mercury V became available. The P.32 also went through a period of officially requested modifications which put back the agreed delivery date from 31st March 1929 to 1st January 1930. However it was not until the 23rd October 1931 that it made its first flight. For the A&AEE trials at Martlesham Heath in February 1933 the engines were changed once again to Bristol Jupiter XFBM radials, but the Authorities appeared to have lost interest in both these aircraft and they were finally broken up and disappeared from the aviation scene.

On 25th February 1927 Mousehold Heath saw the arrival of the Norfolk and Norwich Aero Club, and civilian flying joined the test flying activities. The following day Sir Alan Cobham brought his De Havilland Giant Moth, G-ADEV, 'Youth of Aviation', and this was followed some time afterwards by Captain Barnard's Flying Circus. Also to put in an appearance was the Fokker F.VII, G-EBTA, named The Spider, in which the Duchess of Bedford made a record flight from Croydon to Karachi during August 1929 before she was tragically lost over the Wash. Large crowds visited the airfield on Whit Monday 1929 to see the Alan Cobham Air Circus, and many experienced flight for the first time in a short joy-flight. One of the visitors was the three-engined Beardmore Inflexible experimental all-metal bomber, considered enormous at that time, which had flown over from Martlesham Heath. Others included Miss Amy Johnson with her De Havilland Moth Jason II on 17th March 1931.

During 1932 the Norwich City Council, assisted by the Air Ministry, purchased Mousehold Aerodrome and developed it into Norwich Airport. The airfield surface was fully grassed with four landing strips in use: north to south 900 yards, north-east to south-west 1,200 yards, east to west 1,000 yards and south-east to north-west 1,000 yards. A small airline, Crilly Airways, operated by Mr Leo Crilly, ran daily services to Liverpool, Nottingham, Northampton, Leicester and Bristol. An aerial photography service was also available as well as gliding facilities. The airport was opened on 21st June 1933 by HRH The Prince of Wales who arrived in his De Havilland Dragon G-ACGG. Aircraft present on that occasion were a line-up of the locally made Sidestrands and the one and only Fairey Long Range Monoplane which flew over from Cranwell.

The Bugle, a P.9 owned by Boulton and Paul, De Havilland Gipsy Moths and an Avro 504 seen at Mousehold Heath at the formation of the Norfolk and Norwich Aero Club on 25th February 1927.
Norwich Union

The continuing slump throughout the world forced the Board of Directors of Boulton and Paul to undertake a major re-organisation. After rationalisation only four departments remained: Structural Steel, Aircraft, Woodworking and Wire Weaving. In 1935 Captain Paul relinquished chairmanship of the company and he was superseded by a Norwich business man, Mr Richard Jewson, JP. A few months later Paul retired altogether, thus breaking the long connection of the Paul family with the Norwich company. As the economic climate improved there was a call for all types of wooden buildings from sheds to large prefabricated structures; also for steel clear-span buildings including hangars and workshops. The future looked a little brighter!

With the advance of air travel the movement of the Royal Mail was under review. In order to provide a suitable aircraft for carrying mail, the Air Ministry issued a specification, No 21/28. This demanded the capability of flying one thousand miles non-stop at 150 mph with one thousand pounds of mail. This performance also had to be achieved on one engine running at less than normal rpm. In addition the aircraft was to be capable of being fitted with floats. During this period Guy ffiske, who was the London office manager, died after a short illness and his position was taken by Major Jack Stewart, OBE. One of his first duties was to complete the contract order details for the Air Ministry mailplane.

Avros submitted their single-engined Type 627, Blackburn a twin-engined design and Norwich their design No P.64, a shapely twin-engined biplane. The aircraft, with its airframe constructed in the well-established Boulton and Paul high tensile stainless steel, emerged from the works in March 1933. It was unusual in that although designed to an Air Ministry contract, the aircraft was to be used for civil purposes. Successful against the competition Boulton and Paul won the contract for the P.64 and had the aircraft flying for the first time just thirteen months later.

North and his design team had made full use of the wind-tunnel in order to create the cleanest possible profile. Although of comparatively simple layout, this machine was distinctive for its uncluttered lines. A rounded nose was shaped into the high-set cabin for pilot and co-pilot and the squarish fuselage then tapered down to a somewhat un-Boulton and Paul mono fin, rudder and square tailplane. The pilot's cabin was totally enclosed with dual control and a navigating compartment behind it which allowed room for a chart table and instruments. Large hatches were incorporated in the fuselage sides for the easy stowage of mail. Plans were in hand for the mail to be picked up and dropped by the aircraft whilst in flight. A hook device would snatch the loaded bags from their perch and a hatch would allow mail to be dropped when required. This was similar to the railways' established practice, in use for several decades. Two 565 hp Bristol Pegasus IM2 nine cylinder air-cooled radial engines were mounted on the leading edge of the upper mainplane and drove large two-bladed propellers. Struts ran down to brace the wide track undercarriage which was unusual in that the main wheels were partially enclosed in large streamlined spats. The high mounted power units allowed the P.64 to sit close to the ground, a great advantage for loading and unloading purposes.

Initial ground and flying trials had been conducted at Mousehold. An accident occurred on the second flight due to brake failure, and the P.64 was slightly damaged when it ran into the aerodrome boundary fence. It was soon repaired and flown to Martlesham Heath for official trials. The author recalls paying a Saturday morning visit to 'The Camp' (the local name for Martlesham Heath) on 21st October 1933. The P.64 on one of its test flights was approaching from the west and gradually losing height as it came in to land; the big propellers could be seen slowly turning as the engines were throttled back. Suddenly and for no

The wind tunnel or channel constructed at Norwich to prove design features on aircraft, using models. *B&P*

apparent reason, it turned and dived, recovered and then turned again and dived into the rough heathland. The aircraft crumpled up and the pilot, Flight Lieutenant G.L.G. Richmond of the A&AEE's Performance Testing Squadron, was flung from the cockpit. Fortunately no fire resulted and the once shapely biplane lay in a tangled mass. The pilot, although badly injured, survived. The remains of the P.64 were carefully picked up over the next few days and carried back across the heath for examination by the A&AEE staff. Up to the time of the accident there was no reason to suppose that the verdict of the test pilots would be other than favourable. This was the end of the P.64 and although a passenger version was planned this was also abandoned.

The P.64 Mail Carrier G-ABYK in original configuration. It shows clean lines with high mounted engines and wide track spatted undercarriage.   *Ian James*

The year 1934 was a milestone in the company's history. On the 30th June the aircraft side of Boulton and Paul Limited was hived off to a new public company which had been formed, Boulton-Paul Aircraft Limited.

Also incorporated into the new company was part of Aircraft Technical Services Limited which had been created in 1931. The initial Board of Directors included the Right Honourable Lord Gorell, CBE, MC, MA, as Chairman, the Right Honourable Viscount Sandon, DL, JP, and as Joint Managing Directors, J.D. North and S.W. Hiscocks. Initial share capital was £300,000 but it was raised to £500,000 two years later. A decision was taken to move out of the increasingly cramped premises at Norwich and after full consideration Wolverhampton, in the West Midlands, was chosen as a suitable site. There were various inducements: the erection of a new factory, an abundance of skilled labour, a new airfield to be built adjacent to the factory and help from Wolverhampton Corporation. Plans were drawn up for the new establishment and arrangements made for the gradual transfer of aircraft activities from Norwich to Wolverhampton.

Boulton & Paul P.71A 'Boadicea', G-ACOX, in airline service with Imperial Airways. 'Boadicea' was lost in the English Channel on 25th September 1936.

British Airways

In the meantime work continued on two new aircraft. Imperial Airways, then the national airline, required medium sized, fast feeder liners. Not displeased with the P.64's performance, they approached Boulton and Paul to produce two aircraft. The new design evolved using the basic concept of the Mail Carrier. With a wing span one and a half inches more than its predecessor and a twenty-eight inch extension to the fuselage, the new P.71A looked very similar to the P.64 except for the power units and the tailplane. The Bristol radials were replaced by less powerful 460 hp Armstrong Siddeley Jaguar VIA air-cooled radials. Although fourteen cylinder engines, they were of smaller diameter than the nine cylinder Bristols, and once again they turned large two-bladed propellers. Choice of engines had been dictated by Imperial Airways because they had a number of Jaguar engines in stock left over from their recently redundant Armstrong Whitworth Argosy airliners. Fuselage modifications included accommodation for seven passengers up to the standard of comfort provided in larger airliners. In order to accomplish noise reduction, the cabin sides were covered with corrugated sheet metal, and four square windows were located in each side of the fuselage. Finished in all-over aluminium, the two aircraft were registered G-ACOX on 19th September 1934 and G-ACOY on 14th October 1934. They were named Boadicea and Britomart respectively. Boadicea arrived at the A&AEE for Certificate of Airworthiness trials which were successfully carried out and the two feeder liners went to Imperial Airways for service on the Croydon to the Continent runs. The two new aircraft were not popular with their crews. In service they were found to be slower than the P.64 and not capable of their specified range. Their lives were short: Britomart was damaged beyond repair when it crashed on 25th October 1935 at Brussels; Boadicea was relegated to mail carrying duties after this incident. On 25th September 1936 it disappeared over the English Channel and although the body of Captain A.C. Thomas, the pilot, was washed ashore a month later on the Belgian coast, very little wreckage was ever recovered. Thus ended another venture into the civil aircraft market.

The pioneer work involved with high-tensile stainless steel resulted in subcontract orders from other aircraft manufacturers. The Blackburn Aircraft Company had designed an all-metal two-seat light bi-plane with which it hoped to compete with the popular De Havilland Moth in the club aircraft market. They subcontracted the wing spars for the B.2 to the Norwich works. Later the wing components for the Blackburn Shark torpedo bomber which was being built for the Fleet Air Arm were also made at Norwich. Even larger were the mainplanes for the Saro London twin-engined patrol flying boat, the subject of another contract.

One of the last Boulton and Paul, Norwich, aircraft, the P.75, was in its final design stage, but unlike so many recent prototypes this machine was not a completely new design. Retaining the lines which had originated with the Bourges, the Norwich team continued to develop the very manoeuvrable, twin-engined biplane medium bomber. Although only serving with the Royal Air Force in small numbers, the Sidestrand had gained a reputation for its many qualities both in the air and on the ground. Sidestrand III, J.9186, was withdrawn from service and sent back to the Norwich works for rebuilding to Specification 29/33.

At this time a great deal of thought was being given to the protection of air gunners from the growing force of the airstream as aircraft speeds increased. Experiments were made with various types of shields, mainly in two seat aircraft such as the Hawker Demon, but so often it was found difficult to aim the gun. Also, in spite of protective clothing, the cold penetrated to the gunners' fingers, causing a slower reaction. The protective clothing was also cumbersome and restricted the gunners' movements.

As far back as 13th August 1932 Boulton and Paul had been contracted by the Air Ministry to devise a means of protecting air gunners in exposed cockpits. The Sidestrand was to be the vehicle for this work, but after a few months the Norwich team came to the conclusion that it was impossible, with current gun-mountings and a protection shield, to retain full control and arc of fire. A totally enclosed position seemed to be the only solution. Surprisingly enough the Air Ministry showed enthusiasm for such a device and the company was encouraged to proceed with the design of such an enclosed gun position, or turret as it was to be known. A design emerged, innovative for its day, incorporating pneumatic power for traverse, manual elevation and an ingenious hydraulic balancing for the seat and guns. A working mock-up was built in the Design Department and was accepted by the Air Ministry for fitting to a Sidestrand by June 1933.

After these modifications J.9186 reappeared, still recognisable as a Boulton and Paul design but with several interesting and quite new features. Still a three-seat medium bomber, named Sidestrand V, P.75, it had been re-engined with 555 hp Bristol Pegasus IM3 radials enclosed in polygonal cowlings, with exhaust collectors on their leading edges. These were beneficial for night operations as they reduced the exhaust flame glow as well as keeping the noise down. The strengthening of the original airframe had increased its weight but did allow a greater bomb load to be carried. These greater stresses called for a re-design of the main undercarriage, and the single oleo-pneumatic leg was replaced by a leg of more robust design. A tailwheel on a similar mounting replaced the

Unique in its conception, the new Boulton & Paul front gun turret was installed in the P.75 Overstrand. *John Chambers*

steerable tailskid. Within the fuselage attention had been paid to the comfort of the crew who now had heating ducts which directed warm air from the engine heaters to their hitherto chilled limbs. The pilot was protected by a fully glazed hood, sliding rearwards on rails, and this gave good all-round vision. Within the confines of 'the office' an automatic pilot had been fitted. The dorsal gunner had not been forgotten as a large windshield protected his position, and some modifications had been made to the ventral position as well. The star attraction was a totally enclosed gunner's turret situated at the front of the fuselage. Basically a vertical cylinder, domed top and bottom, it was almost entirely glazed. A bearing fitted to a projecting structural member below the forward fuselage carried the turret whilst a large roller bearing comprised the top fixing.

Armament in the form of a single 0.303 inch Lewis gun was carried on a pivoted bracket with the weapon's barrel protruding out from the turret in a vertical slot which ran the whole height of the turret. An ingenious sealing device shrouded the gun barrel as it moved up and down the slot and this eliminated a great deal of the airflow entering the turret. The gunner sat behind his weapon on a seat which was supported by a hydraulic jack, and two other small jacks were coupled to the elevating gun arm. Variations in the weight of individual gunners was dealt with by adjustment of the leverage of the jacks linked to the gun-arm. This resulted in an accurate balance between the gunner and his weapon. Rotation was effected by a reversible pneumatic motor geared to the turret base. This motor was driven by compressed air at 120 pounds per square inch which was stored in a set of cylinders under the cockpit. The cylinders were topped up by a compressor mounted on one of the Pegasus engines. Even if the engine failed the cylinder storage capacity enabled the turret to be rotated approximately twenty times before the air supply was exhausted. Low down in the front of the turret, offset to port, was an optical flat bomb aimer's panel; when this was in operation, the turret was locked in the mid-position. Bomb sighting gear rotated with the turret and warm air ducting was fitted for the gunner's comfort. Bomb carrying capacity was increased, with two 500 pound bombs stowed under the centre fuselage and two 250 pounders on external racks.

During 1933 the Sidestrand V made its maiden flight from Mousehold and after some minor adjustments and modifications J.9186 was despatched to the A&AEE for performance and armament testing. In March 1934, after evaluation, Martlesham Heath issued their usual report. Although the test pilots praised the performance of the aircraft, there were reservations concerning engine vibration and longitudinal control. The Armament Squadron found the dimensions of the turret too confining for most gunners but they were unanimous in their praise of the additional comfort afforded by the 'greenhouse'. Like so many aircraft both before and after the Sidestrand V, the Royal Air Force immediately gave it a nickname, The Bandstand.

At the Fifteenth Royal Air Force Display held on 30th June 1934 at Hendon aerodrome, J.9186, now revealed as being the prototype Overstrand and based at Martlesham Heath, was programmed as Event F and timed at 14.10 pm. This event was a display of aerial combat between the bomber, flown by Flight Lieutenant A.V.M. Odbert, and three Bristol Bulldog fighters from No 29 Squadron. The Overstrand gave an extremely spirited performance and throughout this event was able to out-manoeuvre its attackers.

Boulton-Paul, now using the new style of name, heeded A&AEE's recommendations and Sidestrand III, L.9770, on Air Ministry instructions, was modified to incorporate a wider front fuselage and a turret of larger dimensions. Engine power was increased by installing Bristol Pegasus IIM3 radials of 580 hp which turned four-bladed propellers. Other modifications included the simplification of the complicated pipework layout behind the engine, and a retractable platform to ease the servicing of the air compressor. After initial trials at Mousehold, J.9770 returned to Martlesham Heath during November 1935. Evaluation trials for both performance and armament were carried out by the two Martlesham Heath Testing Squadrons and a series of diving trials were undertaken by the Performance Testing Squadron to study vibration. During one such dive the leading edge of the fin collapsed but without dire results as the aircraft was able to make a normal landing.

The Air Ministry issued Specification B.23/24 for a contract for twenty-four production version Overstrands; these were constructed at Norwich, the last aircraft to be made there. Like their sister Sidestrands, the Overstrands entered RAF service with No 101(B) Squadron on 24th January 1935 where they were immediately well received. The first machine delivered was J.9185, a converted Sidestrand, and the second, J.9179, was received on 26th February 1935. The first true-built Overstrand, K.4546, was accepted during early 1936 and the type stayed with No 101 Squadron until 1937, when it was replaced by the new monoplane three-seat medium bomber, the Bristol Blenheim.

Popular with air and ground crews alike, the Overstrand was an excellent bombing platform and in bombing trials results surpassed anything achieved previously. Both the Sidestrand and Overstrand inherited the agile manoeuvrability of the Bourges and were able to out-fly many fighters. In squadron service the Overstrand's turret was an immediate success; not only did it achieve all aspects of the contract but gunners, who hitherto were accepting fifteen per cent hits as normal, were now clocking up a startling seventy-five per cent.

Success in this field prompted the Norwich company to delve further into turret design and at the same time consolidate the business side of this innovation. Applying for patents in 1934 they were disappointed to find their application turned down. The basic turret design was taken over by the Government for inclusion within the Secrets List. This news was received with dismay at Norwich, for Boulton and Paul regarded

Sidestrand III J.9186 converted to Overstrand configuration with forward turret, enclosed cockpit, revised undercarriage and Townend ring-cowled engines. *B&P*

international patent agreements as an important facet of their business. However, a few months later when details of the Overstrand's turret were published in an aeronautical magazine, a reply to the article was received from a French source. This contained a design for an hydraulically operated turret, as opposed to the British pneumatically actuated model, which embodied light structural weight but was limited in performance by its power ratios.

In 1936 J.9770 was again employed in an experimental role, this time to be partnered by the Vickers B.19/27, Type 255, J.9131, sometimes known as the Vannock II, in air to air refuelling trials at the Royal Aircraft Establishment, Farnborough. It was thought that if the outcome of this experiment was successful it could be employed by Imperial Airways in their longer overseas routes. On 31st August 1937, J.9770 and J.9131 gave a demonstration at Farnborough to high ranking officials, and later the two aircraft were transferred, as a result of a renewed contract, to Ford aerodrome in Sussex. Flight Refuelling Limited were instrumental in advancing this important work which ultimately led to the refined systems now used as everyday procedures by the Royal Air Force and other air forces throughout the world.

When in due course the Blenheim replaced the Overstrand in squadron service, the latter operated as gunnery trainers, carrying out this important duty until 1941 when they were finally withdrawn. Still maintaining the established biplane design, the Norwich Design Office worked on a successor to the Overstrand to be known as the Superstrand. Fitted with 720 hp Bristol Pegasus IV engines, it would have had a retractable undercarriage and was expected to have a top speed of 190 mph. However, the days of the biplane bomber were over and the project was abandoned.

Norwich-built bomber twins the Overstrand and Sidestrand show their similarity of design and difference in armament. *B&P*

CHAPTER SIX

Pastures New

WHEN BOULTON-PAUL Aircraft Limited took over the aircraft business of the parent company, Boulton and Paul Limited, it was clearly set forth in the prospectus that the business would be moved to the Midlands. Nevertheless the announcement that the company was due to move to Wolverhampton was greeted with dismay in Norwich. For some years the number of men engaged in aircraft construction in the Norfolk city had numbered only a few hundred, but in the early months of 1935 the effect of the Government Aircraft Expansion Scheme had brought immediate benefit to local industries. Several hundred additional skilled mechanics and operators were provided with employment as well as a proportionate number of unskilled and semi-skilled workers. However as all local supplies of suitably skilled personnel had been rapidly exhausted, it was necessary to carry out an extensive search for the right type of worker throughout all parts of England. In the main these were in the north-eastern and north-western counties. It was for this reason, amongst others, that Wolverhampton with its abundant supply of engineering labour proved an attractive proposition.

A plan for the erection of an aircraft factory was submitted by the company to the local council in July 1935. The proposed buildings included hangars, workshops, canteen and offices. The land belonged to Wolverhampton Corporation and lay between the canal and the River Penke adjoining Pendeford Lane, near the site already proposed as an aerodrome. From the plans prepared by Messrs W. Stanley Hattrell and Percy S. Wortley, chartered architects of Coventry, work commenced on the factory at Barnhurst in October that year. The cost was estimated to be around £60,000 and included the erection of a main block covering a floor space of 170,000 square feet. The general building contract was carried out by Wilson Lovatt and Sons of Wolverhampton, and because of the nature of the land—it had previously been used as a sewage farm—a considerable piling operation was necessary. Although local contractors constructed the factory, the light steelwork came from Boulton and Paul in Norwich who were responsible for much of the roof structure. The large hangar doors also came from the same source.

The factory was not completed until December 1936 but was increasingly operative from June that year. By August two hundred families were arriving from Norwich and were settling into vacant houses throughout Wolverhampton and its neighbourhood. They brought with them furniture and all their belongings, including cats and dogs. In due course it was intended that they should all move to new homes closer to the factory, but the houses did not materialise until some forty years later. There was also considerable recruitment of local labour; men and women trekked there on foot and on bicycle in the hope of finding employment. Very soon the factory had its full complement of staff. John North and S. Hiscocks were originally Joint Managing Directors, with H.V. Clarke as Chief Designer.

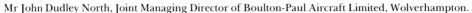

Mr John Dudley North, Joint Managing Director of Boulton-Paul Aircraft Limited, Wolverhampton.

One of the members of staff who decided not to move to the Midlands was Squadron Leader Rea. He left the new company and founded his own business at Mousehold, occupying the same sheds in which the Sidestrands and Overstrands had been constructed. Eventually he bought all the surrounding buildings together with fifteen acres of land and started the manufacture of seaplane floats and other aeronautical components. He had many happy memories of his years with Boulton and Paul and the various personalities with whom he was in regular contact: Doc, or Digger, Odgers, the company metallurgist; the Works Manager, Major Noble; J.B. Purefoy, who later started his own company along with other Norwich personnel; H.A. Hughes, who lost his life when returning from America during the Second World War; W.J. Pickthorn, responsible for publicity; Mr Freeman, involved with the wind tunnel; Mr Williams, the Drawing Office chief; and Mr Clarke, who dealt with cockpit layout. His position as test pilot was taken by Flight Lieutenant Cecil Feather—nicknamed Fluffy—who had been commissioned into the Royal Air Force in March 1924 and who after service overseas had been posted to No 15 Squadron at Martlesham Heath as a test pilot in the Armament Testing Flight.

As with any re-location there were a number of teething troubles. It was several months before the canteen was completed and fitted out, and the nearest shops were at Bilbrook, some distance away. Transport to the factory from the eastern side could only approach through a narrow cart-track. Buses from Wolverhampton were therefore routed from the western end; unhappily there was an unpassable bridge which required the passengers to disembark and walk for some minutes to their destination—in all weathers. Concerted demand ensured the replacement of this bridge so that buses could travel to the factory gates. In early 1937 there was a strike on the factory floor which revolved around the debt system employed by the company. This system was based upon a piece-work bonus given when jobs were completed ahead of schedule but which became a debt when they fell behind. Anyone regularly accumulating a debt was liable for dismissal. After negotiation the management withdrew the system for what was regarded as a fairer method of payment.

All in all the company had settled down remarkably well in their new surroundings, particularly as many of the employees had needed special training to adapt to the high standard of workmanship required. Within a year of arrival the volume of orders had increased so much that a massive extension to the works was under construction.

In Norwich delivery of the remaining Overstrands to the RAF had yet to be completed whilst in Wolverhampton the work in hand was mainly under subcontract. The Saro London mainplanes were constructed from stainless steel and when finished despatched by road to Southampton. After shipping by ferry to East Cowes they were covered by fabric at the Saunders-Roe factory. These mainplanes spanned eighty feet and the first consignment met with disaster whilst in transit and were returned to Wolverhampton for extensive repairs. The Saro London served from 1936 until 1941 when it was superseded by the Catalina.

Twin-engined patrol flying boat, the Saro London, which embodied Boulton & Paul manufactured mainplanes and Townend ring engine cowlings. *Westland A/C*

The largest order however was for the production of the Hawker Demon, a fighter which had been evolved from the highly successful Hawker Hart day bomber serving with the Royal Air Force. As the contract had been negotiated with Hawker Aircraft of Kingston on Thames shortly before the company's arrival in Wolverhampton, the Demons were the first aircraft to emerge from the new production line. The batches were fifty-nine aircraft K.5683–K.5741, ten machines K.5898–K.5907 and thirty-seven aircraft K.8181–K.8217, one hundred and six machines in total. The parent company had built 128 Demons at its own factory but during May 1935 production was transferred to Wolverhampton where it continued until December 1937. In all 234 Demons were built for the RAF, who used them until they were superseded by the Bristol Blenheim.

Hawker Demon two-seat fighter biplanes built by Boulton-Paul Aircraft under contract stand outside the Pendeford Flight Shed. *B&P*

An unequal span two-seat biplane with a swept back upper mainplane, the Demon was a shapely aircraft with the good looks of its forebear, the Hart. These aircraft were of all-metal construction and fabric covered, techniques in manufacture with which Boulton-Paul were well acquainted. In the large Cover and Dope Shop the workers, mainly women, stretched the fabric covering on the Demon components before its initial painting with the red acetate shrinking dope and its final coat of aluminium dope. To supervise the installation of the Rolls-Royce Kestrel engines, the engine manufacturers appointed Jack Hart as Resident Representative at Boulton-Paul Aircraft. Originally armed with twin Vickers guns firing forward through the airscrew, and one Lewis gun in the rear cockpit, from October 1936 all Boulton-Paul Demons were fitted with a Frazer-Nash shielded gunner's turret, known as the 'Lobster-Back'. This was ironic because the company was already developing its own turret, a much more sophisticated product altogether. The first Wolverhampton built Demon, K.5683, made its maiden flight on 21st August 1936, just thirteen days after the main workforce had moved to the factory. At the controls was the new Chief Test Pilot, Flight Lieutenant Cecil Feather. He was later joined by an Assistant Test Pilot, George Skelton, who had been born in Australia, taught to fly in South Africa and commissioned into the Royal Air Force during 1930. He served with No 32 Squadron, flying Bristol Bulldogs at Kenley, and was later posted to No 30(B) Squadron in Iraq. Upon his return to England he transferred to the A&AEE at Martlesham Heath as a test pilot. Owing to his experience with the Defiant, he was recalled by the RAF from Boulton-Paul in 1940 and posted to No 264 Squadron, which was equipped with that aircraft. Shot down over Holland on the 13th May of that year, he was badly wounded, made a prisoner of war and spent much of his captivity in hospital. He was repatriated through neutral Sweden during 1943. After the war he was granted a permanent commission and finally retired with the rank of Air Commodore.

The Frazer-Nash 'Lobster-Back' gunner's shield fitted to the Hawker Demon two-seat fighter to protect the gunner from the slipstream.

Aircraft were not new to the Wolverhampton area: the Midland Aero Club had staged a flying display as early as July 1910 at Dunstall Park. The new flying machines had attracted huge crowds and there had been demonstrations by several well-known aviators including Claude Grahame-White in his Farman biplane. During the ensuing years other flying shows, such as Alan Cobham's Flying Circus, had visited the district.

However, during the 1930s, Wolverhampton had decided to establish a permanent centre of aviation at Pendeford. The new airport covered an area of nearly ninety acres and runways of over eight hundred yards ran in each direction. Buildings comprised a large main entrance, hall, lounge, dining room, kitchen and bar. The first floor contained the Control Room and offices, and the whole complex was managed by the Midland Aero Club who also provided facilities for flying tuition.

In order to encourage local interest in aviation the *Wolverhampton Express and Star* had presented a Wicko monoplane to the Midland Aero Club. Named Wulfrun II, it replaced a De Havilland Moth given by the same newspaper in 1928. The club in return agreed to train four pilots. These scholarships provided a full course of aeronautical training to the 'A' Certificate level.

The Wolverhampton Municipal Airport was not officially opened until 25th June 1938 but Boulton-Paul had been using the airfield for flying off and landing their own production aircraft from a much earlier date. The grand opening by Flying Officer A.E. Clouston, then Cape Record Holder, included displays by a lady parachutist, who nearly landed in the canal, inverted flying by Mr Thorne of Avro and a mock air-raid carried out by a flight of RAF Gloster Gauntletts of No 46 Squadron. Also represented was the new twin-engined Bristol Blenheim, a Fairey Battle light bomber, an Armstrong Whitworth Whitley heavy bomber and Amy Johnson in a Kirby Kite sailplane.

The new Flight Shed at Pendeford with Norwich-built Overstrand K.8175 standing on the threshold. Designed and fabricated at Norwich, both the hangar and the aircraft had now moved to their new home in the West Midlands.   *B&P*

CHAPTER SEVEN

Turret Fighters

UPON COMPLETION of the Hawker Demon order another contract was undertaken at the Wolverhampton factory, this time for Blackburn Aircraft Limited of Brough, East Yorkshire. Blackburn had designed a two-seat dive-bomber for the Fleet Air Arm, the Skua, and at this time were fully involved in the production of this aircraft. However the Fleet Air Arm was badly in need of a carrier-borne fighter to replace their ageing Hawker Nimrod single-seat fighter biplane, the Navy's standard fighter. The Skua was envisaged as the basis for the proposed new fighter. It was to incorporate the very new Boulton-Paul four-gun turret that was being developed for that company's P.82 turret fighter. This was to be an entirely new concept, the world's first deck-landing naval aircraft to be equipped with a multi-gun turret. Boulton-Paul Aircraft received a contract on 28th April 1937 to produce 136 of these machines to Specification 0.15/37, later amended to 0.30/35. Named Roc, the aircraft were to be serialled L.3057–L.3192.

Not an easy aircraft to produce, the Roc had a fuselage of Alclad watertight sections. For a maritime aircraft this would provide buoyancy should it be forced down onto the water. Both the Skua and the Roc looked very much alike, although the latter's centre fuselage had of necessity to be re-designed to accommodate the turret. The modification work for this re-design was carried out in the Wolverhampton Drawing Office. Both machines were low wing monoplanes but differed in that the Skua had upturned wing tips, whereas the Roc incorporated increased spanwise dihedral.

Following the 1938 Munich crisis tremendous efforts were being made by British industry during this uneasy period to improve the RAF's stock of front line aircraft. The new expansion scheme aircraft— Blenheim, Wellesley, Wellington, Battle, Lysander, Whitley, Hampden, Hurricane and Spitfire—were beginning to join the production lines in increasing numbers.

Aerodromes to accommodate them were being hastily constructed, mainly in the Eastern Counties, the new buildings and aircraft appearing in drab camouflage colours. The situation certainly looked grim!

Although located in the West Midlands in what was then regarded as a safe area, the new factory was given the full camouflage treatment.

Gangs of men clambered over the roofs and scaled the walls applying green and brown paint to blend the outline of the factory into that of the surrounding countryside.

The prototype Roc flew for the first time from its parent's airfield at Brough on 23rd December 1938, and after trials L.3057 was flown to the A&AEE at Martlesham Heath for evaluation during March 1939. It was joined there by the next two aircraft so that the A&AEE's policy of simultaneous handling and armament trials could be carried out.

Performance was not up to expectation: the turret caused considerable drag and the Bristol Perseus XII sleeve valve, air-cooled radial engine of 905 hp could only attain 223 mph at 10,000 feet. A cruising speed of 138 mph, a ceiling of 18,000 feet and a range of 810 miles was not sufficient should it be called upon to intercept the new bomber aircraft coming into service on the continent of Europe. Martlesham Heath reported that aerodynamically the Roc was good, for with the use of dive-brakes it could be held steady in a steep dive, a characteristic it had inherited from the Skua. Recommendations caused the makers to fit a larger airscrew as well as several drag reducing modifications, but these proved to be of little assistance to the general performance. Turret modifications, wing folding gear and additional equipment had also increased the total weight to 7,950 pounds. After the A&AEE tests the Roc was passed to the Fleet Air Arm for familiarisation trials. The first four production aircraft were sent to No 806 Squadron at Eastleigh during February 1940, whilst six more went to No 801 Squadron based in the Orkneys.

Completed Blackburn Roc two-seat naval fighters outside the now camouflaged Flight Shed.

Ian James

Blackburn Roc production showing the crowded assembly area involving fuselages, mainplanes and tail units. *BPA*

Its days as an operational fighter were numbered however, and after only four months, during June 1940, No 2 Anti-Aircraft Co-operation Unit at Gosport took charge of sixteen Rocs to replace its ageing Blackburn Shark target tugs.

Squadron Leader D.H. Clarke recalled,

As far as I am aware I flew the very first RAF Air Sea Rescue patrol in Roc L.3131 on 8th August, 1940. This operation was to rescue survivors of the ill-fated C.W.9 convoy which had been severely dive-bombed off St Catherine's Point, Isle of Wight. In conjunction with corvette T.68 I was responsible for the rescue of one German pilot from the sea, one sailor on a raft, and an RAF launch with eight injured on board.

On 26th September 1940, in Roc L.3085, I engaged a Heinkel He.59 twin-engined biplane floatplane about ten miles south of St Catherine's Point when I was searching for British pilots in 'the drink'. The pilot was obviously looking for German pilots who had been shot down in the aerial battles of that afternoon. As far as I am aware, this was the first ever air combat between two opposing Air Sea Rescue aircraft.

I flew a total of 117 hours in the Blackburn Roc. It had the enormous advantage of dive brakes, and these saved my life on several occasions. At these times I was unarmed, no guns in the turret, and was attacked by an assortment of German aircraft. It was then brakes down, dive vertically—yes, ninety degrees was essential—to three hundred feet before pulling out.

Early during the Roc's career four machines had been fitted with twin floats borrowed from the same maker's Shark floatplanes. The first, L.3059, began trials at the Marine Aircraft Experimental Establishment's wartime home at Helensburgh on the River Clyde, having moved to Scotland from Felixstowe at the outbreak of hostilities. Fast running water trials gave an early indication of directional instability and this culminated in the aircraft crashing on take-off on 3rd December 1939. Trials continued with L.3057 with an extra fin fitted beneath the rear fuselage, thus increasing the stability considerably. In this condition the aircraft was cleared for service but pilots were warned against making banked turns at low altitude as the machine had a tendency to drop into the turn. Speed as a seaplane was reduced to 178 mph at six thousand feet and the whole concept was then abandoned.

The Rocs had found their way to many stations in the United Kingdom and some even served with the Fleet Air Arm in Bermuda, all shore based. The last two Rocs were withdrawn from service during August 1943; none was ever employed on carrier duties. The aircraft spanned 46 feet, was 35 ft 7 in. long and 12 ft 1 in. high. Operational maximum speed was 196 mph at 6,500 feet and a ceiling of 15,200 feet was obtained, but the range had fallen to 610 miles. Armament was four 0.303 inch Browning machine guns in the Boulton-Paul powered turret, but no forward armament was carried. Boulton-Paul Aircraft were contracted to produce 136 Rocs but only 105 were delivered to the services.

The Boulton-Paul P.82 turret fighter design stemmed from problems which had been encountered by the Royal Air Force during operational exercises with fighters. The gun mountings employed on 1930s aircraft had originated during the First World War and were not capable of efficient operation at ever increasing speeds. This shortcoming became more and more apparent in successive yearly air exercises. Gunners in both multi-seat fighters and bombers had been in open, wind-swept gun positions. The exception was the Overstrand with its somewhat primitive turret in the front gunner's position. Swinging guns into a firing position, let alone aligning them onto a target, with near-frozen fingers was becoming well nigh impossible. At 150 mph the windstream made changing an ammunition drum of the Lewis gun difficult and in certain attitudes it was not unknown for the drum to be whipped out of the gunner's hand and lost overboard.

Frazer-Nash had designed a folding 'lobster-back' type of protective shield for the gunner, as had been fitted to the Hawker Demon. Whilst affording protection to the gunner, it did not obviate the sighting problems. The gun barrels still protruded into the slipstream, and they still had to be manhandled.

The Bristol Aeroplane Company had also been working upon the protection of the wind-swept gunner, and when their Type 120 two-seat biplane appeared during January 1932, it was fitted with a cupola for the gunner's cockpit. This cupola, or 'parrot cage' as it was nicknamed, was constructed of light metal and completely protected the gunner. It was especially effective when he was standing up and firing downwards.

Boulton-Paul Aircraft recognised that although the Demon was still in squadron service, it was only a stop-gap and a new design was urgently required. Their new concept was a turret fighter with the potential to attack bomber formations. There was to be no forward armament so that the pilot could concentrate on positioning the aircraft suitably for his gunner, who was conducting the offensive role. Its duties were to be twofold.

Firstly, as a day fighter, it would co-operate with Hawker Hurricanes, flying along the flanks of an enemy formation and hopefully engaging any bombers flushed out by the single-seat fighters. At no time was it envisaged that the new turret fighter would be engaged in combat with other fighter aircraft—it was primarily a bomber destroyer. With an estimated speed close to that the Hurricane it would enable the two different aircraft to operate with maximum efficiency. Later events were to show up the 'ifs and buts' of this current thinking and how operational requirements can sometimes dictate unsuitable usage. Secondly, as a night fighter, it would operate as a 'lone wolf', guided to its target by the very secret radio-location from ground stations. However, the electronic element of this scheme was of course still in its infancy.

In 1935 staff of the A&AEE, Martlesham Heath met John North and the Chief Test Pilot from Boulton-Paul to consider a replacement for the Demon incorporating a powered turret. Design work in hand at Norwich was at that time concentrated around the P.81 Army Co-operation aircraft to Specification A.39/34, and a bomber, the P.79, to Specification B.1/35. After April 1935, when the Air Ministry issued Specification F.9/35 for the new fighter, design work on the two former projects was abandoned and the P.82 became top priority.

During August 1935 the Norwich company submitted their final design which in many aspects appeared similar to the Hawker Hurricane. Of clean aerodynamic form it embodied enclosed cockpit, fully retractable undercarriage and all-metal monocoque construction. The wings were deep enough inboard to house the undercarriage yet thin enough outboard to give an efficient low drag. Racks for light bombs were to be enclosed in the lower outer panels and wing de-icing was specified. The gunner was to enter his turret by a car-type door on the port side behind the pilot's cockpit. There was also an alternative layout for dual control. Drag reduction in the turret area was achieved by retractable fairings to operate automatically as the turret rotated. Power was to be supplied by a Rolls-Royce Merlin F twelve-cylinder engine, cooled by a large radiator mounted beneath the power plant, and driving a three-bladed controllable pitch propeller. In fact, the radiator was moved back to a ventral position in the prototype, similar to that of the Hurricane. It was estimated that the maximum speed would be 323 mph at 15,000 feet and that the weight was likely to be around 5,774 pounds; this would give the proposed design a performance very much akin to that of the Hurricane.

Component parts for the P.82 had been made in the Experimental Shop at Norwich during late 1935 and were well advanced by the time of the move to Wolverhampton. Completed parts were transported there in the greatest secrecy.

The Armstrong-Whitworth contender in this field was of mid-wing layout and of all-metal construction and powered by two Armstrong Siddeley Terrier engines. However the design was rejected at an early stage and the project abandoned.

The Bristol Aeroplane Company of Filton, Bristol, were also rivals with a project designated Type 147. An all-metal low wing monoplane with parallel chord wing and retractable undercarriage, it was to be powered by a Bristol Perseus sleeve valve radial air-cooled engine. This would give it an estimated top speed of 280 mph at 15,000 feet. The second option was the larger Bristol Hercules engine of the same type which would give the Type 147 an estimated top speed of 308 mph at 15,000 feet. An enclosed cockpit was provided for the pilot and the gunner, who was positioned closely behind him on a rotating seat. Remote controls in front of the gunner operated a submerged turret which housed four 0.303 inch Browning machine guns. These were capable of 180 degrees traverse and 90 degrees elevation. The movement of the turret was controlled by a reflector sight in front of the gunner's eyes and effected by two handwheels which moved round with the seat. Submitted during August and September 1935, neither of the two versions of the Type 147 were accepted and work on these projects at Filton ceased.

Hawker had also developed the Hurricane into a two-seat light bomber, the Henley, which utilised many of the same components. This in turn emerged with a re-designed cockpit, reshaped rear fuselage and revised tail unit as another prototype, designated Hotspur and serialled K.8308 and to Specification F.17/36. The new turret armament concept was thought important by the Air Ministry but after all designs were considered in greater depth, it was decided to proceed with the prototypes from Hawker and Boulton-Paul.

The Hotspur's first flight was made on 14th June 1938 and on test handled well. In prototype condition it was slightly faster than the proposed P.82. Hawker were at this time heavily committed to Hurricane production and for this reason the Hotspur prototype had been delayed.

In due course it was presented for trials at the Royal Aircraft Establishment during 1940 but was written off after a forced landing at Yateley Common, Hampshire on 12th February 1942.

Boulton-Paul's P.82 was now the only contender and permission was given for a second prototype, K.8620, to be produced. Work on turret development proceeded speedily and the Armament Design Office had to ratify which of the de Boysson turrets should be employed. Boulton and Paul Limited had acquired the full British patent rights for the French designed turrets. The original design used an engine-driven hydraulic pump to power the turret, but when full working details were received from France it was realised that the built-in power unit was a much better proposition.

Hawker Hotspur two-seat turret fighter prototype K.8309, which bore a very close resemblance to its sister, the Hurricane. The turret was only a mock-up. *British Aerospace*

During March 1937 a production order, Contract 622849/37, was received for eighty-seven P.82 aircraft to Specification F.5/37m, the machine to be officially designated 'Defiant'. They were to be serialled L.6950-L.7036. The prototype K.8310 was nearing completion and was soon to be in the Flight Shed prepared for its first flight. To gain experience of the turret's behaviour in the air, a prototype turret was mounted on the old Overstrand K.8175 in the front gunner's position and many problems were solved by this combination of old and new. The prototype aircraft was now ready for flight trials but the turret was not yet available. Permission was given to fly the aircraft as a single-seater, turret-less but with ballast compensation. The original envisaged car door type entrance for the gunner had been deleted and the retractable tailwheel design replaced by a fixed unit.

When it emerged on to the Flight Shed apron at Wolverhampton on 11th August 1937, in its natural metal finish, it looked sleek and purposeful. After test runs for engine and brakes, all was deemed ready for the great occasion. Later that day K.8310 was airborne from Pendeford airfield on its maiden flight in the hands of Flight Lieutenant Cecil Feather. Mr John Chambers, Print Room Manager, recalled, 'I remember watching the aircraft from a vantage point by the railway bridge on Pendeford Lane, and seeing Flight Lieutenant Feather afterwards with black oil from a leaking oil pipe spattered over the legs of his flying suit.' A speed of 302 mph was reached, below the estimated top speed but good enough for development to continue. Stability and general handling were found to be excellent with only a few modifications required. One outstanding feature which showed up the fine design of the Defiant was that the trim remained constant when flaps or undercarriage were lowered.

After arrival at the A&AEE, Martlesham Heath, trials were commenced on 7th December 1937 and continued until the 31st of that month. The programme called for handling, engine cooling and diving trials so that the aircraft would be ready for armament trials when the turret was eventually fitted. In this guise the prototype was considered overweight at 7,113 pounds, but modifications would be made in various areas to reduce the weight by 113 pounds and give a revised maximum permissible weight of 7,000 pounds. Cooling tests showed up areas of concern in the engine radiator and oil cooler, for although adequate for operations in the United Kingdom, they were unsuitable for tropical service. The oil cooler failed during trials and was replaced.

The handling trials were conducted in the usual Martlesham Heath manner with four experienced test pilots flying and reporting on K.8310. The following items were criticised: tailwheel fork failed and replaced by modified unit; difficulty in gaining access to the front cockpit, overcome by fitting strips of non-slip material to the upper surface of the wing centre section; draughts in unheated cockpit, even with cockpit hood closed; elevator trim tabs control which was crank handle operated tended to 'creep', it was suggested that a wheel on the lefthand side of the pilot's seat would be more satisfactory; the indicator also moved contrary to instinctive movement, that is forward for tail-heavy and vice versa; fuel cocks stiff and out of pilot's reach; complicated undercarriage and flap selector lever system needed simplification, and substitution of the electrically operated undercarriage position indicators by mechanically operated ones; battery operated electric pump for undercarriage and flap hydraulics unsatisfactory for Service aircraft, engine driven pump recommended as replacement; better balance needed for ailerons by making them slightly heavier; increased flap movement to allow 90 degrees depression, so allowing steeper approach glide.

One or two maintenance points were raised regarding lubrication of the rudder hinges and propeller, and the engine cowling fastenings were considered unsatisfactory for Service aircraft. A lifting bar was also required to lift the tail of the aircraft, instead of the special sling which necessitated the aid of a crane. The original engine had been changed for a Merlin I, this drove a Lockheed hydraulic pump to supply oil under pressure for the undercarriage and flap systems and thus relieved the electrical load on the battery. Lockheed had also supplied a new set of undercarriage oleo legs. Crew comfort was improved by the elimination of the many draughts emanating through holes in the bulkhead, ruling out the need for special clothing. As a result of these early trials, fairings which had entirely covered the wheels when retracted were found unnecessary and removed. They were replaced by hinged flaps attached to the underside of the fuselage.

Both aircraft and turret were at the A&AEE, but not together; the Defiant was in the Performance Testing Squadron and the turret in the Armament Section. When the turret did eventually arrive back at Wolverhampton it was fitted to the prototype, several small modifications were made, and K.8310 returned to Suffolk during the middle of February 1938 for armament trials. The delay in availability of the turret meant that the official firing trials at the A&AEE's testing ranges at Orfordness needed to be rushed through and were completed in two weeks.

Until the official announcement the Defiant's appearance at Martlesham Heath had remained a mystery. For security purposes, unlike other resident aircraft, it never stood outside the hangar but was always put out of sight between flights.

Rolls-Royce had been further developing the Merlin engine, and the current production model, Merlin II, was to power the second prototype, K.8620. Other modifications incorporated in this machine were improved wheel doors, telescopic aerial masts beneath the aircraft, ailerons of increased chord at the trailing edge and some alterations in the metal cockpit framing. In this guise K.8620 took to the air for the first time on 18th May 1938, to be followed on 30th July by the first production Defiant from the Wolverhampton factory. Production machines were powered by 1,030 hp Merlin IIIs, the introduction of which necessitated some re-design of the engine mountings.

The Air Ministry were confident of the Defiant's capabilities and placed orders for another 202 aircraft during February 1938, followed by 161 more during May of the same year. Other orders were placed during December 1939 for a further 150 Defiants.

During July 1940 the A&AEE, which had moved from Martlesham Heath to Boscombe Down at the outbreak of hostilities, received the first development Defiant, L.6950, for trials with light bomb racks. The Central Flying School carried out handling trials on L.6951, and L.6952 made a brief stay at Northolt to carry out comparison trials with the Hurricanes of No 111 Squadron. After conducting a series of mock combats with the Hurricanes, the squadron's Commanding Officer reported that the Defiant would fare badly in combat with a single-seat fighter. It also became obvious that this new concept of two-seat fighter required very close co-operation between pilot and gunner, particularly if the Defiant should be forced into a defensive situation. Whilst the Merlin III engine had increased power, in-service weight had also risen thus losing any advantage gained by the more powerful engine. There was no doubt, however, that the Defiant would be able to fulfil its design role of bomber destroyer.

In spite of the substantial orders which had been placed for the Defiant, trials were still being conducted to improve the machine's capabilities, and the second prototype, K.8620, was engaged in this work.

Opposite: Now mated with the four-gun turret, K.8310 also displayed new exhaust stubs, revised undercarriage fairings and anti-dazzle paintwork on the upper forward fuselage.   *BPA*

There was still criticism of the lack of visibility when flying in rain, cockpit entry and draughts in the pilot's cockpit. Entry or exit by any but the smallest of air gunners was a problem due to the gun mechanism. Some difficulty was also experienced with the pilot's cockpit sliding hood which could not be opened at speeds exceeding 210 mph. Later aircraft were fitted with a jettisonable version. There was also criticism of the emergency lowering of the undercarriage which called for two hundred strokes of the hand pump. From a performance point of view the initial climb was just within the specification and the landing run rather on the long side for a fighter, but in other aspects it was satisfactory and its night flying qualities were good.

Second prototype P.82 Defiant K.8620 shows further modifications such as wireless aerial masts, and small transparent panels in the pilot's cockpit fairing.   *BPA*

The fairings fore and aft of the turret, which were designed to raise and lower automatically as the guns traversed, were actuated pneumatically and the air supply was inadequate for their continuous operation. This was due to the engine-driven air compressor which was not capable of replenishing the air reservoirs quickly enough. The wheel brakes were also pneumatically operated and lack of air pressure could have had a detrimental effect upon them. To conserve air pressure, the A&AEE suggested that air gunners should lower the fairings before any action and only raise them again when the engagement was over. After the A&AEE trials, K.8620 served with No 5 Operational Training Unit and crashed at Porthcawl on 13th July 1940.

During 1936 the Air Ministry had issued a Specification F.11/37 for a large twin-engined long range escort fighter. On 23rd September 1937 Boulton-Paul Aircraft submitted their proposals for their design. They were eventually selected ahead of six other tenderers for a contract to design a prototype. A further contract was placed during March 1938 for two prototypes: one to be powered by the new Rolls-Royce Vulture engine, and the other by the Napier Sabre, both 24 cylinder in-line units and both untried.

Front aspect of P.92/2 showing single-seat cockpit, fixed troused undercarriage and Gipsy engines. Because there was insufficient room in the cockpit the engine instrument dials were placed on the inside face of the engine cowlings, but visible from the cockpit.   *BPA*

Throughout 1939 extensive wind tunnel tests were conducted on models both at Wolverhampton and the Royal Aircraft Establishment, Farnborough. A half-scale flying model was designed to establish the aerodynamic characteristics of the projected fighter. The Wolverhampton factory was fully committed to Defiant production so the flying scale model, designated P.92/2, was contracted out to Heston Aircraft. It was of all wooden construction and power was provided by two 130 hp De Havilland Gipsy Major II in-line air-cooled engines, because of their close similarity in profile to the Vultures. The outstanding feature of this proposed three-seat fighter was the gun turret, which was to merge into the aircraft's shoulder-mounted wing above the centre section. Of special low drag profile, the turret was mounted in a well in the fuselage. The four 20 mm cannons were housed almost entirely within the body of the turret and only the four barrels protruded. This layout resulted in a remarkably slim fuselage, the crew being seated in tandem. In practice the model could not be scaled down in all aspects with complete accuracy; for instance, a half-scale pilot was obviously not available and so the forward fuselage was larger than scale. Even under these conditions the test pilot, Flight Lieutenant Feather, fitted in with some difficulty and was seated on the cockpit floor.

Considerable research was carried out on the aerodynamics of the turret for, when traversing, the guns might change the airflow over the tail surfaces and consequently affect the aircraft's stability as a gun platform. With a wing span of 33 ft and a length of 27 ft 6 ins, the P.92/2 weighed in at 2,778 pounds. During its extensive flight trials it recorded a top speed of 152 mph and cruised at 138 mph, very creditable considering the low power of the Gipsy engines. An ex-member of the Research Department recalled:

> One problem in the P.92's design was going to be the escape procedures for the pilot, as the engines were in close proximity on either side of the cockpit and immediately behind was the large turret with its guns. The difficulty was to be overcome by a door in the cockpit floor positioned immediately aft of the pilot's seat. To escape from the aircraft, the pilot would operate a mechanism which released the door and swung the seat back and aft through the opening. In this pre-ejector seat action, the pilot would be ejected head first away from the aircraft. To test the apparatus a trial was set up and nets arranged to catch the test 'victim' as he was ejected. Mr North elected to make the test; he actuated the mechanism and all worked perfectly. Unfortunately, owing to a slackness of the nets, he was only partially restrained and hit the floor with some thud, suffering a cut forehead, resulting in a ten day absence from his office.

Serialled V.3142, the aircraft continued trials into 1940, but even before it had flown the Air Ministry was already considering other new aircraft types for the RAF. Equally important they had to take into account the capacity of Britain's wartime aircraft industry to produce them. On tactical grounds it was decided to abandon the P.92/2 and during March 1940 all work stopped on the F.11/37 prototypes. A major cause of the P.92's cancellation was the unreliable performance of the Vulture engines.

Estimated performance of the P.92 was to have been quite outstanding for a machine of 66 ft wing span and a loaded weight of 19,000 pounds. The two Rolls-Royce Vultures, each of 1,760 hp, were expected to give a top speed of 371 mph at 15,000 feet and to cruise at 320 mph. Climb was estimated at 2,900 feet per minute and a ceiling of

37,000 feet would have given it an advantage for bomber attack. Fuel capacity was 328 gallons, but a 2,000 mile range was to be obtained by using additional tanks. It is well worth reflecting what effect this heavy long-range fighter might have had on the course of the war had it ever gone into RAF service.

The Defiants had entered squadron service on 8th December 1939 with No 264 Squadron, and were worked up to operational standard. Details of its career are told in a following chapter but suffice to say it was given tasks for which it had not been designed. The Defiant had been conceived as a bomber formation destroyer and not a daytime dog fighter. It was never utilised in its correct role and although it had fought well against the occasional single-seat raider over Southern England, its day fighting ability was restricted.

The lull in the Luftwaffe's activities after the Battle of Britain was only short-lived for they soon re-directed their efforts towards the night bombing of cities and towns in the British Isles. The only aircraft available for night fighting had been the near obsolete Bristol Blenheim Mark I.F. The Defiants were now coming off the production lines at sixty per month and were considered ideal machines for this purpose. Stable, easy to fly and equipped with the four-gun turret, it appeared that the Defiant could now come into its element: single combat against night bombers, its secondary design role. Other favourable factors were its rapid delivery and a surplus of aircraft ready for conversion. Consequently Defiants now appeared with a number of new squadrons, matt black overall with dark red squadron letters, and designated Defiant NF.Mk I. In this guise they engaged in all the major night battles and notched up an impressive number of kills on enemy bombers.

Defiant Mark IA Night Fighter with Air Interception (AI) Mark VI radar, the aerials for which are located on fuselage and mainplanes. *BPA*

The pilot's cockpit in the Defiant was compact and well laid out. Ex-pilots will recognise the standard blind flying panel in the centre of the instrument board with the compass beneath. The bucket seat accommodated the pilot-type parachute upon which the wearer sat.   *John Chambers*

These aircraft had to cruise around in the darkened skies, guided only by radio and searchlight signals, and stalk their prey where and when they could find them. Things improved when the A.I.Mk IV radar equipment became available, compact enough to be accommodated within the Defiant. This was fitted into the Mk I night fighters which then became known as the Defiant I.A. The new radar was mainly pilot operated, so as well as flying the aircraft he had also to scan the radar screen and give directions to his gunner. Shortly after the introduction of the early A.I. sets, a further developed unit became available and was fitted into new aircraft as Modification 194. These aircraft were designated Defiant NF.II. Further modifications, a 27 gallon tank in the port outer mainplane and a 28 gallon one on the starboard side, increased the range to 550 miles at a cruising speed of 260 mph.

The Defiant was now performing one of the tasks for which it was originally designed and the squadrons operating them could claim the highest rate of kills per interception of any night fighter units. After being later replaced by the twin-engined Bristol Beaufighter and later still the De Havilland Mosquito NF, some Defiants were employed in a radio counter-measure role, flying ahead of Bomber Command mainstream to jam enemy directors. In 1941 the output of Defiants exceeded requirements and a number were towed by road to RAF Cosford, minus outer mainplanes, where they were stored until required.

Although the Defiant was powered by the Rolls-Royce Merlin III of 1,030 hp, the company received instructions during early 1940 to carry out a trial installation of the Merlin XX and the Merlin 24. The Wolverhampton Drawing Office preferred the Merlin 24 but the XX was at a more advanced stage of development. Accordingly N.1550 was modified to take the new XX engine and made its first flight on 20th July 1940. Increased engine torque from this more powerful unit necessitated an increase in vertical fin area. The second trials machine, N.1551, appeared with this modification incorporated as well as an increased rudder area and an adjustable trim tab. To cope with the greater power the two machines were fitted with Rotol airscrews of modified design and larger radiators were installed to ensure sufficient cooling. An optimistic top speed of 345 mph at 21,000 feet had been estimated but in practice only 9 mph was added to the speed of the production models.

Wolverhampton still contemplated production with the Merlin 24 but the July 1940 Defiant contract stipulated the Mark XX, and in this guise, from machine AA.370, the production aircraft were designated Defiant II. There were major changes especially to the front fuselage with new engine cowlings and mountings, larger radiator and oil cooler air intake. The rudder area was also increased but a new turret which had been visualised for this model was not developed.

The Battle of Britain had taken a huge toll of the RAF's fighter resources and several aircraft manufacturers were instructed to modify existing designs speedily in order to produce a stop-gap fighter. Boulton-Paul had a good contender in the P.82 Defiant and so an early Mk I was suitably converted. Designated the P.94 project, it was identical in shape and size to the Merlin XX Defiant but with the turret removed. The finished product resembled the Hawker Hurricane and the Drawing Office estimated a top speed of 380 mph at 23,500 feet. Armament was to be four fixed machine guns in the mainplanes.

Springing from this project was a variant with four 20 mm cannons and four 0.303 inch machine guns in the wings. Unique was the installation of the cannons: they could be selected manually to depress at an angle of 17 degrees and could be operated for ground attack whilst the aircraft remained in level flight. The angle of the cannons could be altered in flight.

The Defiant, having been seconded from its day fighter role and now carrying out night fighter duties, was also used in another capacity, as a top-cover escort fighter for Air Sea Rescue operations. The majority of the ASR squadrons had a Defiant on their strength, and they used to fly out quickly to the scene of a reported 'ditching', maintain radio links, drop smoke flares and sometimes a small dinghy to the unfortunate aircrew or aircrews in the water. This gave them some protection until the arrival of the Westland Lysander with its large dinghies, and eventually the Supermarine Walrus amphibian which was able to alight on the water and pick up the airmen.

Because of the Defiant's good flying characteristics it was considered for another role. After the delivery on 15th February 1942 of the last radar equipped Mk II, the production line was re-jigged to produce the Target Tug version. The first Defiant TT Mk I, DR.863, was accepted for service in early 1942 and was followed by 139 more, the last delivered in March 1943. Others were converted from Mk II fighters, all being powered by the Merlin XX.

In the Target Tug version, the turret was replaced by a rearward facing winch operator's position and a large drogue winch was fitted. Drogues were housed in a stowage box attached under the rear fuselage; internal stowage bins for flag drogues were also fitted. To allow for underneath stowage the radio aerial masts were moved to the cabin top. Operation in tropical conditions was anticipated so items such as air cleaners for use in sandy atmospheres were fitted.

Fighter Command at this time had considerable numbers of Defiant Mk I aircraft which had been withdrawn from operational service. Consequently a contract was placed to convert 150 of these, designated Mk III, into Target Tugs. Basically the NF.Mk I, less of course the turret, they were fitted with larger radiators, as used on the NF.Mk II, and a new

Defiant TT. Mark III converted from Mark I fighter for target towing duties.   *BPA*

design of oil cooler which gave a greater operating range. The prototype, N.3488, passed service trials but the conversion contract was given to Reid and Sigrist at Desford, Leicestershire.

In spite of the aircraft's high approach and landing speeds, Defiant pilots were full of praise for their mount with its stable handling characteristics and many forgiving ways. With these qualities the Defiant was in the forefront of experimental and research work and its duties were indeed many and varied.

Specification N.7/43 had been issued for a carrier-borne naval fighter aircraft and the Defiant was again involved. The test aircraft for the project was designated the Defiant Special Features, and was powered by a Rolls-Royce Griffon liquid-cooled engine or a Bristol Centaurus air-cooled radial. Estimated performance was 463 mph for the Griffon powered version and 435 mph for the Centaurus, but the project was dropped and passed into obscurity.

The Defiant was declared obsolete as an RAF Type during July 1945. One of its last contributions to aircraft research concerned DR.944 and the development of the Martin-Baker ejector seat. The trial seat was fitted where the turret had previously been located. When ground tests had been successfully completed, the aircraft was flown to Wittering, Northamptonshire, for air firing trials on 11th May 1945. Later that day Rotol's Chief Test Pilot, Mr Brian Greenstead, made the first dummy ejection in flight. During the next week further dummy ejections were made at speeds up to 300 mph. Since these pioneering trials the Martin-Baker ejector seat system has been fitted to service aircraft throughout the world and saved countless lives.

The Defiant may be considered to have failed in its main operational function, but it was a sound, reliable and easy to fly aircraft. Doubtless if more time and training had been available before the aircraft and its crews were thrown into action, it could have proved a formidable opponent. Many of the derogatory statements about the aircraft have been made more from hearsay than from actual experience. An ex-No 264 Squadron member wrote, 'There was no question of new methods of night interception outmoding the Defiant with its most up-to-date equipment for night interception. The lack of foresight shown in laying aside a machine which could easily, with some improvements, have been a formidable weapon' was regrettable. Squadron Leader D.H. Clarke who flew a considerable number of operational aircraft during his RAF career regarded the Defiant as 'a steady gun platform. I would have liked the Defiant for ground strafing in the Western Desert, but with eight 0.5 inch machine guns in the wings. Used for the wrong job, it never really stood a chance.'

CHAPTER EIGHT

'Diffy' in Service

A S DEFIANTS, or 'Diffies' as the RAF nicknamed them, became available in December 1939, they were allocated to No 264 (Madras Presidency) Squadron, which was commanded by Squadron Leader Stephen Hardy. It had been formed on 30th October of that year and was based at Sutton Bridge in Lincolnshire. The unit's aircraft were a mixed bunch of semi-obsolete Fairey Battle light bombers and Miles Magister two-seat basic trainers. These were replaced by Defiants L.6957, L.6968, L.6970 and L.6972.

On 8th December 1939 No 264 Squadron moved south to Martlesham Heath where it commenced working-up and familiarisation exercises with their new aircraft. After the Battle and the Magister, the Defiant was a lively aeroplane, but airborne hours were limited as there were frequent engine faults and malfunctions with the hydraulic systems which resulted in all their aircraft being grounded on 28th January 1940. Teams of specialists from the engine makers, Rolls-Royce, and hydraulic test engineers from Lockheed Hydraulics investigated the troubles. Within two weeks the problems had been overcome and the grounding restriction lifted. Unlike the prototypes with their all-over natural metal finish, the new arrivals were in 'B' Scheme camouflage, earth and brown topsides, and black and white undersurfaces.

Although the aircraft was not designed for the purpose, dive-bombing trials were carried out at nearby Orfordness to evaluate the aircraft's capabilities as a ground attack aircraft. The machine employed for these trials was L.6950, which had been fitted with Light Series underwing bomb racks. Defiant L.6968 also carried out trials in an Army Co-operation role and this resulted later in the year in No 2 Squadron receiving several Defiants for this work. They were not considered suitable, however, and were eventually withdrawn without carrying out any operations. The tactical use of the Defiant, the only fighter with a turret and no forward armament when operational, required considerable thought and application. The success of these aircraft in action was largely due to the preliminary planning as well as the skill and inspiration of Squadron Leader Phillip Hunter who had assumed command during March 1940.

Defiants awaiting delivery at Pendeford. This batch are in day fighter camouflage of brown and green with the early style roundels and fin flash. *BPA*

It came as a surprise when the Air Officer Commanding, Air Vice-Marshall Leigh-Mallory, arrived at Martlesham Heath and ordered the commencement of night flying. With a high stalling speed and a landing speed above 100 mph, the Defiant did not appear the most suitable aircraft for this role. This was a period of unusually wintry weather and the grass at Martlesham Heath, without hard-surfaced runways, had become soft and badly rutted. This new order to carry out night flying training on a dimly lit airfield and with unfamiliar aircraft seemed inopportune. The object of the new order was to get the 'Diffy' operational, and the night flying did take place and the majority of the squadron's pilots mastered the art of night operations. Working-up had reached the stage where on 20th March 1940 two sections each of three aircraft were declared at operational readiness, and the following day No 12 Group posted them to Wittering for operational duties, designated No 264 Squadron (Detachment).

A few coastal patrols were flown off the East Coast during April but the squadron as a whole was not declared operational until 8th May. Two days later the entire squadron moved to Duxford, Cambridgeshire, just as German troops were beginning to attack the Low Countries. The squadron was divided when 'A' Flight moved to Horsham St Faith, near Norwich, on 12th May as an advanced detachment. Almost immediately it was called into action, six aircraft in conjunction with Spitfires of No 66 Squadron, who were flying top cover, were sent to patrol the Channel off The Hague with the intention of catching German troop-carrying aircraft, Ju.52s, before they had time to land their cargoes. Unfortunately they were too late. On the way home a Junkers Ju.88 was encountered and promptly shot down, the squadron's first kill.

At dawn the following day 'B' Flight, with a Spitfire escort, made their first patrol to attack troop movements along the Dutch coast. During this patrol they encountered a flight of Junkers Ju.87B Stukas and shot down four of them. However they were caught by the escorting Messerschmitt Bf.109Es and badly mauled. Five of the Defiants were destroyed in the attack. Only the damaged L.6974, flown by Pilot Officer Kay, escaped. He managed to reach an airstrip at Knocke in Belgium where he re-fuelled, made temporary repairs and flew the crippled machine back to Duxford that evening. Two other pilots and their gunners survived and returned to base a few days later. It was now becoming painfully evident that when forced into defensive combat, Defiant pilots were finding great difficulty in positioning their aircraft for the gunner to have an effective field of fire.

The Defiant's likeness to the Hurricane had lured several Luftwaffe pilots into attacks from the stern and had paid the price for their mistake. New aircraft and crews joined the depleted unit, and from 23rd May No 264 Squadron flew from Manston, Kent, each day for operations along the French coast to support the Allied withdrawal from Dunkirk. Squadron Leader Hunter's plan for mixing Defiants and Hurricanes paid off and the squadron records read, 'Opposition increased day by day with one German being shot down on 24th May, five on 27th, six on 28th, thirty-seven on 29th and nine on 31st. The score of 37 enemy aircraft destroyed in one day by a squadron for no loss was an achievement which remained unequalled throughout the war.'

Squadron Leader Phillip Hunter's Defiant I of No 264 Squadron.

Extracts from the Squadron Log-book for this period make interesting reading:

Duxford. May 28th, 1940. Squadron Leader Hunter and twelve Defiants again patrolled Dunkirk-Calais. Early in the patrol the squadron encountered twenty-seven M.E.109s and in the ensuing engagements six M.E.109s were shot down and three Defiants were lost. Three parachutes were seen descending into the sea.

May 29th, 1940. Squadron Leader Hunter and twelve Defiants patrolled Dunkirk-Calais in conjunction with three Hurricane squadrons. We were detailed to look for enemy bombers, with one of the Hurricane squadrons leaving the remainder to engage the fighters. After the squadron reformed it was attacked by twenty-one M.E.110s, fifteen of the enemy were shot down and also a Ju.87 which was brought down by Sergeant Thorne and Leading Aircraftman Barker, who were momentarily detached from the squadron. Pilot Officer Kay's aircraft was badly damaged by an M.E.109 and his gunner, Leading Aircraftman Jones baled out when his turret was hit, but the aircraft successfully landed at Manston. In the evening the squadron made a second patrol and engaged about forty Ju.87s, which were bombing Dunkirk. Eighteen Ju.87s were destroyed and one Ju.88. Sergeant Thorne's machine was badly damaged and had to land with one undercarriage leg stuck down. The squadron remained at Manston for the night.

May 29th, 1940. The following signal was received from No 11 Group: 'The Air Officer Commanding sends sincere congratulations to No 264 Squadron on their magnificent performance in shooting down over thirty enemy aircraft without losing a single pilot, one of whom brought back his aeroplane minus both elevators and an aileron.'

May 30th, 1940. The squadron returned to Duxford and was released for the day.

May 31st, 1940. Squadron visited by the Air Officer Commanding, No 12 Group.

After these operations Lord Beaverbrook of the Ministry of Aircraft Production wrote to Mr Strickland of Boulton-Paul Aircraft:

I send you a message for all the workers at Boulton-Paul. It is a report from your front of battle, a record of the result achieved by the Boulton-Paul staff and their emissaries between the 12th and 31st of May.

Thirty-five Junkers bombers, thirteen Heinkel bombers and thirty Messer-
schmitt fighters fell to the guns of the Defiants. That was the bag! That was the fruit of your labours, of the skill and devotion which has made the Defiant so formidable a defender of our homes and our liberty. It is a magnificent achievement. The pilots in the RAF rejoice in the splendid weapon which you have given them. I send my warmest congratulations to you all.

Notes taken from the official combat reports of Fighter Command Headquarters were forwarded to the company as being of particular interest to those producing the aircraft:

May 29th, 1940. I was Leader in the formation of Defiant aircraft when patrolling the coast near Dunkirk. At Dunkirk we observed about four Ju.88s delivering dive bombing attacks on vessels around the harbours and along the beach and when giving chase to one, ran into about ten Ju.87s. We attacked one Ju.87 and gave two bursts of about 30 rounds at 150 yards when it burst into flames and fell into the sea. We immediately closed up below and between two other Ju.87s giving three 50 round bursts at one, which immediately dropped its bombs (almost on another Defiant) and then burst into flames. This, however, was fired on by at least one other Defiant and we do not know who finally brought it down. We gave another Ju.87 one 50 round burst and this also burst into flames and crashed into the sea. A Ju.88 was then sighted going out to sea at about 500 feet and we gave chase accompanied by two other Defiants. The aircraft dropped right down to sea level and when about ten miles out to sea turned round and proceeded back east. I managed to cut him off and made a cross-over attack around the front of and slightly above him at a range of about 50 to 75 yards. We gave him a long burst and could see the incendiary bullets going into the pilot's cockpit. We were met with a burst of fire from the gun in his nose. As our ammunition was almost exhausted we retired and returned home, landing at 20.30 hours. Our aircraft had one bullet through the tail fin and rudder, caused apparently by one of our own guns.

During the month sixty-seven enemy aircraft had been destroyed with an unrecorded number damaged, all for the loss of seven crews and fourteen aircraft. This led to the award of the Distinguished Service Order to the Commanding Officer, Squadron Leader Hunter, as well as awards of the Distinguished Flying Cross and Distinguished Flying Medals to other members of the squadron. Unfortunately, as records show, the Luftwaffe had recognised the new fighter's Achilles heel, its total lack of forward armament, and this resulted on 31st May in the loss of seven Defiants through low astern attacks. New problems had arisen from the combat experience: difficulties in operating the aircraft flown to the gunner's dictates, the gunner's inability to escape from the lower hatch, and lack of gun depression which prevented defence against low attacks from the stern by enemy fighters.

During June 1940 No 264 Squadron received replacement aircraft and crews, and worked up once again to an operational state. A few night patrols were carried out during this period, but the majority of the work comprised East Coast patrols flying from Martlesham Heath and Debden in Essex before the squadron moved north on 23rd July to Kirton-in-Lindsey, Yorkshire.

A publicity photograph much used as a Defiant advertisement in the early part of the Second World War. The aircraft, though, are portrayed still in the pre-war aluminium finish.   *BPA*

A second Defiant unit, No 141 Squadron, received its first aircraft on 4th April 1940; on 3rd June the squadron was declared operational at Grangemouth, Scotland, as part of No 13 Group. On 10th July the unit moved into No 11 Group and sixteen aircraft were ready for action at West Malling in Kent as day fighters. Their operational forward base was Hawkinge, also in Kent, and No 141 was at readiness at that base on 19th July 1940. Action came quickly. At 12.30 pm they were scrambled, but so swift was the call that only nine aircraft had time to become airborne when they climbed to 5,000 feet off Folkestone. Here they were bounced by Me.109s diving out of the sun. Two Defiants fell to the enemy's first pass, and then two more attacks from below. Another was lost near Dover and yet another near Hawkinge, and only a badly shot-up L.7014 managed to make home base. Four pilots and five gunners were killed, but four Me.109Es were shot down in the engagement. Once again the Defiant had proved its inability to compete in fighter to fighter combat, and after two days in the south of England No 141 was withdrawn to Prestwick on the west coast of Scotland. There they awaited raids on the north-west by unescorted Luftwaffe bombers.

With the Battle of Britain approaching, air battles over southern England increased in intensity and No 264 prepared for further action. 'A' Flight was detached to Ringway, Manchester, for the defence of that city, and 'B' Flight to Coleby Grange. The remainder flew North Sea patrols from Kirton-in-Lindsey. On the night of 15th August a few of the squadron aircraft took off to intercept enemy bombers operating over north-west England. At this time fighters on night patrol showed coloured downward lights for recognition by the Observer Corps. Pilot Officer Whitley and Sergeant Turner in L.6985 suddenly witnessed tracer flashing past them when an enemy bomber fired at their identification light. Following the tracer to its source the fighter's crew discovered a Heinkel He.III which was promptly destroyed, the Defiant's first night fighting success.

During the thick of the Battle of Britain, No 264 Squadron moved down to Hornchurch in Essex and used Manston, Kent, as its forward base. On 24th August it was scrambled to engage fifteen Junkers Ju.88s. Two Defiants were shot down for a claim of three of the enemy bombers and a Bf.109E fighter. During this action their much respected commander, Squadron Leader Hunter, was lost. Later that day, at Hornchurch, seven Defiants were being re-fuelled when an enemy bomber formation appeared. One machine, L.7013, was damaged on the ground, four aircraft took off, one of which, L.6967, was lost, but the remaining three claimed victories. L.7003 destroyed a Ju.88 and a Bf.109E, L.7005 a Bf.109E, and L.7025 two Ju.88s. On 26th August 1940 the enemy was engaged again when three Dornier Do.17s were claimed, but the veteran Defiant, L.7025, was lost. Two days later the squadron was at Rochford, near Southend, when the airfield was attacked by enemy bombers. The Defiants managed to get away just in time and engaged the enemy. Escorting enemy fighters shot down two of No 264's aircraft and damaged another four. During the eight days' operations from Hornchurch they destroyed fifteen enemy bombers confirmed, and one unconfirmed, but lost five pilots, nine airgunners and eleven aircraft in so doing.

By 31st August 1940 some one hundred and twenty aircraft had been delivered, but over half this number had been lost and clearly day fighter operations with the Defiant could not be continued. A few days later Lord Dowding instructed that the two squadrons should be transferred to night fighting duties, No 264 in No 12 Group and No 141 in No 13 Group. The former retired to Kirton-in-Lindsey and the latter to Turnhouse in Scotland. As a night fighter the Defiant depended on visual sightings of enemy aircraft, either illuminated by searchlights or in an area of anti-aircraft fire. It was expected, however, that the arrival of the Defiant IA with its Air Interception Radio-Location would give them a greater measure of success. On 22nd November No 264 Squadron moved to Debden to protect the eastern approaches to the capital and from this base night fighter patrols were carried out under the control of North Weald until the end of the year. The other Defiant unit, No 141 Squadron, moved south of London, when 'B' Flight took up residence at Biggin Hill. It had an almost immediate success when two Heinkel He.IIIs were destroyed on the night of 15th/16th September. Three days later 'B' Flight moved to Gatwick, where it was joined by 'A' Flight.

This was the period of the Luftwaffe's heaviest night attacks on London, but ground control was limited, and although the night fighters flew over blazing London with bombs bursting beneath them No 264 could claim only six enemy aircraft actually destroyed between September 1940 and April 1941.

Another move was made during April 1941 to Biggin Hill and then to West Malling, from where, during three nights in May, intruder work was carried out which resulted in the destruction of four enemy aircraft. During a heavy assault on London, 9th/10th May, two enemy aircraft were disposed of by 'A' Flight.

On 23rd December 1941 Flight Lieutenant S.R. Thomas, acting Squadron Leader, received a silver salver on behalf of No 264 Squadron from Boulton-Paul Aircraft. This was to commemorate the action at Dunkirk when thirty-seven enemy aircraft had been destroyed and the fact that one hundred enemy aircraft had been destroyed between May 1940 and November 1941.

During April 1941 No 141 Squadron was based at Biggin Hill and Manston but on the 29th of that month moved north to Ayr in Scotland, with the unit's 'B' Flight deploying to Acklington in Northumberland. With the arrival of the new Bristol Beaufighter IF the squadron was declared operational on 5th August 1941 using both aircraft types, but the Defiants were withdrawn a few weeks later.

The Defiant IA was a standard machine fitted with the rather crude and heavy Air Interception Mark IV Radio Location gear which was pilot operated. This apparatus left much to be desired as it had a limited range of four miles maximum and a minimum of six hundred feet. Air Interception equipped Defiants could be identified by the H-type aerial on the starboard side of the fuselage just ahead of the cockpit and the arrow-head aerials on each wing. The AI Mark VI provided an improved reception but the problem was not fully solved until the Centimetre Wavelength Air Interception came into operational service.

With the delivery of additional Defiants, further squadrons were formed, one of the first being No 307 (Polish) which was based at Jurby on the Isle of Man. Other new squadrons engaged in night fighting duties with the Defiant were Nos 85, 96, 151, 255 and 256. Several of these were now operating with detection equipped Defiant IIs. More power was available, as the Defiant II was fitted with a Merlin XX of 1,260 hp. Crews experienced in night fighting operations were posted to the new units, one such being Wing Commander A.T.D. Sanders, DFC, who became the Commanding Officer of No 85 Squadron. He was replaced at No 264 by his namesake, Squadron Leader P.J. Sanders, DFC.

By the middle of May 1942 many of the squadrons were beginning to re-equip with the Beaufighter and then the De Havilland Mosquito NF, and so the Wolverhampton machine was phased out once again.

Wing Commander Deanesly of Edgbaston had flown Spitfires during 1940 and had been shot down twice into the English Channel. From early 1941 to the middle of 1942, as a member of No 256 Squadron, he flew the Defiant:

> They were a very stable and comfortable aircraft to fly—much easier than either the Spitfire or Hurricane. The night fighter squadrons were largely formed from inexperienced pilots. To expect these people to fly by night in the blackout, without initially even VHF radio, was cruel and resulted in a fearsome number of casualties. But with better weather and more experience the casualties dropped.

On 10th April 1941 Flight Lieutenant, as he then was, Deanesly with his gunner, Sergeant W.J. Scott of the New Zealand RAF, took off from Fernhill at 21.55 hours. With reports of large fires below, he had climbed to 20,000 feet searching for condensation trails, when both he and his gunner saw an enemy aircraft 600 to 800 yards ahead and about 200 feet below. However, within half a minute the distance closed rapidly and the pilot was able to throttle back, drop below and to port. When in approximately beam position the gunner opened fire. The first burst registered on the engines and after a second short burst the aircraft caught fire. There was no return fire but the enemy aircraft closed towards them in a quick movement. This reduced the range, originally 200 yards, to 50 yards and a further burst set the whole fuselage alight. This showed up the transparent nose and confirmed the aircraft to be a Heinkel He.III. They followed down to 10,000 feet and watched the aircraft, still well alight, descending, but the pilot did not pursue further as he feared balloons. The subsequent location of the burnt out wreck showed that his apprehensions were well founded, for after colliding with a barrage balloon cable, the Heinkel crashed between Nos 281 and 283 Hales Lane, Smethwick, on the site of what is now Nos 23 and 25 St Mark's Road. Seven people in these houses were killed, whilst two of the Heinkel's crew died in the crash and two parachuted down to be captured by local police and military. The crew of N.1771 were awarded the DFC and DFM respectively.

Presentation of a silver salver on 23rd December 1941, on behalf of Boulton-Paul Aircraft, to S.R. Thomas, Acting Squadron Leader of No 264 Squadron, in recognition of their exploits over Dunkirk and destruction of 100 enemy aircraft between May 1940 and November 1941. *BPA*

An ex-member of No 141 Squadron, Flight Lieutenant F.C.A. Lanning, DFC, remembered his days with the squadron as a pilot officer. During May 1941 he was flying as gunner with his pilot, Flying Officer R.L.F. Day, DFC, from Acklington. Their job was to intercept German bombers attacking Durham, Newcastle and Middlesbrough from their base at Stavanger in Norway. At 10,000 feet they spotted a twin-engined Heinkel III immediately above them. Closing to less than 100 feet he carefully criss-crossed both engines and undersurfaces with a long burst. The Heinkel became a flaming mass and crashed in the grounds of Morpeth hospital. Short of fuel, they returned to base and after re-fuelling and re-arming took to the air again in Defiant T.3957; no sooner had they levelled out than they saw a Junkers Ju.88 on the skyline, obviously heading out to sea for the long journey back to Norway. It was about 2 am, and after catching up with the aircraft, they managed to engage it at 400 yards and head it off. They then chased it northwards along the coast, never being able to catch it for the *coup de grâce* and having to contend with its sporadic, panicky tracer, which mostly went wide. It finally crashed on Holy Island and burst into flames. The Defiant returned to base but with only a few gallons of fuel left. It was for this action that Pilot Officer Lanning was awarded his DFC.

During the spring of 1942 with the arrival of the Beaufighter into squadron service many of the Defiants were released from night fighting duties. In February trials had been conducted with Defiants Mark I and II regarding their suitability for an Air Sea Rescue role. During March official permission was given for their conversion to this work. When a signal was received that aircrew were down in the sea, the Defiant's role was to leave its coastal airfields as swiftly as possible and fly out to the area. It would then drop one or more dinghies and provide aerial protection if needed. By using radio Defiants were also able to guide in the slower rescue aircraft such as the Supermarine Walrus, Westland Lysander and Avro Anson.

At the end of March No 281 Squadron (ASR) was formed and based at Ouston with a detached flight at Turnhouse, whilst during May four more Air Sea Rescue squadrons received the Defiant. No 277 Squadron had a complement of twelve Defiants and four Lysanders for their extensive duties on the south coast, particularly on 19th August 1942, when all twelve aircraft gave ASR cover for the ill-fated Dieppe landing.

Useful as they proved, there were drawbacks operating the Defiant in this role; their high stalling speed made observation difficult and the wide turning circle proved a problem. The Lysander was able to overcome these difficulties and, although it remained in service, was much slower. The Spitfire took over from the Defiant in the ASR 'Quick Action and High Cover' role and by the end of 1942 the Defiant had been phased out of service once again.

About fifty Defiants had been converted to the ASR configuration and served with the squadrons Nos 275 (coded PV), 276 (AQ), 277 (BA), 278 (MY) and 281 (FA). For ASR duties many of the ex-Fighter Command Defiants had been finished in green and grey camouflage.

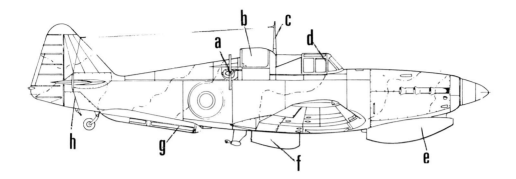

Defiant Target Towing aircraft
a. Winch; b. Winch operator's cockpit; c. Radio mast; d. Pilot's cockpit; e. Revised air intake;
f. Enlarged radiator; g. Target stowage box; h. Anti-fouling wire to protect tailplane.

In the United Kingdom the Target Tug Defiant Mark I replaced the Lysander Target Tug in Anti-aircraft Co-operation Units. However, they were also to be seen world-wide including in the Middle East and Far East. Target towing fell into two categories, ground-to-air for the Anti-aircraft Co-operation Units, and air-to-air for gunnery training. In the latter many Air Gunnery Schools employed the Defiant for turret training. Air Observers' Schools, Advanced Flying Units and the Central Gunnery School all had their quota of the now ex-operational fighters. The majority of Bomber Command Operational Training Units had a Defiant on their strength for target towing or turret training.

During 1943 the Royal Navy had employed the Defiant Target Tug all over the world, and their bases ranged from Gibraltar, Algiers, Dekheila, Malta, Trincomalee, Minneriya, Freetown, Kilindini, and Trinidad to several stations in the Far East. Outwardly their machines were identical to those of the RAF except that they carried yellow code letters and 'Royal Navy' above the aircraft service number.

American Forces in the United Kingdom were issued with two Defiant Target Tugs, DR.944 and DR.945, for use by the Combat Crew Replacement Centre, Bovingdon, as part of the United States Army Air Force.

No 1692 Flight based at Drem in Scotland was involved in training aircrews in the mysteries of the 'black box' coded 'Serrate', which was a homing device to detect the Luftwaffe's FuG 202/213 Lichtenstein Air Interception radar. In this secret work of countermeasure electronics the Defiants, for training purposes, were fitted with a suitable transmitter to simulate the German radar signals.

The last of these aircraft to see operational service were the Defiant Flight which was originally based at Northolt. The aircraft, Defiant IIs, were fitted with an electronic device coded 'Moonshine'. This was a transmitter/receiver capable of receiving transmissions from the enemy's Freya Early Warning radar. It then amplified the signals and transmitted them again as a much boosted signal which appeared on the enemy Freya CRT radar screens as a greatly exaggerated echo signifying large formations of Allied aircraft airborne. A small number of Moonshine equipped aircraft could have a surprising effect upon the enemy's control defences.

This was the RAF's first operational jamming device and took a while to settle down. It was not used until the night of 6th August 1942 when eight Defiants gave Moonshine an outing, flying in a set formation over the English Channel, south of Portland. It must have been gratifying for radar operators in the UK to see some thirty Luftwaffe fighters scrambled to intercept the large formation of hypothetical intruders. Moonshine was used again in daylight on 17th August 1942 when they 'boosted' an 8th Air Force mission against Rouen in France. Thirty 'spoof' missions were mounted to support daylight operations against enemy targets by the Flight up to 1st October 1942 when the Flight was re-designated No 515 Squadron. The Defiants were joined in this work by Beaufighters and the two types carried out 202 sorties up to July 1943 when the Defiant was retired.

The morning after. Sad demise of Defiant N.1795 of No 141 Squadron after crashing into a hillside, killing the two crew members. *John Chambers*

The Defiants found themselves operating in all manner of places over the years, sometimes as Station Flight runabouts. DR.990 was employed by No 1566 Met. Flight at Khormaksar and others lingered on in remote stations for some time, but as an RAF type it was declared obsolete during July 1945. Various airframes remained in Technical Training Schools, trainee fitters and metal workers cutting and patching them until they eventually found their way to the scrapyard or the Fire Dump. A Defiant Mark I night fighter, N.1617, can thankfully still be seen in the Royal Air Force Museum at Hendon. This aircraft, unlike so many other exhibition aircraft, actually saw operational squadron service. Mr Chambers recalled, 'The aircraft was at St Athan and was an ex-fighter converted to a target towing machine. It had to be converted back to a fighter version for display purposes.'

A Defiant crew member is remembered in a most unusual manner and place—a plaque on a channel marker in the picturesque north Norfolk harbour of Blakeney:

> In memory of Flt. Lt. Nicholas Gresham Cooke, D.F.C. A keen sailor in Blakeney Harbour, British Dinghy Team 1934. Killed in action over North Sea 31.5.1940. Pilot of Defiant L.6975. No. 264 Squadron

Flight Lieutenant Cooke was born at Blakeney. After Marlborough College and Cambridge, he joined the Royal Air Force in 1936. Posted to the Defiant Squadron No 264 he was responsible, together with his gunner, for destroying eight enemy aircraft over Dunkirk. He was awarded the DFC but was lost on 31st May 1940.

Defiant Mark I NF. N.167 stands proudly in the Royal Air Force Museum, Hendon, the sole survivor of this once numerous breed. Note Polish Air Force insignia on fuselage side beneath pilot's cockpit canopy.

CHAPTER NINE

War Work

HOSTILITIES brought all manner of restrictions to the Wolver-hampton factory, as the West Midlands was now no longer regarded a safe area. One precaution that had been taken to mislead the enemy was the construction of a dummy or decoy factory about two miles north of Pendeford and, to add to the deception, this decoy at Coven was built alongside a canal, exactly the same as the real target. Only four such decoys were built to protect aircraft factories, their cost being considered the ruling factor. The deception was successful, for the Coven decoy was bombed on three occasions by enemy aircraft whilst the Pendeford factory remained unscathed. The Luftwaffe was not ignorant of its existence, for German target maps dated October 1940 have 'FLUG-ZEUGWERKE BOULTON AND PAUL' accurately located. These maps are interesting as although the heading and description are in German, the name of Boulton and Paul in English is out of date, being that of the old Norwich company.

Blast walls were constructed between the aircraft assembly lines within the factory to reduce any effect of bomb blast within the interior. When the factory had first been constructed, a metal partition had been erected between the Flight Shed and the rest of the works. This had been removed so that during the winter months, when the hangar doors were opened, the ensuing blast of cold air penetrated deep into the works. Complaints were made but it was not until the foreman was struck down with pneumonia that the partition was eventually restored to its former position.

At first air raid shelters were dug into the hillside by the eastern end of the factory, some hundreds of yards from the place of work. As these shelters had to be approached over a narrow wooden bridge, there would obviously have been a terrible bottleneck in times of emergency. Later, underground concrete shelters were built at the front of the factory and these, together with surface shelters and a decontamination room, would have provided additional refuge in the event of any raid or gas attack. The large areas of glass panels in the factory roof were removed and replaced with asbestos sheets in what proved to be a major operation. Shortly afterwards many of the glass windows in the offices were replaced by solid materials.

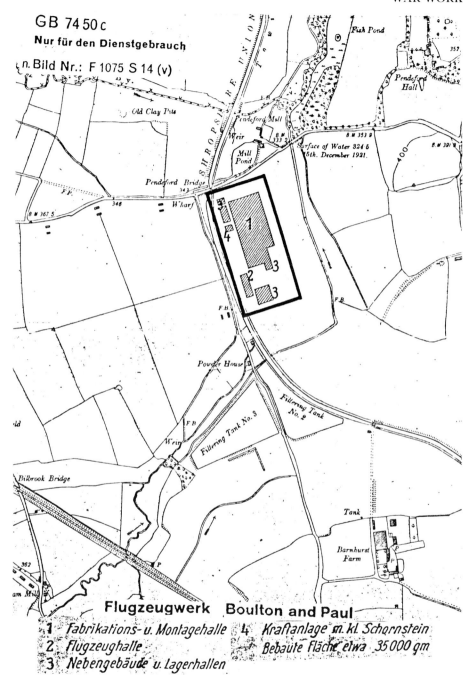

GB 74 50 c

Nur für den Dienstgebrauch

n. Bild Nr.: F 1075 S 14 (v)

Flugzeugwerk Boulton and Paul

1 *Fabrikations- u. Montagehalle*   4 *Kraftanlage m. kl. Schornstein*

2 *Flugzeughalle*   *Bebaute Fläche etwa 35 000 qm*

3 *Nebengebäude u. Lagerhallen*

The Drawing Office, where a vast amount of secret and irreplaceable documents were stored, was made secure. At this time a great deal of modification drawing work was under way for the Defiant; also in the offing was a design for a large twin-engined heavy bomber. Spanning 87 feet and 61 ft 3 in. long, this design was faintly reminiscent of the DC.3 with its monoplane wing, radial engines and forward retracting undercarriage. Gun turrets of Boulton-Paul design, mounting Lewis drum-fed machine guns, were to be located in the front, dorsal and tail positions. The bomb load would be stored internally in rotary racks, a fore-runner of modern design. Carrying Boulton-Paul Design Number P.79, the new bomber was to be tendered for Air Ministry Specification B.1/35, butt after initial drawing work the project was dropped.

During the week night shift personnel were in the buildings but at the weekends fire-watching duties were expected of the employees. Mr Chambers recalls, 'Invariably I ended up with a Saturday night spot. It was an eerie experience walking around a deserted factory, only partially lighted.' A special factory Fire Service was formed and Jack Shelton became the Chief Fire Officer. Not over equipped, their task was to contain any fire until the Fire Brigade arrived.

From the onset the Defiant production line had been laid out on the 'Flow System', three tracks being set out down the length of the Assembly Shop to take wheeled trolleys. These tracks ran in between the blast walls. The aircraft's centre section was positioned on the trolley, then the complete assembled fuselage was lowered onto it and secured. Other components were attached to the growing assembly as it moved along the track. Progressively taking shape, the finished aircraft eventually reached the end of the assembly line minus outer wings and airscrew, which were added in the Flight Shed.

The expansion of the labour force was so rapid that a shortage of skilled men developed and teams were despatched as far afield as Scotland and Northern Ireland to recruit suitable labour. To fill other vacancies, large numbers of unskilled men and women were also brought into the factory. In order to increase production, several small premises were taken over in the Wolverhampton district and these served as dispersal units and stores. Over this period the main works grew to almost three times its original size. Mr L. R. Jones of Sedgley remembered, 'We worked seven days a week on two shifts, 8 am to 7.30 pm and 7.30 pm to 8 am.' A bonus scheme was operated in the factory and Boulton-Paul workers were by far the best paid in the area.

Another test pilot, Robert Lindsay-Neale, joined the company on lst January 1940 as assistant to Flight Lieutenant Feather. He had learned to fly at Croydon in 1931 and acted as an aviation consultant in London before joining the Royal Air Force at the outbreak of war. Robin, as he was known at Boulton-Paul, was a popular figure and there was never any lack of volunteers for a flight with him. He preferred to take up live men rather than ballast as it gave a better weight distribution. However there were times when the human ballast had some misgivings if the test developed into an aerobatic display.

At the beginning of the war troops with fixed bayonets guarded the factory but a determined enemy would have had little trouble in gaining access to the works from the southern end which was next to the airfield. Everyone had to wear a badge and carry a pass although usually a person could walk through the gate unchallenged. Later the troops were withdrawn and the police were armed.

Owing to the enlarged workforce the canteen facilities were badly strained and a new separate canteen was built at the front of the buildings for use by the staff. Car parking at the factory was not permitted; those with a petrol ration had to take their cars past the factory and park them under the trees. There was a special bus service, and every evening a fleet of buses lined up on the road outside the works.

Wartime camouflage applied to the Pendeford buildings.   *John Chambers*

Land Army girls worked on the hillside to the east of the factory and pigs were kept on some spare land. Canteen scraps were boiled up to provide swill for the animals in a boiler close to the offices, forcing the staff to endure the unpleasant and all pervasive aroma.

Lunchtime concerts were arranged from time to time with touring concert parties. At least one was broadcast on the radio under the 'Workers' Playtime' programme from an aircraft factory somewhere in the Midlands. Some talented entertainers were discovered from the among the workforce. There was a special lunch and concert at Christmas and the Managing Director would make a speech thanking everyone for their efforts during the past year.

Because the Government placed the contracts it was not really surprising that they should appoint some of their own personnel to oversee the company's own Factory Inspection Department. The Aeronautical Inspection Directorate (AID) was resident in the works and financed by the Air Ministry. An investigation some years later into the production methods of various large aircraft manufacturers resulted in the appointment of Mr R. Beasley from Armstrong Whitworth Limited as director and General Manager of Boulton-Paul—much to John North's utter disgust as this greatly reduced his authority.

The Defiant was fitted with Rolls-Royce Merlin engines and two service engineers from that company were resident in the factory. Their function was the final tuning and adjustment of the power plants after the Merlins had been fitted by Boulton-Paul fitters.

His Majesty King George VI shows interest in a twin gun turret, installed in the Lockheed Hudson patrol bomber, whilst an operative carries on with his work.   *BPA*

Their Majesties King George VI and Queen Elizabeth stand at the entrance to the Flight Shed during their visit to Pendeford. 19th April 1940. *BPA*

When on 19th April 1940 King George VI and Queen Elizabeth visited the factory, an impressive line-up of Defiants awaited them. Arriving at Wolverhampton Airport at 10 am, they were entertained by an Auxiliary Fire Service display, followed by a low flying demonstration by the test pilot in a Defiant. Reaching the factory at 11 am, they then inspected the aircraft and the company officials conducted them on a tour of the works. The official hand-out read,

> Their Majesties will visit Boulton and Paul Aircraft Limited where Lord Gorell, CBE, MC, (Chairman), Herbert Strickland, Esq., (Managing Director) and Viscount Sandon, DL, JP, (Director) will be presented. The factory, which specializes in the production of Fighter Aeroplanes and aircraft Gun Turrets, was built three years ago, and now covers 60,000 square yards and employs 3,600 people, the majority of whom were previously employed in the local hollow-ware trade.

The tour moved through the various offices, to the factory, finally arriving at the Defiant assembly line and the apron outside the hangar where completed aircraft were inspected. The royal party then left for a visit to the large RAF station at Cosford.

115

The Pendeford factory had to date escaped the attention of the Luftwaffe but on Sunday, 29th September 1940 at 6.45 pm a lone Junkers Ju.88 appeared on the scene and dropped its bomb near the works. Mrs Phyllis Perry of Wolverhampton remembered the occasion, 'I was working in the canteen one Sunday afternoon, my friend and I were carrying tea from the canteen to the works. Suddenly a German aircraft came over and the men who manned the guns on the roof opened up on the raider. The bombs from the 'plane missed the factory and hit the sewage farm. Always, after that day, if we went into the open yard we had to exchange our white overalls for green ones.' None of the bombs caused any damage although if one of them had landed six feet the other way it would have breached the banks of the Shropshire Union Canal and flooded the factory. The bomber was later shot down and crash-landed near Nuneaton—to the bewilderment of the crew. They thought that the factory they had bombed had been the Rolls-Royce plant at Hucknall, near Nottingham.

A wartime *Daily Telegraph* article on J.D. North stated

North is an outstanding personality in more senses than one. I would not like to guess his weight, but he is well over six feet tall. When at work, which is nearly always, for he eats and often sleeps in the factory, he wears heavy horn rimmed glasses. He is fair and clean shaven. The company's Managing Director, Mr Herbert Strickland, told me the other day that ever since the Air Ministry arranged the entry of the Defiant into action against German 'planes, the workers have been puffing out their chests. Every mention of the Defiant is cut out and pasted up on the walls of workshops and canteens. And beneath the clippings they have written 'Our Work'.

Changes were made within the Drawing and Technical Offices because, as all contracts were now received direct from the Ministry of Defence, the usual sales procedure had altered. Mr W. J. Pickthorne, who had been responsible for sales and publicity, became Commercial Secretary in the Drawing Office. Mr Clarke had departed, Dr Redshaw had been appointed, and Mr J.W. Batchelor had been made Chief Designer—Aircraft, with Mr Cooper as Chief Draughtsman—Aircraft (Experimental).

Two large notice boards were erected on the hangar walls near the apron, warning employees that aircraft might arrive at the factory loaded with live ammunition. Visiting machines arrived and departed daily. They collected parts, carried official visitors, or came in for trial installations. In the latter case, one of the first to arrive was the American-built Lockheed Hudson which was to have a Boulton-Paul turret fitted in the dorsal position. The Hudson came to Pendeford for assessment as the actual turret fitting was carried out elsewhere, although the turret was of Boulton-Paul manufacture. Other arrivals, but mainly by road transport, were severely damaged Defiants which, due to the shortage of aircraft, were still required. Under normal circumstances many of these semi-wrecks would have been written off, but now they had to be repaired and returned to front-line service as soon as possible.

Wolverhampton Airport, which was the departure point for Pendeford built aircraft, was put to another use during 1941. Due to a great shortage of pilots for the RAF, strenuous efforts were being made to make good the shortfall. Part of this effort was the establishment at Wolverhampton of No 28 Elementary Flying Training School. The unit was under the control of No 51 Group Flying Training Command and was formed on 1st September 1941. Just ten days later the first pupils arrived. The school was operated by Air Schools Limited and from the outset thirty De Havilland Tiger Moths were taken on charge; a year later there were 108 aircraft engaged on training duties.

In order to accommodate this large number of aircraft taking off and landing, Relief Landing Grounds (RLG) had to be organised. These were established at Penkridge and Battlestead Hill and mainly used for night flying training. During this period the skies over the district must have echoed with the chatter of Gipsy engines for twenty-four hours a day when the weather was suitable. An interesting facet of the school was that during 1942 a contract was won with neutral Turkey to train their pilots for duty with the Turkish Air Force.

Mr K. J. Knowles of Bushbury remembered an amusing incident in 1942:

His Royal Highness the Duke of Kent stayed at Himley Hall as the invited guest of the Earl of Dudley. The Duke had particularly requested to visit the factory of Boulton-Paul Aircraft at Wolverhampton, where I was employed in the Transport Department. Mr North, the Managing Director, asked me if I would like to be the Duke's chauffeur for the duration of his stay at Himley—the Earl's chauffeur being indisposed. I accepted and became temporary chauffeur for five days. In the late afternoon of Friday, I set out on my last journey with the Duke to the Hall. On arrival the Duke asked his equerry, a Royal Air Force officer named Fielden, if he had any money on him. The equerry put his hand into his pocket and pulled out a ten shilling note which he handed to the Duke, who in turn gave it to me. I thanked the Duke and asked him if he would mind signing it for me. 'Certainly,' said the Duke, and asked his equerry for the loan of his pen. He placed the note on the gleaming Humber Snipe and was about to sign when I interrupted him. 'Excuse me, sir,' I said, 'please don't sign on the car, it will scratch the surface.' 'I am very sorry,' said the Duke, 'how thoughtless of me.' He then signed the note on his equerry's back and handed it to me. A fortnight after this incident the Duke was tragically killed in a 'plane crash.

As part of the 'Sister Firm' arrangement Boulton-Paul Aircraft were responsible for the American-built Douglas Boston and Havoc twin-engined aircraft. Here Boston IV BZ 435 is receiving attention from the Pendeford crews. *BPA*

Mr Charles Kenmer of Wolverhampton recalled his wartime days in the factory, 'At one period we became the "daughter firm" for the Douglas DB.7 Boston and Havoc. I had very little to do with the Boston but I remember the drawings which came from the United States as these were all very long, four or five times as long as the standard British ones.'

A British aircraft company was responsible for service, modifications and so forth for each type of lease-lend machine supplied to Britain. A.V. Roe of Manchester had the contract for the DB.7 Boston and Havoc at first—the Havoc was the night-fighter version of the Boston——but it was later transferred to Boulton-Paul Aircraft. The American drawings for these aircraft were nearly forty inches wide and twenty or more feet long. Apparently when they prepared a general arrangement drawing this occupied the first four feet or so, then came all the detail parts on the same roll of material. These massive drawings were almost impossible to track through a copying machine but were eventually replaced by micro-film reductions in book form.

Over the years there had been a great advance in the company's research and development. Many of the problems of forming large sheet metal panels had been overcome at the Pendeford works where heat treatment processes had been perfected to allow more complex pressings to be made. Part and parcel of the large panel manufacturing process was the employment of big rubber presses, the forming faces of which gave the finished work a very high degree of accuracy and surface finish. Working with a variety of metals, light alloy, stainless steel and many

118

others, these presses worked almost continuously, night and day, forming panels for not only the company's products but numerous others in the industry.

As the Defiant production line began running down in 1942, further aircraft assembly work was sought. At first it appeared that the Bristol Beaufighter twin-engined heavy fighter would be built under contract. This, however, never materialised and the next contract was to manufacture the Fairey Barracuda for the Royal Navy. The Barracuda had been designed by Fairey Aviation Limited as their Type 100 to meet Specification S.24/37, which had been issued during 1937 for a monoplane torpedo bomber to replace the Fairey Swordfish and Albacore. Originally it was to have been powered by a Rolls-Royce Exe 24 cylinder engine, but this had been discontinued by the Derby company and Fairey's airframe was re-designed to take the Rolls-Royce Merlin.

Of stressed skin construction, the layout was that of a shoulder wing monoplane with Alclad skin covering. This material was resistant to salt water corrosion and hence very suitable for a naval aircraft. Unfamiliar were the outboard mounted Fairey-Youngman, three-position flaps, which could be moved to high-lift depressed angle, fully depressed for landing and moved to a negative angle for dive bombing. The crew of

Boulton-Paul Aircraft built Fairey Barracuda II DP.860, one of a batch of 300 produced at the Pendeford factory. *BPA*

pilot, navigator and gunner/radio operator were housed in a long glasshouse atop the fuselage, although the middle man had his chart table and other tools of his trade in a spacious cabin located in the centre fuselage. This section was fitted with large windows for observation purposes. Armament was an externally slung 18 inch torpedo, or bombs, depth charges or mines. Its defence comprised a pair of flexible mounted Vickers 'K' guns in the rear cockpit. Only twenty-five of the Mark I version were built.

Fairey Barracuda production line at Pendeford during August 1942. These were larger aircraft than the Defiant and incorporated several unusual features. *BPA*

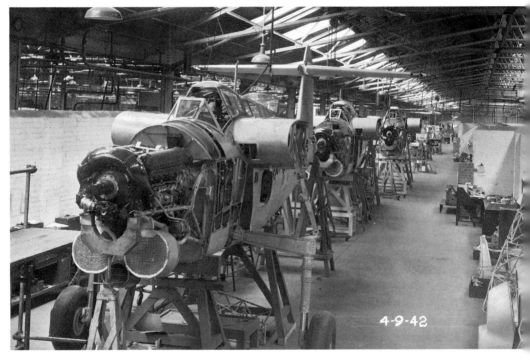

Boulton-Paul Aircraft were contracted to produce three hundred Barracuda Mark IIs and seven hundred Mark IIIs, but in fact only 692 were built as the remainder were cancelled. The Barracuda Mark II, as built at Wolverhampton, was the torpedo bomber version and the prototype, P.1767, had flown on 17th August 1942. Production was then started at the parent company's factory at Stockport, Blackburns at

120

Brough and Boulton-Paul at Wolverhampton. The Westland Aircraft Company at Yeovil joined them later. The Mark III was generally similar, but was intended for anti-submarine reconnaissance duties and for this work carried the Anti-Surface Vessel (ASV) Mark XX radar with a scanner under the rear fuselage. The prototype for this variant was a Boulton-Paul built Mark II, DP.585, and first flew during 1943.

Through no fault of its designers, the Barracuda was a much maligned aircraft. It was called upon to carry torpedoes, rockets, mines, bombs, lifeboats and clutters of radar equipment and their attendant masts. One unit even had to contend with containers under the mainplanes to carry secret agents to occupied Europe! Its required ability to be catapaulted or rocket-assisted into the air from vessels at sea presented the Barracuda with many difficulties. Nevertheless, this aircraft carried out numerous daring and shattering raids on the enemy and left its mark in the annals of naval aviation.

One of the varied jobs carried out by the Drawing Office during the early part of the Second World War was detail design work for the outer wings of the Gloster E.29/39, or Pioneer as it was sometimes called. This was the first jet to be built in this country and it made its first flight during the evening of 15th May 1941 at Cranwell.

Another project which never got under way was the construction of a large number of metal canoes for the Normandy invasion. Pendeford works' people recall thousands of paddles, which had been made by another contractor and intended for these craft, being received and held in stores.

Mr R.O. Jones of Franche recalled the trials of long range tanks which had a capacity of 250 gallons and were made at Wolverhampton in the Sheet Metal Section. 'They were fitted with a quick release mechanism so that they could be ejected if the machine was intercepted by enemy aircraft. The tank was slung into position under a fighter, but at this trial was empty so the camp commander was approached and permission given for a water bowser to fill the tank with water. It took a considerable time for us to convince the bowser crew that it really had to be filled with water and not aviation fuel.'

CHAPTER TEN

In from the Cold

IN ORDER to maintain continuity, the history of the powered aircraft gun turret has to be contained in one chapter and spans the period 1930 until the 1950s. This was a sphere of activity in which both the Norwich and Wolverhampton companies were engaged and they carried out the pioneer work on these products.

The origins of the hydraulically operated turret for aircraft lay in a small French company, SAT, which was engaged in the manufacture of a variety of mechanical devices. One of the licences held by the company was for the production of hydraulic pumps of Hele-Shaw design. Antoine de Boysson was an engineer working for SAT in 1930. Hydraulic power was a speciality of his, particularly as it applied to aircraft design. Recognising the difficulty of protecting air-gunners as aircraft speeds increased, he designed a gun turret to overcome this problem. The operating medium was by means of a variable flow hydraulic pump. His next step was to patent his invention in France. The French Air Ministry had shown interest and he cherished high hopes that his employers would take up his patent and manufacture the turret. For some reason SAT decided against manufacturing the turret so de Boysson took his design to another small French company, Société d'Application des Machines Motrices (SAMM). Here, at the age of forty, he was accepted and installed as the firm's consultant engineer. The company abandoned their other products and began the design and manufacture of hydraulic systems mainly for the aviation and armament markets. From these small beginnings they gradually expanded and became one of the leading designers and manufacturers of aircraft armament systems.

The first turret design incorporated twin drum-fed Lewis machine guns and was designated AB.1 after the initials of its designer, this form of designation following right through the entire range of turrets. One innovation was that the power supply for the turret was independent of the aircraft's main hydraulic power system. Perfected also was the control column or 'joystick' system which allowed the operator to control the movements of the turret with one hand. More ideas poured from the brilliant brain of de Boysson and over the next few years he patented remotely controlled turrets, automatic control of firing angles, shock-proof armament mountings, gunner controlled sights and continuous armament feeds.

Apart from the technical design work, de Boysson was also responsible for the marketing of SAMM products. Thus it was that during the mid-1930s negotiations took place between SAMM and Boulton and Paul Limited which culminated in an agreement for the Norwich company to manufacture the SAMM turret designs. The licence obtained gave Boulton and Paul Limited exclusive manufacturing rights in Great Britain and the British Empire as a whole.

On 23rd November 1935 two quadruple turrets were ordered from the French company, differing only from their own design in that they would mount Browning machine guns instead of the French designed Darne weapons. Options were also taken up on a powered turret capable of mounting a 20 mm cannon. The two French made turrets arrived at Norwich during July and August 1936, and one was installed in the front gun position of Overstrand K.8175. After development flying, various modifications were made to the turret with the incorporation of the design into the forthcoming Boulton and Paul P.82 two seat fighter in mind. Another Overstrand, K.8176, joined the Armament Development Trials and this was fitted with a pedestal mounted 20 mm Hispano shell-firing cannon. This was not an enclosed turret like the machine gun variant. So successful were the evaluation trials of the turrets that the newly formed Boulton-Paul Aircraft was confident enough to sign definitive licence agreements in April 1937.

As a result of the trials with the four gun turret, the Air Ministry issued a revised specification, F.9/35, which was virtually drawn up around the new armament feature. The basic turret which would be produced in England for installation in the P.82 was designated the Type A Mark II. It differed only from the French supplied SAMM AB.7 in some improvements for operational use, such as interconnections, the electrically operated firing mechanism and other small details.

The specimen turret of SAMM AB.15 type had been sent to Norwich and this mounted a Hispano-Suiza HS.404 20 mm cannon. This turret stood up well during trials and Boulton-Paul Aircraft seriously considered production. However, in the light of later events, it was fortunate that they did not proceed for there were difficulties in the production of the cannon after the fall of France in 1940. Many of the component parts were manufactured in France and of course the jigs and tools were lost after the German occupation.

Work went on apace in the Experimental Department to bring the turret up to production standards: many modifications needed to be incorporated into the final production model. The hydraulic control system of the four gun turret was new to the British design team. The original Boulton and Paul turret was a pneumatically operated system. It was quick and smooth but had its drawbacks, the chief of which was its limited power supply. Rapid use of the turret exhausted the air supply storage cylinders and it took a few minutes for the engine-driven compressor to charge them up to supply pressure again. The hydraulic system was compact, simple and gave good sensitivity of control and response. It was also superior so far as installation was concerned. Most important was the fact that the hydraulic system was contained within the rotating section of the turret. Also fractures and leaks caused by vibration were almost eliminated. The electric supply to power the self-contained hydraulic system was fed into the turret via a slip-ring on the axis of rotation. Maintenance crews were to appreciate this feature, for it only involved the turret being lowered into position, lined up and then bolted down, with electrical leads and external oxygen supply all feeding through the centre.

Type 'A' four-gun powered turret as fitted to Blackburn Roc and Boulton-Paul Defiant turret fighters. The unit was self-contained and required only external electrical supply.   *BPA*

The Type A Mark II gun turret mounted four Browning 0.303 inch machine guns and was more or less self-contained, requiring only external electrical supply. It was capable of full 360 degrees rotation, and when it was installed in fighter aircraft retractable fairings allowed the gun barrels to pass over the pilot's cockpit canopy. A special parachute pack was devised, of slim design, to allow the gunner to wear this essential piece of equipment within the confines of the turret.

The turret was constructed around a large casting and comprised a fixed ring, 43 inches in diameter, bolted to the aircraft's top longeron. Affixed to its inside perimeter was a gear ring for the drive pinion to engage. Integrated with the fixed ring and running on it, supported on ball bearings, was a rotating ring which carried the whole of the turret including the gunner and the cupola. The guns, two each side, one above the other, could be elevated or depressed by an hydraulic jack. If the hydraulics failed, pressure on the rear end of the guns caused them to elevate or depress. Rotation of the whole was achieved by an hydraulic motor directly mounted on the gear ring; once again, in the event of power failure, a hand operated gearbox and handle allowed rotation.

An electrically driven hydraulic generator or pump was plumbed via pipe lines to the drive motor and the gun operating jack. Control of the pump was via a direct mechanical link to a control column. This was slightly offset to the right of centre to suit the gunner's right hand. The control column moved in all axes; full forward movement depressed the guns at maximum speed whilst a backward movement achieved the reverse. Movement of the column to the right or left rotated the turret in either direction. Partial movement in any direction resulted in the same movement of the turret. Suspended under the casting were four ammunition boxes holding 600 rounds per gun, and canvas bags to receive the empty cartridge cases. An oxygen cylinder was also contained within the turret. The cupola incorporated sliding panels for access at the rear, and was fully glazed. A small instrument panel mounted hydraulic pressure gauges, and linked to the guns was a gyro gunsight, although reflector sights could also be fitted. A piece of armour plate provided some protection for the gunner's face. The guns were fitted electrically by means of solenoids and wired into firing cut-out devices which stopped the guns if directed towards any part of the aircraft's structure. A large door under the gunner's seat allowed access and exit. This lower door was also used for maintenance purposes. The turret weighed in at 361 pounds less guns, sights and accessories.

Operation of the turret, from the gunner's point of view, was quite complicated but it soon became second nature. The turret had to be entered in the correct manner or else the result would be a tangle of arms, legs and parachute. Correct stowage of the specially designed parachute was essential before entry in order to ensure its easy removal when required. Once the feet and legs were over the edge of the turret, the two upright struts within the turret had to be grasped to take the gunner's weight, not the glazed structure of the cupola as this was liable to cause distortion of the sliding turret doors. Positioning of the feet in the foot rests was also vital because if left dangling beneath the seat there was every chance of their being removed, at the ankle, when the turret rotated. Ample adjustment of the gunner's seat was provided. It was most important that this was correctly set up for the gunner to line up with his gun sights and for an even distribution of weight.

Cocking the four guns was a time consuming chore as each gun had to be cocked twice separately. This was to ensure that the first round of ammunition on each belt from the ammunition boxes below the turret was securely fed into the gun breeches. Intercommunication leads were then coupled, oxygen pipes connected, and a series of switches operated for the reflector gun-sight, power pump, control column and firing controls. If this operation was not carried out in the correct sequence, it would result in the main turret fuse blowing. The rotation of the turret was checked through 360 degrees, also the lowering and raising of the fairings fore and aft. Only after all these procedures had been carried out to the gunner's satisfaction was he able to call up his pilot and report that he was ready for take-off. After flight check-down was carried out with very much the same procedure.

There was a precise series of procedures for the armourers too. The ammunition belts had to be carefully positioned in the four ammunition boxes, and then loaded into the bottom of the turret via a detachable hatch in the fuselage bottom. The belt ends were then passed up, one at a time, to a second armourer sitting in the turret above. The canvas bags for collecting the spent cartridge cases also had to be secured.

Often referred to as the 'Defiant Turret', even in France, the Type A went into production at the new Wolverhampton factory. Full collaboration on all modifications was carried out with de Boysson's knowledge and assistance. A full set of drawing prints was sent from France but the translation and re-drafting to Imperial standards and measurements was carried out at Norwich before the move to Wolverhampton. The Armament Section was headed by Mr 'Pop' Hughes with Mr A. Doe as his Chief Draughtsman.

Impressed into service with the RAF and engaged on maritime patrol duties, the ex-Imperial Airways Short 'C' and 'G' Class four-engined passenger flying boats were some of the first aircraft to be fitted with Boulton-Paul turrets. Cousins of the famous Short Sunderland, they

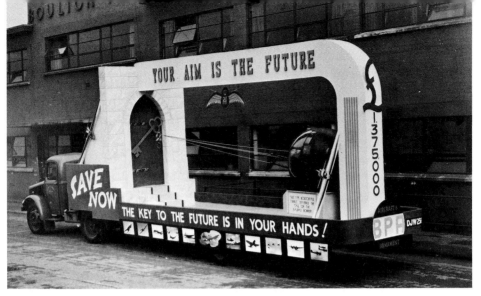

To boost the war effort and raise funds from the public, Boulton-Paul Aircraft converted one of their articulated lorries into a display vehicle which toured exhibitions and displays.

John Chambers

were able to be converted for their wartime work. The 'C' Class or Empire flying boats, *Clio* and *Cordelia*, were taken into RAF service during July 1940, and flown to Short and Harland's factory at Queen's Island, Belfast, to be converted for Coastal Command operations. This included the fitting of two Type A Mark II four gun turrets, one amidships and the other in a new position astern of the tailplane, in the same manner as the Sunderland. The two aircraft were then serialled AX.659 and AX.660.

Larger than the 'C' Class Empire boats, the 'G' or *Golden Hind* Class had been launched prior to the Second World War but like the 'C' Class were now being converted for military duties during the summer of 1940. *Golden Fleece*, not yet registered, *Golden Hind*, G-AFCI, and *Golden Horn*, G-AFCK, became X.8274, X.8275 and X.8273 respectively and were converted by Blackburns at their Dumbarton works on the River Clyde. They were each fitted with three Type A Mark II four gun turrets, located amidships on the upper hull, one halfway back towards the tail unit and the other in the stern aft of the tail unit. The last installation necessitated a new rear fuselage section to replace the streamlined tail cone. Each gun was provided with 600 rounds of ammunition. With the conversion of plough shares to swords the air merchant fleet went to war.

This turret was also used by fast motor patrol boats and air-sea rescue launches. Here a problem arose: the main turret member was cast from magnesium alloy, very susceptible to sea water corrosion. The

127

difficulty was overcome by the use of light alloy. Other turrets also armed with four 0.303 inch machine guns were designed for use on mine-sweepers.

The early versions of the four-engined Handley-Page Halifax to enter RAF Bomber Command were armed with Boulton-Paul designed power-operated turrets. In front was a Type C Mark I, mid-upper, a Type C Mark V, each with two 0.303 inch Browning machine guns, and the tail turret was a Type E Mark I four gun unit.

Lockheed Hudson N.7208, the third aircraft to be delivered to the RAF from the USA, is measured up in the new Pendeford Flight Shed prior to having the first 'C' Type turret fitted.

Colin Manning

The American designed and built Lockheed Hudson twin-engined maritime patrol bomber had been the subject of a purchase agreement with the USA just prior to the Second World War for service with the RAF. It was fitted with the Boulton-Paul Type C Mark II or IIA in the dorsal position. Fully glazed with a specially contoured cupola, it was capable of covering the whole hemisphere, and mounted two 0.303 inch Browning guns. It proved to be very effective during many encounters with enemy surface and undersea vessels, as well as hostile aircraft. Later, during the Second World War, the Hudson's big brother, the Lockheed Vega Ventura, was fitted with a similar turret in the same position; in this aircraft either two or four 0.303 inch Browning guns could be fitted. This turret, the Type C Mark IV, provided 2,000 rounds per gun and the Ventura, although not widely used by the RAF, did carry out several notable operations including the daylight bombing of the Philips Radio and Valve Works at Eindhoven in Holland, during the course of which a crew member was awarded the Victoria Cross.

Another United States designed and built aircraft which operated mainly in the Middle East was the Martin Baltimore, a twin-engined medium bomber fitted with a Type A four gun turret mounted in the mid-upper position and capable of complete rotation. The Consolidated B.24 Liberator, a heavy four-engined bomber, was also of American design and manufacture. It served with the RAF Coastal Command and was equipped with two Boulton-Paul turrets, Type E Mark IIA and Mark IIE, mounting four 0.303 inch Browning machine guns located in the mid-upper and tail positions. These machines proved very successful with long range maritime patrols over the North Atlantic and the Bay of Biscay in search of enemy U-boats.

The Armstrong-Whitworth Albemarle was also fitted with a Type A Mark II four gun turret in the dorsal position. Only forty-two examples were built as bombers but many more as glider tugs and transpsort aircraft, some even seeing service in Russia.

Much later the big brother of the Avro Lancaster, the Lincoln, was equipped with a Type F turret which mounted two 0.5 inch machine guns in the nose position and was remotely controlled. The rear turret was of the Type D and carried two 12.7 mm guns and was aimed and controlled by a radar scanner in the extreme rear end of the fuselage. In line of succession, the Lincoln developed into the maritime patrol aircraft, the four-engined Shackleton.

Avro Lincoln RE 418 fitted with remotely controlled Type 'F' turret in the front gun position and a Type 'D' radar scanner controlled turret at the rear.   *British Aerospace*

In the early days of the Second World War until the fall of France, the Americans had been interested in de Boysson's turret designs. During 1941 they entered into negotiations with Boulton-Paul, who offered manufacturing rights to the American company, Emerson. This firm then produced two gun, 12.7 mm turrets, many of which were fitted in the B.24 Liberators employed by the United States Army Air Force. As a reverse form of lease-lend, John North and Pop Hughes, the Chief Armament Designer, had gone to the United States to impart their specialised knowledge of the turret to the American aircraft and armament industry. For their return journey North travelled by air but Hughes preferred a sea crossing. North arrived safely but Hughes lost his life when his ship was torpedoed.

Once war had been declared the Wolverhampton company expected a much greater demand for their turrets, and to allow for the increased production a new building was constructed to house their manufacture. It was completed in 1940 but before the equipment was installed the Ministry of War Production decided to switch manufacture to other sources of supply. The reason for this decision was to allow Boulton-Paul to concentrate on aircraft manufacture, as well as the design and development of new turrets. The turrets were manufactured by Joseph Lucas Limited at Birmingham.

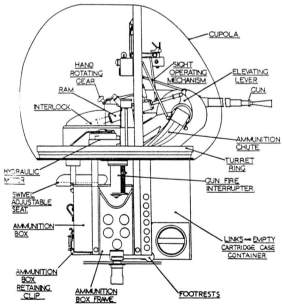

Operating diagram for the 'C' turret showing the all-round visibility available to the gunner.

BPA

In February 1940 Lucas received orders for 4,242 turrets and 3,982 cupolas, destined for the Defiant, the Lockheed Hudson, the Halifax and the Albemarle. To meet this demand a 'shadow' factory used for stores at Formans Road was immediately equipped for gun turret production. More than 20,000 Boulton-Paul electro-hydraulically operated aircraft gun turrets were made by them during the Second World War. They also made large numbers of hydraulically operated turrets of Frazer-Nash design, for Lancasters and Wellingtons.

The range of Boulton-Paul turrets followed similar lines but were engineered for their specific duties. The Type C turret was a two gun version of the Type A for fitment in the front gun position and allowed sufficient room below the turret for the bomb-aimer's position. With the reduced number of guns, ammunition was increased to 1,000 rounds per gun. Another modification was that only partial rotation was required but gun depression was essential. The glazed cupola was tailored to fit its environment with access doors in the rear, opening into the fuselage. They could also be opened when in the fully sidewards rotated position to allow emergency escape for the gunner.

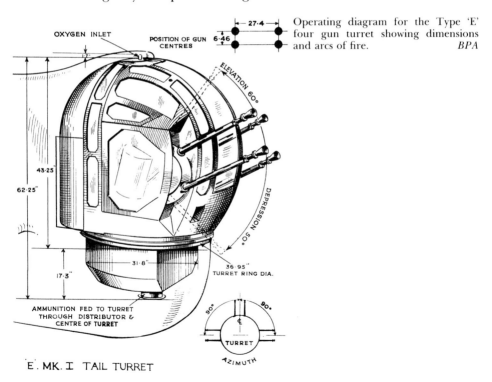

Operating diagram for the Type 'E' four gun turret showing dimensions and arcs of fire.   *BPA*

The Type E, designed for the rear position in a bomber, was a four gun unit and once again the cupola was tailored to fit the existing fuselage profile. One big change was that the ammunition was stored in the rear fuselage instead of in the turret. Fixed steel tracks installed along the fuselage sides conveyed the ammunition in its belts to the guns via a roller bar at the base of the turret. As the turret required only partial rotation, this arrangement saved considerable weight at a crucial position so well aft of the centre of gravity. It also allowed additional ammunition to be carried, 2,000 rounds per gun in the boxes and 695 rounds in the carrying tracks. Access doors, escape arrangements and parachute stowage were the same as the Type C.

Later the four 0.303 inch guns were replaced by two 0.5 inch guns. These more powerful weapons necessitated a more robust gun mounting, and with the heavier ammunition the number of rounds was reduced to 750 per gun in the boxes and a further 350 in the tracks. In this form the unit was re-designated Type D and, when later modified to fit on the Avro Lincoln, it was fitted with a special radar sight which locked the turret onto a receiver signal. Other turrets were designed for a variety of aircraft, but orders failed to materialise. All the 0.303 inch and 0.5 inch machine guns were of Browning manufacture and the 20 mm cannons of Hispano design.

Boulton-Paul were involved with the research and development of various items of equipment associated with their turrets: gun mountings for 0.303 and 0.50 inch guns and 20 mm cannons, for both two and four gun, hydraulically controlled recoil units, and remotely controlled babettes. They also established a Turret School for RAF personnel to be trained in the correct maintenance of the turrets.

In the late 1930s the Hispano-Suiza 20 mm cannon was regarded as an ideal weapon for future bombers. Many designs for suitable aircraft were prepared but never accepted. Boulton-Paul were given a contract to install the weapon in a Defiant prototype. On 28th July 1939 it duly arrived at the A&AEE. It was air tested but there were too many problems; the project was shelved and the turret stored. The idea had not, however, died completely. A battle-damaged Defiant arrived at Wolverhampton in 1941 for repair. This machine, N.1622, was rather special, for when serving with No 141 Squadron it had claimed a Heinkel He.III, destroyed at night. Because the single cannon turret was still in the works, and was interchangeable with the current Type A Mark IID unit, permission was sought and received to continue the programme using N.1622 as the trials aircraft. These trials progressed through 1941 and early 1942, when another Defiant, N.3397, joined the test programme. Although the turret rotation torque was greatly reduced, the standard hydraulic system was not capable of turning the turret more than 30 degrees from the astern position into the airstream. It was considered impractical to install extra hydraulic power for this purpose and once again the single cannon turret fell by the wayside.

Turret School at Pendeford with Hudson turret at left front, and installed in a mock-up fuselage at left rear; a Defiant turret is at right front.   *BPA*

During the period 3rd September 1939 to 15th August 1945, the company produced 1,597 gun turrets and 207 sets of special turret equipment for test and training purposes. Many thousands of turrets

133

were also manufactured by outside contractors. Towards the end of the war the demand for turrets dropped dramatically. Not only had the quantity of turrets for current aircraft types decreased, but new types coming into service were no longer employing turreted guns for defence. The designs for new heavy bomber aircraft came as a surprise, for all defensive armament was absent, the aircraft's speed and altitude hopefully making it almost immune to fighter interception and attack. The Mosquito was the first example, and that was followed into service by the jet bombers, the twin jet Canberra, and four jet Valiant, Victor and Vulcan, all fast, high flying and unarmed. During the latter stages of the war the wing-mounted rocket projectile had come into service and in many instances was replacing the gun in both fighters and bombers.

The supply of spares for those turrets still in service kept that department busy for a brief spell. When Boulton-Paul's competitor in this field, Parnells, who made the Frazer-Nash (FN) turrets fitted to many bombers such as the Lancaster, Whitley and Wellington, ceased production, the Wolverhampton company took on their spares responsibility too. All Frazer-Nash drawings were sent to Wolverhampton so that continuity of spares could be maintained. The Ministry of Defence had thought it wise to have an alternative range of powered turrets available for its aircraft. The Boulton-Paul electro-hydraulic system was preferred, but as this system was patented by the Wolverhampton company, the Frazer-Nash turrets had to use an hydraulic power supply from engine drive pumps. The engines were mounted out on the mainplanes so it required long hydraulic pipelines; these were prone to leakage and, in an operational aircraft, damage from enemy fire.

Boulton-Paul turrets can still be seen in the Lincoln bomber at the RAF Museum, Cosford, and on the Defiant in the RAF Museum, Hendon, where there is also a tail turret salvaged with the Halifax from the bottom of a Norwegian lake. Originally conceived in the Norwich Design Office, where far-sighted men were able to see the future requirements of the Royal Air Force, the design and development of the turret as defensive armament was a most interesting phase.

In conclusion, Mr J.D. North always held positive views regarding the aircraft turret and a memorandum written by him during September 1940 fully expressed these:

> Although the importance of speed, climb and manoeuvrability has in no way diminished, since superiority in these characteristics ensures the power of initiative, armament and armour play an essential part in the make-up of the fighting qualities of military aircraft. In the provision of effective armament, the technical equipment of the Royal Air Force has attained a higher standard than that in any other Power. This has been achieved not only by high fire

A wartime exhibition mounted by Boulton Paul Aircraft and designed to raise funds from the public. This particular one gave the 'man in the street' a chance to operate an aircraft powered turret.

BPA

concentration but also by the use of power operated gun turrets which allow accurate aiming at high speeds.

The use of turrets in aircraft has been the subject of much public discussion, not to say controversy, among writers on military aeronautics, particularly in France. Bougeron, who was at one time the head of the armament division of the French Air Ministry, in his book confidently stated that turrets could not successfully be employed in aircraft. Firstly, because it would be impossible to maintain an adequate standard of performance in any aircraft fitted with turrets and, secondly, because the relative velocity of the aircraft would make it impossible to obtain a hit with a gun not firing along the direction of the flight. Other writers expressed their equally confident opinion that it would be impossible to fire broadside from an aeroplane because the stability of the bullet would be so disturbed by the relative wind that any sort of accurate shooting would be unlikely. It is even supported by some alleged experiments carried out at the French gunnery experimental station at Caseaux, as a result of which it was said that bullets fired broadside from aeroplanes travelling at a high speed had been found to turn over in flight with loss of all directional accuracy. Although it was known from other sources that these statements were incorrect, I was interested to hear as recently as last May from the lips of the chief experimental gunnery officer at Caseaux that this story was complete fiction and that this phenomenon to which the writers had not even hesitated to give the special name of the 'Caseaux effect' was quite unkown to them.

From the many accounts of air operations which have appeared in the press everyone will now be familiar with the fact that British bombers are equipped with gun turrets, and this has been done whilst maintaining a high standard of performance and providing a defensive armament which enemy fighters have learned to hold in great respect. The weapon so forged is not only for the immediate present, but for the future as well, and in its allotted role the turret fighter is playing, and will play, its part.

CHAPTER ELEVEN

First Again

ALTHOUGH the company was very busy at this period, the design of new aircraft had not been abandoned: several interesting projects were under preparation. One such was the P.105, a single-engined deck landing aircraft which was proposed during 1944.

Designed round the Bristol Centauras sleeve valve radial air-cooled engine, this type would have been unusual because the basic airframe could have been quickly adapted for several different roles by means of a field conversion kit. The fuselage was capable of conversion by adding or removing components to accommodate a pilot only or pilot and observer. It could carry a varied complement of armaments—torpedo, bombs or reconnaissance equipment. It could also be armed as an interceptor or strike fighter. Designed to be the smallest deck-landing naval high performance aircraft, the P.105 could be converted to any of these roles aboard its parent carrier. The estimated performance was quite spectacular: at an average all-up weight of 12,500 pounds, the speed of the fighter version at 25,000 feet was 455 mph, whilst the torpedo carrying variant was only 5 mph slower. However, with the cessation of hostilities in sight, the proposed design was abandoned.

The end of the war resulted in the termination of many contracts, and others were drastically cut back. As a consequence the workforce was substantially reduced, more than two-thirds going within the first month or so. Mr Chambers remembered 'large queues of people lining up to get their cards. My staff of fifteen went down to three or four and the new canteen was closed and used for other purposes'.

Mr Ian James, once Technical Librarian for the company, recalled his days during this period:

Many of the leading figures at Boulton-Paul were known by their initials or by contractions of their surnames. Mr North was always J.D.—but not to his face. As I remember, there was also Mr B.F. Clarke—B.F., and Mr V.J. Johnston—V.J., always dapper and with a fresh carnation in his button-hole every morning. The Technical Director, Mr F.F. Crocombe, co-developer of the Monospar construction technique and later designer of the Hamilcar heavy glider and Beverley transport, was very much a gentleman and always referred to as 'Croak'.

Mr F.F. Crocombe, Technical Director, co-developer of the Monospar aircraft construction system and later the designer of several large aircraft. *John Chambers*

J.D. took a great interest in the Technical Library which he considered almost as his private preserve, and he had a very good knowledge of its contents. When sending his secretary for a book he could not always give the full title but could always give some information about it. For instance, 'It's a thick blue book and the name of the author is P.S. Barnes.' What is more, he was always right!

On 15th January 1946 Boulton-Paul Aircraft were successful in signing a contract to re-furbish and convert Vickers Wellington bombers into trainers for bomber crews, mostly navigators. The twin-engined geodetic frameworked monoplanes were flown into Wolverhampton and at one time a line-up of these aircraft, awaiting conversion, stretched down the edge of the runway, sometimes to be bogged down in the mud!

Upon entering the works they were completely stripped down, all the old equipment was discarded and new systems built in. When the 'new Wimpys for old process' was completed, they emerged from the factory as new aircraft. The Wellington was a fabric covered aeroplane and when the trainers came out from the Flight Shed they had a totally different appearance. The turrets of Frazer-Nash manufacture had disappeared from the nose and tail, and the aircraft was doped aluminium over all except for trainer yellow bands on the mainplanes and fuselage. The first Wellington T.10, as the type was then designated, was delivered on 20th June 1946 and the last on 15th November 1950. Records show that 154 Wellington bombers were converted to the trainer version. Officially designated as a post war trainer, the T.10 had provision for two pilots, three navigators, two signallers and one instructor, and were used by a number of training units including No 1 Air Navigation School, South Cerney, and No 201 Advanced Flying School at Swinderby. The last Wellington in RAF service was flying until 1953. The only Wellington preserved at present, apart from that salvaged from Loch Ness, is the T.10 proudly displayed in the RAF Museum at Hendon and now converted back to the bomber version. This aircraft, MF.628, was one of the Boulton-Paul conversions.

137

Armstrong-Vickers Wellington twin-engine bomber after conversion at Pendeford to Heavy Trainer T.10 configuration. This entailed complete refurbishment with an unfamiliar finish—all-over aluminium with yellow bands.   *John Chambers*

With the end of the war there was less call for new pilots, and tuition ceased at the school on Wolverhampton Airport. However, it continued to run refresher courses and to instruct pilots of foreign air forces. A few months later the RAF reviewed its training requirements and decided to combine the Elementary Flying Training Schools into the Reserve to provide refresher training courses for pilots and navigators. Under this ruling, on 26th June 1947 No 28 EFTS, Wolverhampton, became No 25 Reserve Flying School (RFS) and was operated by Air Schools Limited using civilian flying and ground staff. The unit complement of aircraft was twelve De Havilland Tiger Moths and one Avro Anson.

When Flight Lieutenant Feather retired as Chief Test Pilot from Boulton-Paul Aircraft in September 1945, his position was taken by Robert Lindsay Neale. His new assistant was Kingsley Peter Henry Tisshaw. Tisshaw was born at Putney, London, on 25th September 1923, and received his education at St Paul's School and Aberdeen University. He joined the RAF in 1941 and after training in the USA served as a flying instructor at a number of RAF home stations. In 1945 he was posted to Turkey, returning to this country in January 1947. He joined Boulton-Paul Aircraft in August of that year.

The Boulton-Paul Board of Directors lost one of its members when Mr N.R. Adshead died during 1948 and Mr J.D. North became sole Managing Director. A month later Dr S.C. Redshaw was appointed to the board as Chief Engineer and Mr G.C. Haynes joined as Director and Secretary.

Mr F.A. Jackson recalled post-war days:

During the war I was trained in electronics for maintaining radar equipment so when I returned to the factory in 1946 I joined a newly formed Electronics

Department of four persons. In charge of the department was Peter Lee, a young physics graduate who later became Professor of Physics at Toronto University, Charlie Jones, an amateur radio enthusiast who was an expert in the construction of small pieces of intricate metalwork, an apprentice, Ron Whitehouse, and myself.

We developed the earliest galvanometer recorder for in-flight measurements, a pressure recorder for distribution of pressure across the wing surfaces in flight, and this led to the development of an hydraulic system for automatic correction for gust alleviation. I left Boulton-Paul for another electronics firm, but on paying a visit to Pendeford twenty years later, it did not have the same excitement as my return during 1946. On that occasion I found my tool box had stood in the same spot for seven years whilst I was away at the war and the mug of tea I had been drinking at the time of my call-up had turned into a hard green mess!

On 3rd May 1948 a young draughtsman, Rex Farran, who worked in the Drawing Office at Boulton-Paul Aircraft Limited, lost his life in most tragic circumstances. A parcel bomb addressed to Captain Roy Farran, his elder brother, was delivered at his Codsall address. It exploded when Rex Farran opened it, causing him injuries from which he died at the Royal Hospital the same day. The explosion occurred within three days of the first anniversary of the disappearance of the Jewish youth, Alexander Rubowitz, a member of the Stern Gang, with whose murder Captain Roy Farran had been charged and acquitted on 2nd October 1947.

An Airspeed Oxford AS.10 ex-RAF twin-engined trainer, now carrying the civil registration G-A.HTW, had been acquired by the company and was used at Pendeford as a general runabout. It was taken out of service during December 1960 and, after repainting in RAF training Command colours, was re-serialled with its former number V.3388. It eventually found a home at the Imperial War Museum at Duxford. Now resplendent in pre-war trainer colours it is available for viewing by the thousands of 'sprog pilots' who once spent their advanced flying training in the 'Oxbox'.

Airspeed AS.10 Oxford twin-engine trainer which was used as a company runabout by the Chief Test Pilot, Robert Lindsay Neale. *John Chambers*

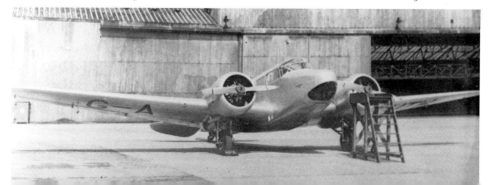

The Air Ministry had drawn up a Specification, T.7/45, for an advanced trainer with a turbo-prop power plant for the RAF. It was also unusual in that it called for a three-seater aircraft instead of the customary two. Boulton-Paul Aircraft tendered their design, P.108, and three prototype aircraft were ordered to be powered by the then untried Armstrong Siddeley Mamba turbo-prop unit. The design which emerged from the Wolverhampton Drawing Office was a low wing, all metal monoplane of clean lines with side by side seating for instructor and pupil with the third occupant in the centre behind the two front seats. The third seat became affectionately known as the 'rumble seat' or 'dicky'. This arrangement was thought the most satisfactory for advanced training.

A problem to be overcome was the requirement of a very short landing run, for after passing over a fifty foot screen, the run was to be a mere 750 yards. In fact, during later flight trials, the P.108 was able to achieve 650 yards! The aircraft's operational duties were taken into consideration for in the hands of pupils the machine was prone to damage caused by heavy landings, taxiing accidents and so on. To achieve these features, Boulton-Paul used the experience of maintenance specialists in the Ministry of Supply and the Air Ministry on all these points which had proved a source of trouble. Selective controls in the cockpit regulated heating and ventilation, and the sliding cockpit hood and the windscreen wipers were electrically operated. Fuel was carried in three tanks, one in the fuselage and one in each wing and all were crash proof.

Construction proceeded well on the P.108—this was Boulton-Paul's 108th design—but when the airframe was almost complete there was no sign of the turbo-prop power unit. Plans were made to replace it with the Rolls-Royce Dart turbo-prop unit which was expected to weigh around 600 pounds and develop some 1,000 bhp. Unfortunately the Dart also failed to arrive in time. For this reason the Drawing Office had to look around for another power unit in order to get the P.108 into the air for aerodynamic testing. The choice eventually made was something quite different, a nine cylinder air-cooled Bristol Mercury 30 radial engine of 820 hp. This engine could be installed without major change and with this engine the P.108, VL.892, made its maiden flight on 30th May 1947. Initial results were encouraging and many hours were clocked up in the intensive flight test programme which had been prepared for the P.108. The Balliol, as it was designated after the famous Oxford seat of learning, made its public debut at the Society of British Aeroplane Constructors (SBAC) Show held at Handley-Page's aerodrome at Radlett, Herts, on 9th–12th September 1947. Aeronautical writers of the day were enthusiastic about the aircraft and mentioned as a side issue that this aircraft marked the return of Boulton-Paul as designers. It was their first original aeroplane since the days of the Defiant.

Boulton-Paul P.108 Balliol VL.892 airborne with a temporary Bristol Mercury air-cooled radial engine, prior to the arrival of the intended turbo-prop unit.   *BPA*

The Dart turbo-prop unit was still delayed, but the Armstrong Siddeley Mamba had become available. However, a new problem presented itself for the Mamba was an axial compressor design, whereas the Dart was a centrifugal one. This meant that in practice the Mamba had a faster idling speed and the aircraft wanted to run away across the airfield. This was overcome by re-designing the propeller.

The first flight of the Mamba powered P.108, VL.917, was made on 24th March 1948 from Pendeford airfield, with Robert Lindsay Neale as the pilot. All went well until the final approach, when there was some malfunction of the propeller. This resulted in a very steep rate of descent and the aircraft hitting the boundary fence and crashing onto the airfield. The pilot escaped with some broken bones, including a broken leg. This flight was memorable as it was the first flight in the world of an aircraft solely powered by a single turbo-prop unit. The next Mamba powered flight was made by the second P.108 prototype, VL.935, on 17th

Balliol VL.935 fitted with Armstrong Siddeley Mamba turbo-prop power unit. This was the first type of aircraft in the world to fly powered solely by this form of propulsion.   *BPA*

May 1948 from Armstrong Siddeley's airfield at Bitteswell, Coventry, by their Chief Test Pilot, Squadron Leader Waldo Price-Owen. Considerable test flying was carried out by the four prototypes, VL.892, VL.917, VL.925 and VL.935, and at a later stage the Mercury powered P.108 was re-motored with a Mamba. The Mercury piston engined prototype was capable of a top speed of 280 mph whilst the Mamba versions were able to attain 307 mph. The turbos were heavier though, weighing in at 7,845 pounds against the piston engined version at 7,575 pounds

The Avro Athena had been designed to the same specification and bore a striking resemblance to the P.108, with the same power plant and layout. At one time the two aircraft types were evaluated side by side by the A&AEE at Boscombe Down. The Manchester firm had received an order for three prototypes. The first aircraft was Mamba powered, the second Dart and the third Mamba. Also in the running was another aircraft to the same specification, the Percival Prentice.

Not unusually, the Air Ministry had a change of heart and decided that the third seat was no longer required; they also changed their minds regarding the power units to be used. Incredibly, a new specification, T.14/47, was issued, calling for some minor alterations, including, surprisingly, a piston engine. After so much pioneering work with the turbo-props, it was bewildering to learn that the design was now to revert to a Rolls-Royce Merlin. Both Boulton-Paul Aircraft and Avro received a further order for four prototypes each to the new specification, the Wolverhampton machine to be designated Balliol T.2 as opposed to the previous prototypes of T.1 classification, and the Athena T.2 likewise. The Balliols were serialled VW.897–VW.900, and the Athenas VW.890–VW.893. Power in both machines was to be the 12 cylinder, liquid-cooled Rolls-Royce Merlin 35, derated to 1,245 hp and employing a single stage blower instead of the two speed unit.

All went well and a considerable number of tests were carried out, and the hours mounted up until on 3rd February 1949 disaster struck. The *Wolverhampton Express and Star* reported:

> Two of the country's leading test pilots were killed instantly yesterday evening when the 'plane they were flying crashed into a potato field at Coven, near Wolverhampton. Robert Lindsay Neale (37), Chief Test Pilot of Boulton-Paul Aircraft Limited, Wolverhampton, was one of the men, and the firm's second Test Pilot, Peter Tisshaw (25), was the other. Both men were so badly burned as to be almost unrecognisable. Immediately after the crash their bodies were taken to Coven mortuary. Wreckage from the 'plane was strewn for a radius of 200 yards in the field and last night men from Pendeford RAF Training Sector remained on guard. Both men were married and both have young children. The crash occurred shortly after 4 o'clock. The 'plane they were flying was a Balliol Mark II trainer fitted with an orthodox type piston engine. The trainer had been designed to be powered by a gas turbine driving an airscrew and was the first airscrew turbine trainer aircraft to fly in any country.
>
> When the crash occurred Mr John Barnes of Coven Lawn Farm was working in the field with a tractor. Accompanying him was 17 year old Ivor Brinlow. Mr Barnes told an *Express and Star* reporter, 'It hit the ground about 40 yards from where we were working and burst into flames.' Less than a fortnight ago, Boulton-Paul Aircraft Limited announced that their Balliol Mark II fighter-trainer had attained a speed of 540 mph—nearly twice the normal cruising speed—in dive tests over the Wolverhampton district. These speeds were reached by Neale and Tisshaw, not actually to find the 'plane's maximum speed, but to test the security of the sliding cockpit cover over the pilot and pupil.

A joint funeral service was held at Coven Church on 9th February 1949. After the tragic crash, one of Neale's colleagues wrote, 'As a test pilot he was outstanding. Completely fearless and quick at decision in emergency, he brought to his task a cool detachment from the purely mechanical business of flying. Always serious in discussing official business, Robin was a light-hearted companion in his leisure hours. He retained a boyish sense of fun – almost frivolity – and was a tireless addition to any company.'

Merlin powered Balliol I VW.897, redesignated T.2 and to Specification T.14/47.   *BPA*

Another colleague wrote, 'Peter Tisshaw belonged to a generation of up and coming young test pilots and his skill in flying and reliability of judgement had always commanded the respect of his colleagues. Quiet in manner and very likeable in disposition, he was happiest when in the air.'

Two points of debate arose from this tragic accident: why did both the Chief Test Pilot and his assistant need to be in the aircraft at the same time, and why had the aircraft apparently exceeded its design speed? It had been reported that while carrying out strain gauge testing of the Balliol windscreen, the glass had broken at 80 per cent full load. After consideration it was decided that the wrong method of testing had been employed. Subsequently, under a different form of test, the full load had been reached without problems. Soon after, however, during the fatal test flight at full speed, the windscreen had failed again at 80 per cent load.

As the company was now without a Chief Test Pilot, urgent arrangements were made for a replacement and Mr A.E. 'Ben' Gunn was appointed. Joining the RAF, he had gained his wings at the RAF College, Cranwell, in 1943 and after further training was posted to No 501 (F) Squadron, flying Spitfires. Later in No 274 Squadron, he flew Hawker Tempest 5s, but after D-Day was posted to the A&AEE at Boscombe Down. In December 1948 he had just completed the Empire Test Pilot's Course at Farnborough when the Air Ministry requested a service test pilot to be seconded to Boulton-Paul following the sad loss of both their

144

own test pilots. He jumped at the opportunity, with the continuing task of clearing the prototype Balliol for its service trials at the A&AEE as his immediate objective. He realised the potential of becoming a civilian test pilot and left the Royal Air Force in February the following year to join the Boulton-Paul payroll.

The newly appointed Chief Test Pilot, Mr A.E. 'Ben' Gunn seated in the cockpit of a Balliol when evaluating this aircraft.   *John Chambers*

A considerable amount of test flying was necessary before the Merlin engined prototype reached the standard required for service trials. The aircraft was pleasant to fly and ideal for the role of advanced trainer but troublesome handling characteristics had been noticed. By dint of much hard work in the Experimental Shop the major modification of 'cocking down' the tailplane two degrees was accomplished. This proved most effective and the aircraft was delivered to Boscombe Down.

An ex-naval pilot, 'Dickie' Mancus, who had been carrying out test flying with the Aero Flight at the Royal Aircraft Establishment, Farnborough, joined Boulton-Paul early during 1949 to assist 'Ben' Gunn in test flying. His experience of naval flying procedures was invaluable as the Balliol was being offered to the Royal Navy as a sea-going trainer. In this sphere he carried out the test flying and Acceptance Trials for the Royal Navy ordered machines, the Sea Balliol T.21. He also tested the Balliols that had been ordered by the Royal Ceylonese Air Force. This was to be carried out after the aircraft had been shipped to what was then Ceylon, now Sri Lanka.

Trials continued, one of the four prototype Balliol 2s making a 5,000 mile flight to the Tropical Experimental Unit, Khartoum. The aircraft was equipped with drop tanks for the flight from Boscombe Down to

Eastleigh (Nairobi), where further trials were made after the pause at Khartoum. Squadron Leader P.P.C. Barthropp, DFC, flew the Balliol and his navigator was Squadron Leader D.M.T. McRae, DFC. The route taken was Boscombe Down–Istres–El Aovina–Castel Benito–Benina–El Adem–Fayid–Wadi Haifa–Khartoum–Malakal–Juba–Eastleigh. The flight was accomplished without incident.

One of the pilots testing the Balliol at the A&AEE was Squadron Leader R. G. Woodman, DSO, DFC, who remembered his Boscombe Down days:

> After the war I graduated at the Empire Test Pilot's School (ETPS) then spent the next six years flying at Boscombe Down where I became Deputy Superintendent of Test Flying. There I was indirectly responsible for Boulton-Paul getting the contract for the Balliol. The Balliol and the Avro Athena were sent to us for test evaluation in direct competition. I started test flying them in March 1949. In May we took them both down to our Tropical Test Unit at Khartoum where I did performance tests on both aircraft types. We were already convinced that the Balliol was the superior aircraft as an intermediate RAF trainer, but the 'boffins' and bureaucrats insisted that we continue testing the Athena which we considered to be a waste of the public's money.
>
> Roly Falk, Chief Test Pilot for Avro, was test flying one of their delta wing aircraft at Boscombe Down at this time and must have conveyed our feelings to his management. When I arrived back from Khartoum in the Athena, I was met by Sir Roy Dobson, Avro's chief, who asked if he could drive me up to the Mess. We stopped alongside the Athena and he asked me for an honest opinion of the two aircraft. The next day he contacted the Ministry of Aircraft Production and told them he was dropping all further development work on the Athena. The 'boffins' and bureaucrats still went ahead and ordered thirty Athenas.

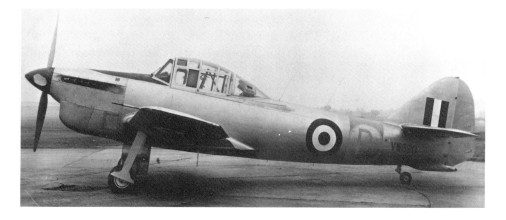

As the test programme proceeded the Balliol prototypes were equipped for the wide variety of duties, which included navigation training, gunnery practice with the aid of a single Browning 0.303 inch machine gun in the port wing, bombing training with four 60 pound underwing mounted rockets and glider towing. Personnel from the RAF who had inspected the new machine were impressed with a feature unusual for a service trainer—manually folding wings. This was a great innovation as it allowed more aircraft to be housed in a given space. The 39 ft 4 in. wing span was reduced to 12 ft 8 in. in the folded position.

Boulton-Paul Aircraft Limited received a contract to construct 138 Balliols and, because of the considerable demand, arrangements were made with the Blackburn Aircraft Company to build a further 120. It was ironic that Boulton-Paul, having built the Blackburn Roc and components for the Shark and B.2, would now have their design built by Blackburns.

The first service allocation was made to the Central Flying School when VR.591 and VR.594 were delivered to that unit for evaluation and familiarisation by the instructors. Later the two aircraft were transferred to Ternhill Station Flight during July 1950. They made their public debut during September at the 1950 Society of British Aircraft Constructors' Show at Farnborough, where they gave an acclaimed display of joint aerobatics.

Further service trials were carried out at Manby, Lincolnshire, by the RAF Handling Squadron who put VR.595 through its paces. These trials showed that lift-off occurred between 86 and 98 mph and the climb away was made at 138 mph. When landing under normal powered approach with flaps and undercarriage extended, the Balliol came in at 98 mph. Other trials were made with two fuel drop tanks carried under the wings; these increased the fuel capacity from 125 gallons to 215 gallons, but the aircraft suffered severe buffeting at speeds exceeding 200 mph. Towing equipment was experimentally fitted, the hook located in the tail cone, and no serious difficulties were encountered in its use, but due to the reduced airspeed resulting from the drag of the target drogue there were slight oil cooling problems. For this reason drogue towing was not permitted under tropical conditions. Owing to carbon monoxide fumes from the exhaust, the canopy was to be closed at all times in flight unless flying with oxygen equipment in use.

Opposite: Avro 701 Athena T.2 VW.890, which was in contention with the Balliol for the Specification T.14/17 contract. *British Aerospace*

The three Balliol prototypes lined up outside the Flight Shed: VL.897 Merlin powered, VL.935 Mamba powered and VL.892 Mercury powered. All three aircraft carry the yellow P in a circle on the fuselage side denoting that they are prototypes. *BPA*

The first units to receive the Balliol were No 7 Flying Training School, Cottesmore, and No 2 Flying Training School, Hullavington, who received VR.598 and VR.596 respectively during June 1950. The majority of the production aircraft were transferred from the factory to No 9 Maintenance Unit (MU) at nearby Cosford, awaiting distribution. During August 1951, VR.597 was despatched from the A&AEE to the Winter Experimental Establishment (WEE) at Alberta, Canada, for cold weather experiments. The Balliol was allotted various duties with numerous units. Typical examples were the Central Gunnery School, Leconfield, the Armament Practice School at Acklington, as well as the Flying Training Schools where they replaced the ageing North American Harvards.

During 1951 the Balliol fell victim to RAF training policy change when the decision was taken that all advanced training would be carried out on jet aircraft. No longer employed in its correct role, it served in such obscure units as the Institute of Aviation Medicine at Farnborough, the School of Control and Reporting at Middle Wallop, the Ferry Training Unit and various Station Flights as far apart as Upavon and Bahrein.

At the Coronation Review which took place at RAF Odiham during July 1953, twelve Balliol T.2s from No 7 Flying Training School, Cottesmore, flew past in four diamond boxes. Some 639 aircraft took part in this massive review of the RAF by Her Majesty Queen Elizabeth II, and the roar of the Balliols' Merlins must have brought back nostalgic memories to many of the assembled company. A few minutes of glory was bestowed on the Balliol on 16th June 1954 when HRH The Duke of Edinburgh, who was carrying out his flying training, made a thirty minute flight in a Balliol from White Waltham.

The largest operator of the aircraft was the RAF College at Cranwell, which was allocated no fewer than 56 Balliols, many of them coming from Flying Training Schools. Unfortunately, nine were written off in accidents during 1954 whilst another four were lost the following year before they were withdrawn by December 1955. Only one University Air Squadron had a brief encounter with the Balliol, the Durham UAS at Usworth, and it only remained with that unit from May 1958 until October of the same year.

The last RAF flying unit to receive the Balliol was the Flying Training Command Communications Squadron, who received three machines during March 1959, but by August they had gone to a storage Maintenance Unit. The last Balliols in RAF service were WG.173, WG.212, WG.225 and WN.509, serving with the School of Fighter Control, from which they were retired on 19th April 1960. The majority of the now redundant aircraft were transferred to No 22 Maintenance Unit at Silloth, where they lingered, awaiting buyers as scrap. When this occurred most of them were processed by the Aluminium Refining Company Limited and Lawton Metals.

Boulton-Paul Aircraft company demonstrator Balliol T.2 G-ANSF, resplendent in all-over red finish, as it appeared at the 1954 Farnborough Air Show.   *John Chambers*

Sea Balliols on the production line at Pendeford. This naval trainer was supplied with four-bladed propellers instead of the three-bladed version for the RAF.   *John Chambers*

Running parallel with the RAF's training programme was that of the Royal Navy. As a consequence, VR.598 was loaned to the Royal Naval Air Station (RNAS) at Arbroath during July 1950, but was returned to its makers at Wolverhampton three weeks later for navalisation and fitting of deck arrester gear. When these modifications were completed, VR.598 was flown down to the A&AEE, where simulated deck landing trials were carried out from November 1950 until April 1951. RNAS Arbroath received another Balliol for trials during October 1950 when VR.596 arrived and stayed for a fortnight before leaving for the Royal Aircraft Establishment at Farnborough.

The first real navalised Balliol, now designated Sea Balliol VR.599, was employed in maker's trials from June 1950 until February 1951. Two more were used for seaborne trials aboard the carrier HMS *Illustrious* when VR.596 and VR.598 were flown by Lieutenant Pridham-Price and Lieutenant Commander Orr-Ewing. After the successful completion of these trials, an order was placed with Boulton-Paul during April 1951 for a production run of the Sea Balliol T.21. Thirty Sea Balliols were taken on charge by the RNAS and were used by Nos 702, 750 and 781 Squadrons aboard the training carrier HMS *Triumph*. The aircraft were flown on the Junior Officers' Air Course based at Lee-on-Solent. WP.333 was the last of the type to be produced on 7th December 1954 and was in fact the last production aircraft to be made by Boulton-Paul Aircraft.

The Balliol had a short life much in the style of its predecessor, the Defiant. Only remembered by a few in the history of Flying Training Command, the Balliol nevertheless made an impact during its service days. One machine still exists, in Sri Lanka, where CA.310 is preserved at the Defence Headquarters at Colombo.

Group of Royal Navy pilots with Sea Balliol. Chief Test Pilot 'Ben' Gunn on left of group and Assistant Test Pilot R.B. 'Dickie' Mancus in centre.   *BPA*

CHAPTER TWELVE

Deltas, Jets and Odd-Balls

JOHN NORTH now steered the company towards hydraulic power control. This resulted in a contract for not only the power controls but an experimental delta winged research aircraft which would incorporate them. Although some of North's colleagues left for pastures new, he still commanded the Design staff and led them onward with ardent zeal. Whilst the production work was in progress on the Balliol and Sea Balliol, the Experimental Department was busily engaged, behind wraps, on a machine of a totally different concept.

Boulton-Paul Aircraft tendered to the Ministry of Supply to design and build a small, experimental aircraft to Specification E.27/46 to research delta wing characteristics at trans-sonic speeds. This resulted from a visit to Wolverhampton by a party of experts from the Royal Aircraft Establishment, Farnborough. It was not a competitive tender but a request from the Air Ministry to design and build. The Boulton-Paul P.111, as it was called, was designed by a team led by Mr F.F. Crocombe. Serialled VT.935, it was to be the sole example, and the contract stipulated that it would be flown at the A&AEE, which had the longest runway in the country at that time, by an RAE pilot.

The tiny delta aircraft took about four years to complete and when it emerged from the Flight Shed, it taxied around the grass airfield at Wolverhampton making noises as yet unheard by the local populace. It was then taken by road to Boscombe Down, quite a formidable task, for the wing did not break in half and the tiny aircraft had to be transferred in one piece. A team of Boulton-Paul fitters and engineers at Boscombe Down prepared the aircraft for its first flight, a jointly operated test flight programme by Boulton-Paul technicians and members of the Aero Flight, Farnborough.

In the hands of one of their pilots, Squadron Leader Smith, Officer Commanding the Aero Flight, the first flight was made on 6th October 1950. The P.111 was found to be extremely sensitive, for without a tailplane there was very little damping in pitch, which could result in rapid pitch oscillations, and with the aid of the powerful ailerons a very fast rate of roll was possible. To allow the pilot to de-sensitise the aircraft as speed increased, a variable gear between the control column and the input power controls was fitted. Experiments were carried out by

152

requesting pilots to choose a gear setting for each speed and then plotting the result. However, flight trials were interrupted when the P.111 landed at Boscombe Down with its undercarriage retracted, but its robust construction allowed it to resume trials again once repairs had been made.

Side view of the P.111 VR.935 illustrating its squat lines, sharply pointed fin and prototype insignia on nose.   *BPA*

Whilst still based there the P.111 was flown by 'Ben' Gunn at the SBAC Show at Farnborough during September 1951, and it greatly impressed the assembled crowds with its incredible rate of roll and climb. The Chief Test Pilot recalled,

As the P.111 had been initiated by RAE, Farnborough, under direct contract, I did not have the privilege of carrying out the first flight, although I subsequently joined in the research programme. It was impossible, because of the runway length, to carry out the test pilot's 'confidence builder' before first flight—commonly known as 'hops'. Great credit must therefore be given to Squadron Leader Smith for his confidence in the work of my company when taking this aircraft on its first flight. During its stay at Boscombe Down, the aircraft met with the usual prototype teething problems and expected problems. It was pleasant to fly, but as speed increased it became difficult to

153

handle due to the extremely sensitive control arrangement. It was quite evident by this time that a major modification was required to the pilot's simulated feel system, and the aircraft was duly grounded and returned to Wolverhampton.

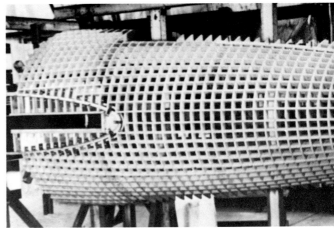

Nose section of P.111 in assembly jig, showing the very rigid structure for this small research aircraft.

John Chambers

    During 1953 the P.111 was modified at Wolverhampton but its original profile was retained. The one visible alteration was the fitting of petal-type air brakes consisting of four rectangular sections, hinged at their forward edges and equally spaced around the fuselage, aft of the cockpit. Another small identification feature was that the double front undercarriage doors on the P.111 were exchanged for a single one on the modified aircraft, which was now designated P.111A. With a new colour scheme of chrome yellow, natural aluminium and patches of black, its maiden flight was made on 2nd July 1953, and in January the following year, after successfully completing maker's trials, it was handed over to the RAE, Farnborough. During trials there it attained Mach 0.93 in level flight at 35,000 feet. The test programme concluded on 20th June 1958, and the P.111A then stood idle until the next April, when it was purchased from the Ministry of Aviation by the College of Aeronautics at Cranfield, Bedfordshire.

    It was used there by their Department of Aircraft Design to demonstrate variable geared power flying control systems and general hydraulic services. Space restrictions forced the college to return the P.111A to Wolverhampton. When Dowty Boulton-Paul severed their connection with aircraft production, there was no demand for apprentice training at the Pendeford factory, and during 1975 it was moved by road to the Midland Air Museum. At this time there was no helicopter in the

United Kingdom with a sling-load capacity to move the aircraft. Assistance came from the Ford Motor Company, who agreed to transport the P.111A provided permission was obtained. Once the Department of the Environment had given their approval, the Ford Motor Company in co-operation with their agents, C. H. Soans & Sons Limited of Leamington, set the operation in motion. Eased onto a transporter on Saturday, 12th July, the load moved off at 4 o'clock the following morning and eventually reached its destination safely. This was a major operation requiring policemen from three areas to close part of the M1 motorway and a stretch of the A45. It was the culmination of eighteen months' effort by members of the Midland Aircraft Preservation Society to transport the 25 foot wingspan jet to the museum at Coventry Airport, Baginton.

Front view of the P.111 with Chief Test Pilot 'Ben' Gunn and his assistant.   *John Chambers*

On 20th August 1952 it was announced that a new Boulton-Paul delta research monoplane had made its maiden flight two weeks earlier. Designated P.120 and serialled VT.951, it was similar in overall appearance to the P.111A but differed in that it was fitted with a variable incidence triangular tailplane. This was adjustable for trim at high

155

speeds, and was operated by an hydraulically activated screw-jack. The power unit, a Rolls-Royce Nene turbo-jet of 5,200 pounds static thrust, was as used in its predecessor. Originally in natural metal finish, it was later changed to all over high gloss black with standard service markings. Sadly, after only eleven exciting hours of test flying, disaster struck on 29th August when the P.120 crashed.

Its pilot, 'Ben' Gunn remembered,

On a bright August morning in 1952, I found myself again at Boscombe Down. On the flight apron was the black shape of the P.120 research delta, referred to jokingly by Boscombe pilots as the 'Black Widow-maker'. On that morning I did not realize how near the truth this remark would be. With the experience gained on the P.111, I was not in the least worried about the first flight—that is, until I had used up approximately three-quarters of the long runway at Boscombe Down and found myself, at 175 knots, still firmly on the ground. I shall never forget the look of startled amazement on the faces of a group of potato pickers at the far end of the runway as the black shape scraped over their heads, clawing frantically for altitude.

A general miscalculation both by our men and the RAE regarding the tailplane setting was responsible for this extremely nerve-wracking take-off. The general flying characteristics were more pleasant than the P.111, and the aircraft at high speed did not have that sitting-on-a-knife-edge feeling. Unfortunately, the life of this machine was extremely short. On 28th August 1952 it was my doubtful privilege to be the first to eject successfully from a delta aircraft. An intense flutter had been initiated on the port elevon and this resulted in a complete hinge failure and loss of this important part of the aeroplane. Some hard work using the remaining elevon and trimming tailplane kept the aircraft in the air for half an hour, but it was obvious that even to attempt a 'wheels up' landing was impossible, and yet another aircraft made its mark on Salisbury Plain.

Professor S. C. Redshaw writes

The Balliol and P.111 deltas were my responsibility and I signed the Design Certificate in my capacity as Chief Engineer. I mention this because the delta was built purely for research purposes to obtain information regarding transonic flight. It had to conform to a strict RAE specification; it was not designed by them and we had the difficult task of putting their requirements into effect. Scientists sometimes think that after de-fusing a problem, it is simple for the engineer to do the rest!

Construction of the P.120 was very much the same as the P.111A except that it was slightly longer at 29 ft 7½ ins. When wing tips were fitted the span was 33 ft 6 ins. Performance was similar to the P.111A.

Following a review of its training requirements, the RAF concluded that it was unprofitable to train National Servicemen as pilots, for only a few remained in the service after their period of duty was finished. In this context, No 25 Reserve Flying School at Wolverhampton was the first to be disbanded on 31st March 1953. After the RAF had departed the school buildings were occupied for several years by various industrial concerns and remained so until the 1970s, when they were demolished.

During August 1951 the wraps were taken off another new Boulton-Paul design, a jet conversion trainer which they had prepared as a private venture aircraft. The P.119 full scale mock-up was pleasant to look at with a wide, well shaped, side-by-side cockpit, swept wing and low, broad undercarriage. Although specifically designed as a jet trainer, it could be employed as a fighter armed with two 20 mm guns and carriers for external bombs and rocket projectiles. Rolls-Royce turbo jets were intended and it was envisaged that with the Derwent, with normal tankage and taking everything into consideration, flight duration at 30,000 feet would be 1 hour 45 minutes at a normal operating speed of approximately 400 mph. Manoeuvrability would be of a very high standard—superior in fact to that of the standard front line fighters of that period. A good view, essential for a trainer, could be obtained from the pressurised cockpit which was also heated and fitted with jettisonable hood and twin ejector seats. All flying and engine controls were duplicated and provision made for amber or blue synthetic instrument flying screens. Advanced training would be possible in day or night flying, gunnery, navigation, bombing and rocket attacks. A naval version was also foreseen, whereby the one-piece wing of the land version, which was a simple fixing to the fuselage centre section by four pin-joints, would be changed for wings folding at half span with either manual or power operation.

The P.119 would employ pneumatic operation for main services such as wheel retraction, flaps, dive and wheel brakes. Altogether a simple structure, it would be easy to maintain and repair, essential for a trainer, which was subjected to harder treatment than a squadron machine. Of light alloy stressed skin construction, the underside fuselage panels, those most likely to suffer in a minor mishap, were designed for quick and easy replacement. Fuel tanks were arranged centrally near the centre of gravity so that when emptying there would be little change of trim. Twin air intakes on the fuselage sides fed the plenum chambers and the turbo jet's position required only a short tailpipe. The mounting of the power plant was positioned immediately aft of the rear wing spar attachment. For maintenance purposes, the complete rear fuselage could be withdrawn on a cradle, and it was estimated that the power unit could be changed in one hour. Unfortunately, this promising venture only reached the full scale mock-up stage and was then abandoned.

The P.119 full scale mock-up of this two-seat fighter trainer. The serial number is only Boulton-Paul's design number. *Ian James*

With the demise of the delta wing experimental aircraft, Boulton-Paul Aircraft Limited ceased production of their own aeroplanes. The unit which had prepared so many designs for new machines during the past thirty or so years now had their endeavours channelled into other areas, but areas still associated with aircraft production.

Experiments with gust alleviation included trials with a specially adapted Avro Lancaster bomber ME.540. Turbulent air when encountered not only causes discomfort to passengers and crew but exerts heavy loads, momentarily, upon the aircraft's structure. A Boulton-Paul system comprised an electro-manometric transducer mounted at the front of the aircraft which provided signals at the appropriate time to an electro-hydraulic power unit and superimposed the required gust correction on the ailerons, independent of the normal control by the pilot. A pilot who was involved with flying the experimental bomber remarked that it was startling to see ailerons 'cock upwards' both together when under normal circumstances they moved in opposite directions – one up, the other down.

Fuselage parted to show ease of maintenance for the turbo-jet power unit of the projected P.119 fighter trainer. *John Chambers*

Other experiments included a modification to the air intake of the De Havilland Vampire and a programme of research into vertical take-off. This considered the possibility of city centre to city centre vertical take-off and landing (VTOL) airliners. The design and manufacture of the huge wing flaps for the Vickers Vanguard was also completed at Wolverhampton.

A subcontract for De Havilland involved a frangible canopy for their Vixen twin-engined carrier-borne naval fighter. Pilots had been lost when their aircraft had run off the carrier and plunged into the sea when either taking off or landing. Water pressure had held the canopy firmly in position, resulting in the crew's death. A new canopy was designed to disintegrate on impact with the water, allowing escape for the crew before the aircraft sank.

Group of Design Staff in the early 1950s.
Back row, L to R: L.G. Prout, K.F. Townsend, J.A. Beesley, F.A. Surman, H. Hill, J. Chambers, G.A. Lowe, J. Grimshaw, E. Stewart, W. Morral, J. Tovell, J. Clarke, T.M. Lowe.
Centre row: E. Gapp, R. Payton, G. Clayton, A.H. Lines, A.J. Morgan, F. Holmesmith, H. Dixon, J. Dawkins.
Front row: B.F. Clarke, J.C. Cooper, J.D. Williams, J.D. North, J.W. Batchelor, D.J. Millard, V.T. Johnston.   *John Chambers*

Mr F.A. Jackson of Shifnal remembered the period. 'This was the beginning of electrical signalling, or "fly by wire" as it is now known, and a great deal of complementary equipment had to be developed for use with this system.'

The *Aeroplane* of 9th August 1957 reported:

For many years, hidden from the public eye, the Tay Viscount is once more back in the news, as the test-bed for a combined electrical signal powered control system by Boulton-Paul Aircraft Limited and Louis Newmark Limited. Boulton-Paul Aircraft test pilots, R.R. 'Bob' Mancus and G. Dunworth, have flown the aircraft with a control system in which only electrical signals connect the pilot's control column with the aircraft control surface actuators. They report very satisfactory functioning with immediate response and a complete absence of backlash.

During the Second World War a method was devised to confuse the enemy radar by dropping long metallised strips—code-named 'Window' —from our aircraft. Dispensing the bundles from a wartime bomber was a comparatively simple task as a member of the crew just launched them into space down a chute, but as the speeds of modern jet bombers advanced, launching problems arose. Boulton-Paul Aircraft designed a launcher for this purpose and this was fitted on a Gloster Meteor twin-jet fighter for trials.

Avro Lancaster III ME.540 modified by Boulton-Paul Aircraft for Gust Alleviation Trials, sporting a large instrument probe from under the front gun turret.   *BPA*

A major contract had been obtained from English Electric for their Canberra twin-jet bombers in the late 1950s and early 1960s. Twelve B.2s, eighteen PR.3s, six T.4/11s, eleven B.6/7s, six PR.7s, a B.15 (Nord A.30) were overhauled and other contracts for Commonwealth air forces also processed. Typical of this work was the design and construction of prototype gun packs incorporating 20 mm cannons which were to be fitted in the Canberra's bomb bay, and the installation of special cameras for photographic reconnaissance duties at high altitudes. Special equipment was also designed and manufactured for an Italian Air Force contract.

English Electric Canberra at Seighford, the satellite airfield for Pendeford where all post-war test flying was conducted. *John Chambers*

Earlier it had become obvious that to remain in the aviation field it was necessary to find larger flying facilities, for the Wolverhampton airfield was a grass one and unsuitable for jet aircraft. It was decided to re-surface the main runway at Seighford, Staffordshire, and the Flight Test Section moved there in 1956. The increased workload due to the English Electric contract demanded additional test pilots so 'Ben' Gunn and 'Dickie' Mancus were joined by 'Loopy' Dunworth and John Power.

The Lightning supersonic fighter from the same manufacturer was also contracted for modification to Boulton-Paul Aircraft, and a number of Mark 2s were part of the Datalink navigational development programme. Structural changes on the fin and wings were designed and manufactured, and Red Top missile installations were also designed and fitted.

161

During 1961 Boulton-Paul Aircraft Limited became part of the Dowty Group based at Cheltenham. This caused some concern at Wolverhampton, for it was known that powered flying controls were already being designed by the new parent company, Dowty Rotol, and that they were manufacturing the tailplane actuating unit for the Indian designed Hindustan Aircraft's HF.24. The fears, however, were unfounded, for the Dowty Group had decided that all flying control design and production would be the responsibility of the Wolverhampton factory, now to be regarded as the Electronics Division of the group.

There were four main categories within this group; aircraft hydraulics, cable laying equipment, naval equipment and electronics. It soon became apparent that the Dowty Group had a very progressive attitude towards new products. Dowty Boulton Paul, as they were now called, despatched technicians to Bremen in Germany where the Focke-Wulf aircraft company, known as VFW, were designing a revolutionary vertical take-off fighter. The British team's task was to design power controls for this machine, but the aircraft design was dropped and the team returned home.

The following year another team was sent to the Fokker aircraft works near Amsterdam, hoping to clinch a contract associated with their F.27 aircraft. For various reasons the mission proved unsuccessful. There was, however, success at Bangalore in India, where an order was placed for five prototype sets of power controls for the Hindustan HF Mark II. A visit to the Fiat works at Turin, Italy, culminated in a contract to supply equipment for their G.222 machine. Also there was good news from Toulouse, in France, where units were ordered for the Anglo-French supersonic aircraft, the Concorde.

Work on the Concorde commenced during 1963 but development of the pre-production models continued until the early 1970s. Basically a fly-by-wire machine, it uses mechanical signalling as a stand-by system. In the prototype, Dowty Boulton Paul designed the electronic amplifier for the electrical signalling system, but in production aircraft the electronics were incorporated into the auto-pilot units and manufactured by Marconi.

The then styled 'European Fighter', the multi-purpose combat aircraft, or MRCA—known to its critics as 'Mother Riley's Cardboard Aeroplane'—and now designated the Tornado, was evolving during the late 1960s. Hydraulic system work was under the jurisdiction of the German consortium, Messerschmitt, Bolkow, and Blohm, and this involved the Wolverhampton team in many journeys to Munich, where the design work was in preparation. The British company teamed up with the German firm Liebher Aerotechnik of Lindenberg and together they bid for the MRCA's flying control systems and the air intake ramp actuators. They were successful with the ramp actuators but failed to obtain the controls contract.

The company continued fly-by-wire research and it was realised that if aircraft were aerodynamically unstable, they could be made more manoeuvrable and with reduced drag. This meant having one hundred per cent reliable fly-by-wire systems, enabling the pilot to signal the aircraft his required movement, but retaining stability by means of the auto-pilot. The Americans, ahead of the field in this technology, had produced the F.16. British Aerospace at Warton were thinking along similar lines and as a result Dowty Boulton Paul received an order to produce flying controls for a fly-by-wire Jaguar. This aircraft was fitted with the Wolverhampton designed system and carried out a successful test programme.

Mr D.J. Millard, Technical Director and later Managing Director of Boulton-Paul Aircraft. He was responsible for the company's 'fly-by-wire' programme. *BPA*

When the much discussed TSR.2 supersonic bomber was cancelled by the Government, all English Electric contract work was recalled to their own factories. This created a problem for Boulton-Paul Aircraft, and in January 1966 they closed Seighford, where so much of their contract work for English Electric had been carried out.

'Ben' Gunn remembered: 'As the amalgamation of the larger aircraft manufacturers began to take effect, it grew increasingly difficult to obtain subcontract work and in the event it became necessary to reduce the test flying staff. "Dickie" Mancus elected to take early retirement, John Power

163

obtained a flying post in the south of England, and "Loopy" Dunworth returned to his market garden. "Dickie" Mancus had become the victim of a crippling disease, and he transferred to the firm's office, where he brought his experience to bear on everyday matters, even whilst confined to a wheel-chair. As an ex-naval officer he was invaluable in dealing with naval contracts in his new capacity as Sales Liaison.' The *Wolverhampton Express and Star* newspaper reported on 3rd May 1977, 'Former Wolverhampton test pilot, Mr Robert Mancus, aged 57, died at his home in Wightwick Hall Road, Compton, on Sunday, 1st May, 1977. He had suffered from multiple sclerosis for many years. Mr Mancus, Assistant Liaison Manager with Dowty Boulton Paul, joined the company as a test pilot in 1949. In 1974 he received the MBE for outstanding service to defence contracts.'

Seen at Wolverhampton Airport during the filming of 'Man in the Sky', in which the late Jack Hawkins starred. Auster J/1 N Alpha G-AIGT standing in the background.

Wolverhampton Express & Star

'Ben' Gunn remained with Boulton-Paul. Later as test pilot for Beagle Aircraft he arrived at Shoreham Airport. When in 1970 the company ran into financial difficulties, he was asked by the Receiver to remain and was later appointed Manager of Shoreham Airport. His leadership and management ability were recognised in 1988 when Shoreham Airport received the Aircraft Owners' and Pilots' Association Sword awarded to the best airport, and Mr A.E. Gunn received the Aerodrome Owners' Association Silver Medal for outstanding services to airports.

Once the war was over civil flying returned as a popular sport, and the Wolverhampton Aero Club was formed on the 1st January 1946 using ex-RAF Miles Magister two-seat monoplane trainers with Gipsy engines. Club meetings and public air displays were given and a general atmosphere of activity prevailed.

One business on the airfield, Wolverhampton Aviation, was appointed Miles service agents, and apart from servicing the Magisters, when the Miles organisation failed in 1948 they acquired several twin-engined Miles Gemini airframes and spares. Five Miles Geminis were completed by this local firm and sold to civil owners.

During the 1950s aeroplanes of many types could be seen on the Wolverhampton apron and in the hangar. However, once the wartime airfield at Halfpenny Green, not far away, had been turned to civilian use, several of these aircraft departed to the new site. When used as a base for the film *Man in the Sky*, starring Jack Hawkins, in 1955, the airport had a brief moment of glory. Unfortunately, the Bristol Freighter employed in the film bogged down in the soft ground and badly damaged a mainplane. Boulton-Paul Aircraft had originally secured a 99 year lease on the Wolverhampton airfield. However, with the end of aircraft production at the factory the company made no objection when the Wolverhampton Corporation decided to withdraw the licence to fly from there.

The decision of the Wolverhampton Corporation to close down the airport in 1970 was reinforced by a tragic accident which occurred on 9th April of the same year. The *Wolverhampton Express and Star* reported,

Three people died today when an executive twelve-seater aircraft crashed on a council estate at Fordhouses, Wolverhampton, and burst into flames. The victims were the two man crew of the aircraft and 51 year old Mrs Nell Hilton who was asleep at the rear of the end terrace house, No 76, Redhurst Drive. Her son, Paul, and his wife, spending a short holiday with her, had a miracle escape in the crash, leaping fifteen feet from the front bedroom window of the blazing terrace.

The 'plane, a blue and silver De Havilland Dove, G-AVHW, belonging to Dowty and operated by McAlpines, had taken off from Luton Airport, Bedfordshire, and was due to pick up two directors of Dowty Boulton Paul, the aircraft component firm at Wolverhampton. Both men, Mr A.W. Turner, Managing Director, and Mr F.A. Jewitt, Production Director, have been working on the Concorde project and were due to have flown to France for business talks. As the £250,000 aircraft came in to land at Pendeford, its engines appeared to fail. It swooped down over gardens on the housing estate, before crashing into the house at Redhurst Drive. The lady killed in this tragic incident worked in the canteen at Dowty Boulton Paul and was on a day's holiday from her work.

Although the airfield licence was withdrawn and all official flying ceased, several illicit flyers continued to use the field until the deposits of local scrap made this too hazardous, even for them.

At Mousehold Heath, Norwich, the airfield remained in constant use after the departure of the aircraft design and construction units to Wolverhampton. The old established Norfolk and Norwich Aero Club continued to fly regularly until the war curtailed their activities. Along

Wrecked buildings at Riverside Works, Norwich, after a German 'blitz' air raid. Considerable damage was suffered throughout that ancient city. *Alan Hague*

with many other open areas, stakes were driven into the ground to deter any possible landing by enemy forces. Later on when Norwich was severely bombed, the airfield suffered too.

Boulton and Paul at Norwich were soon at full stretch when the Second World War made its demands upon all departments. Military contracts ranged from portable buildings in wood, buildings in steel, Summerfield wire netting track for airfields and tank transporters to air-raid shelters and radio masts. In 1936 they had absorbed Stephens and Carter Limited, operating from several bases within the United Kingdom, and in 1942 the Midland Woodworking Company of Melton Mowbray joined the group. A return to their former association with the aircraft industry was a contract for manufacturing nose sections for the Airspeed Horsa heavy glider and fuselages for the Airspeed Oxford advanced twin-engined trainer at the Melton Mowbray factory.

After the war the engineering departments, based at the Riverside Works, were involved with the fabrication of structural steelwork—including such buildings as the Heathrow Air Cargo Terminal, the Pressed Steel factory at Swindon, the Royal Enclosure Grandstand at Ascot racecourse and the reactor building for the United Kingdom Atomic Energy Establishment at Winfrith. Alas, in recent years the company has reluctantly closed the steel erection plant.

During 1962 a £1.5 million joinery factory and quay were constructed adjoining the Inner Harbour at Lowestoft, Suffolk, where timber could be received direct from the ships. Of modern design, extensions and improvements have kept this factory at the forefront of joinery products. To increase the timber product range, the group acquired, during 1968, the old established firm of John Sadd and Sons Limited, of Maldon, Essex.

At Norwich, Boulton and Paul's aircraft manufacturing activities are remembered. In the Bridewell Museum there is a display of aircraft relics, whilst Wensum Lodge has murals depicting Norwich built aircraft. The main doors of Norwich City Hall embrace engraved panels of local trades including one of men working on an aero-engine. By happy coincidence the company still has a presence—a sales office—at Martlesham Heath, where so many of the Norwich built machines were tested to the full.

John Dudley North died on the 11th January 1968; a memorial service was held on lst March at St Peter's Collegiate Church at Wolverhampton. The address was given by Lord Kings Norton and the service was attended by the Secretary of State for Air.

In 1913, at the early age of 20 years, he had been accepted as an associate member of the Royal Aeronautical Society. Forty-eight years later an honorary fellowship was conferred on him at the same time as his contemporary, Sir Sidney Camm of Hawkers. Among his appointments were council member of the Society of British Aerospace Constructors (SBAC) from 1931 to 1962, Vice President (Aircraft) from 1941 to 1943, and Chairman of the society's Technical Board in 1944–45 and 1947–48. He was a member of the council of the Air Registration Board from 1942 to 1960, and Chairman of the Design and Construction Panel from 1943 to 1960. His influence on the requirements of the board is thought to have been greater than that of any other single member, and this showed up in the policies on which the requirements for the British Civil Airworthiness Certificate were formulated. North's work with the SBAC led to his nomination as a Governor of the College of Aeronautics at Cranfield, a task which he performed with dedication, remaining in office until 1960.

John North was a founder member of the Operational Research Club, which later became the Operational Research Society, and in this capacity he was approached by the Air Ministry to look into military aircraft reliability. The task took him five years to complete (1948–53) and under the title of *Design for Reliability* it ran to thirteen volumes.

Mr J.D. North receives a Georgian silver salver to mark the 40 years he had spent with the Norwich and Wolverhampton companies. Mr T. Sanders (Personnel Manager); Mr & Mrs North; Bert Harris (Factory Convenor); Mr G.C. Haynes (Secretary).

In 1967 he was made an Honorary Doctor of Science (DSc.) by the University of Birmingham. Five years earlier he had attended Buckingham Palace to receive his Companion of the Order of the British Empire (CBE) from Her Majesty the Queen.

The survival of the company that he had nurtured over many years was a constant worry for John North in the post-war period. Gigantic resources, both technical and financial, were necessary for research and development programmes of new designs. For this reason he welcomed the approach by his life-long friend, Sir George Dowty, in April 1960. By its association with the Dowty Group the future of Boulton-Paul Aircraft, in one form or another, was assured.

Frontal view of the present day Pendeford offices and works. The lawn in the foreground was the previous site of wartime air raid shelters. *BPA*

169

During the 1960s the company was successful in winning a contract with the Royal Navy for supplying control systems for HMS *Intrepid* and HMS *Fearless*. Resembling miniature floating docks, their ballast tanks could be flooded or pumped out to lower or raise the craft in the water in order to launch or retrieve their assault craft. Dowty Boulton Paul supplied the hydraulic jacks for valve control, as well as tank water level instrumentation.

Other contracts won from the Royal Navy involved winches for the Hunt Class mine counter-measures vessels, pumps, power packs and hydraulic propeller pitch control and stabilisation units for Type 21 and Type 22 frigates and the Type 42 destroyers, including HMS *Exeter*.

Contracts were gained from the Army in the field of hydro-static four-wheel drive systems and hydraulic steering. Development contracts were also obtained for the tank hull motion simulator for tank crew training, which functions in much the same way as simulators for aircraft flight training.

Orders were also received from abroad: for the Italian Augusta 129 helicopter; for the joint Jugoslavian-Romanian fighter aircraft known unofficially as the Jurom; from Airbus Industries and from Boeing, Lockheed and McDonnell-Douglas of the USA. One of the Dowty Boulton Paul technical team, Mr C. Kenmer, had the unique experience of manning the Dowty Group stand at the British Technology Exhibition held in Peking, China, where he lectured to the Chinese on fly-by-wire techniques.

Although still closely associated with the industry, it is many years since the company were in aircraft production themselves. It is to their credit that they have been able to adapt themselves to the needs of an ever-changing aerospace industry. A Dowty Boulton Paul spokesman summed up the situation:

A policy of diversification does not automatically result in success. Much depends on the quality and type of basket in which one's eggs are put. Unless their selection is made with care, the bottom can fall out of too many, even for a company of the calibre of Dowty Boulton Paul. It was in the choice of baskets that the skill and judgement of Mr J.D. North, CBE, the company's Chairman, was of immeasurable value.

As an important member of the Dowty Group, Boulton-Paul can call upon the resources of their group companies for design or production facilities. It is a wide organization which is constantly seeking new markets for its activities and industrial products, and it is against a background of a half century of endeavour and achievement in the aircraft industry that Boulton-Paul advances towards its next fifty years of operations.

The fiftieth anniversary of the initial flight of the Defiant fell on 11th August 1987. Because the company was no longer involved with the design and manufacture of aircraft, the management decided it was inapplicable to commemorate the event. Mr John Chambers, however, decided that this anniversary should not go by unnoticed and mounted an exhibition at the Wolverhampton Public Library. Displays of photographs and a model and other items relating to the Defiant were exhibited and were well received by the local populace, many of whom had, of course, been associated with this aircraft.

Exhibition mounted by Mr John Chambers, a staff employee of long standing at Wolverhampton, to commemorate the 50th anniversary of the first flight of the Defiant aircraft.   *John Chambers*

Additional Technical Details

BOBOLINK It was a double bay biplane but with N-type interplane struts which were a new feature. It was of wooden and wire-braced construction, fabric covered except for the forward fuselage engine panels. Two fixed Vickers machine guns were mounted on the upper forward fuselage, firing through the airscrew disc. A Lewis gun could be mounted on the trailing edge of the centre section and this fired forward over the arc of the airscrew. An ingenious innovation was the fuel tank arrangement, which was located behind the cockpit and which, in an emergency, could be jettisoned through an aperture in the fuselage floor.

Test flights showed up a lack of lateral control which was cured by fitting ailerons to the lower wing, and further modifications resulted in a new horn-balanced rudder of larger proportions being fitted. Struts connecting the upper and lower ailerons were also removed and replaced by an arrangement of cables.

BOURGES The front gunner's gun ring mounting was fitted sloping forward; this gave him an increased field of fire over the nose. There was considerable backwards rake to the bomb-aiming compartment windows, and transparent panels were fitted for all round vision. A sliding panel in the fuselage floor allowed downward vision for the bomb-sight. The bomb doors were later replaced by shutters which were coupled to laths and tensioned rubber cords. Modifications to incorporate a bomb stowage arrangement consisted of a rotary shaft attached to vertical guides. When rotated it released the bombs one at a time. The bomb in the lowest position passed through the guides and then the shutters until it was free of the aircraft.

Equal span, unstaggered mainplanes were supported by a three bay strut layout with ailerons on both upper and lower surfaces. Short interplane struts carried the cowled engines at mid-gap and the wide track undercarriage, which was to be a distinctive Boulton and Paul design feature, was located beneath each engine. The tailplane layout was of orthodox design and the fin carried the serial number F.2903 on the drab Nivo green doped fabric covering. Nivo, or Night Varnish Orfordness, was a camouflage conceived at RFC Station Orfordness.

The suffix 'A' to the Mark II denoted that the mainplane configuration was with the conventional centre section mounted above the fuselage, whilst 'B' applied to versions with a gull wing layout. The only significant difference in the Mark IA airframe was that the mainplanes now carried non-balanced ailerons, upper and lower, and the rudder had been re-profiled and enlarged. F.2903 was fitted with large diameter spinners on the airscrews which streamlined into the tapered engine nacelles. However, it became apparent that these spinners deprived the engine cylinders of air cooling necessary to avoid overheating. The spinners were removed and the engines fitted with close fitting circular cowlings.

On the Mark IB the upper mainplane was now 'gulled up' from the centre fuselage. This was to give the dorsal gunner a much greater arc of fire. Horizontal tailplane surfaces were now rigged at dihedral angle, the angle matching the gull angle of the upper mainplane centre section. A modified fin, of smaller area, was also fitted but the enlarged rudder of the first prototype was retained. Positional changes were made to the Dragonfly engine mountings when they were fitted directly on the upper surface of the lower mainplane over the wide track undercarriage. This was lengthened to give greater airscrew clearance with the ground.

Details of the Bourges: Mark I:

Span:	54 ft (57.3 ft with balanced ailerons)
Area:	738 sq. ft
Gross weight:	6,300 lbs (empty 3,420 lbs)
Max. speed:	124 mph at 10,000 ft
Landing speed:	50 mph
Climb:	10,000 ft reached in 11 mins

Mark II As for Mark I except gross weight was 6,800 lbs

P.8 Atlantic

Span:	61 ft
Length:	40 ft
Weight:	(ready for journey) 7,000 lbs
Top speed:	149 mph at 10,000 ft

P.6

Span:	25 ft
Length:	19 ft
Weight:	1,725 lbs (loaded)
Max. speed:	103 mph at 1,000 ft
Landing speed:	45 mph

It was registered on the Civil Register on 20th May 1919 as K.120/G-EAJ but never carried these markings.

P.9 It was a two-seat light 'plane developed from the P.6. Spanning 27 ft 6 in. and 24 ft 8 in. long, it was an unstaggered single bay biplane with equal span mainplanes and was powered by a 90 hp RAF 1a engine. Weighing in at 1,770 lbs loaded and 1,440 lbs empty, top speed was one mph faster than its predecessor at 104 mph. Climb to 5,000 ft took 8 mins 30 secs whilst the ceiling was 14,000 ft and range 3 hours at full throttle.

P.10   Estimated performance was:

Speed:	104 mph (fully loaded) at 1,000 ft
Climb:	8 mins to 5,000 ft
Ceiling:	14,000 ft
Weight:	(loaded) 1,700 lbs (empty) 1,104 lbs
Duration:	5 hours at 90 mph
Span:	30 ft
Length:	26 ft
Height:	12 ft
Wing gap:	5 ft 6 in.
Wing cord:	5 ft 6 in.
Fuel capacity:	26 gallons
Oil capacity:	3 gallons
Engine:	Cosmos Lucifer radial of 100 hp

BODMIN P.12   It had two 450 hp Napier Lion water-cooled in-line engines mounted on the fuselage floor, in tandem, which drove, via transmission shafts and gearboxes, two tractor and two pusher propellers, mounted outboard of the fuselage, at mid-gap of the mainplanes. Clutches enabled the propeller drive to be disconnected should an engine fail, the propellers then being allowed to windmill until the fault had been rectified. When power was restored again, the clutch would be re-engaged and normal drive resumed. The forward mounted engine drove the tractor propellers and the rear mounted one, the pushers. To tend his charges, the 'engineer' could move around in the 'engine-room', where he could stand upright; large windows gave him adequate light by day, whilst electric lighting was provided for night operations.

Radiator cooling was by means of six separate coolers, any one of which could be shut off in the event of a leak. Mounted in the slipstream, on the horizontal drive shaft housings, they had sufficient cooling capacity for tropical operations. Enclosed in aluminium fairings, they were one of the first examples of ducted radiators. Like the cooling system, fuel tanks could be isolated if necessary. The exhaust manifolds and silencers were fabricated from welded stainless steel. The front cockpit was provided with a duplicate set of flying controls for emergency use. As well as the wide-track main undercarriage, a pair of auxiliary wheels were carried under the front fuselage to prevent nosing over.

Main details:

Wing-span:	70 ft
Length:	53 ft 4 in.
Wing area:	1,204 sq. ft
Weight:	(loaded) 11,000 lbs (empty) 7,920 lbs
Speed:	at ground level 116 mph
Ceiling:	16,000 ft
Climb:	9 mins to 6,500 ft
	16 mins to 10,000 ft
Service ceiling:	16,000 ft

BOLTON   Looking very much like the Bourges, it embodied the latest tensile steel methods of construction. The wing-span had been increased and the two 450 hp Napier Lion water-cooled engines were mounted on raised beds, part of the upper surface of the lower mainplane. The engines were located just inboard of the innermost set of interplane struts of the three bay wing configuration. They were left uncowled, which assisted cooling and allowed the use of smaller radiators. Four-bladed propellers were fitted and hand cranking gear permitted the engines to be started from the rear of the nacelle.

The Bolton's silhouette featured equal chord mainplanes with square tips and a tailplane of the same profile, whilst the angular rudder had a horn-balanced portion forward of its hinge line to assist the pilot with its movement. A square box-like fuselage with a triangular top decking aft carried a dorsal gun position behind the top mainplane. Forward of the mainplanes were the pilot's cockpit and the front gunner's position. Its wide-tracked undercarriage, of typical Boulton and Paul design, was located under the engines; the oleo-pneumatic shock struts were of Norwich design. Protruding forward from the main undercarriage was a system of struts with a small wheel mounted at its forward apex, in the manner of the now familiar tricycle undercarriage. Span was 62 ft 6 in. and the loaded weight 9,500 lbs. No other details are available as the records were lost.

BUGLE P.25 Larger than the Bourges, it spanned 65 ft 6 in. This wing-span was slightly reduced when the original horn-balanced ailerons were replaced with those of plain form, upper and lower components being linked by struts. Mainplane configuration was three bay with the engines mounted on struts at mid-gap. Inner interplane struts were of steel whilst the others were of duralumin. It had equal span unstaggered mainplanes of square outline. The wide-track undercarriage mounted under the engines employed a simple arrangement of drag struts and radius rods attached to Boulton and Paul designed oleo shock struts. The large horn-balanced rudder was hinged onto an angular fin and the large tailplane was mounted on the rear fuselage top and braced to the lower fuselage longerons by two substantial struts on each side.

Mark II

Wing-span:	62 ft 6 in.
Wing area:	932 sq. ft
Weight:	(gross loaded) 8,760 lbs
	(disposable load) 3,681 lbs
Top speed:	120 mph at 10,000 ft reached in 15 mins 30 secs
Engine:	Bristol Jupiter 400 hp radials

SIDESTRAND Mark I It was a three-bay equal span biplane, staggered with square end plates and slight sweepback. Of constant chord, the high aspect ratio mainplanes were particularly efficient. A new wing section was used in the design and this combined a high lift co-efficient with only a small centre of pressure movement. Exceptional stiffness of the mainplane structure was brought about by the use of steel strip fabrications, nickel chrome fittings for high loaded locations, aluminium tubings and aluminium-silicon alloy die castings.

Originally designed around two Napier Lion water-cooled engines, these were replaced by two Bristol Jupiter VII nine-cylinder, air-cooled radials of 425 hp. The three fuel tanks were located in the centre fuselage and carried a total of 260 gallons. The engines were semi-cowled with only the cylinder heads protruding and, owing to the shortness of the direct drive shaft, large two-bladed propellers turned close to the front of the cowling. Mounted on a structure atop the lower mainplane, the engine mountings were unconventional in that they could be swung out to allow maintenance on the back of the engines.

Attached to the lower mainplane main spar were the Norwich designed oleo-pneumatic undercarriage legs for the wide-track undercarriage assembly, which was of normal layout. The fin and rudder had what was now typical Boulton and Paul profile, and together with the broad chord angular tailplane were mounted on top of the rear fuselage. Of slim lines, the fuselage provided accommodation for the front gunner forward of the offset to port single cockpit for the pilot. The third member of the crew was in the dorsal position. Span 72 ft; length 40 ft 8 in.; wing area 943 sq. ft; speed at sea level was 125 mph and at 5,000 ft 130 mph; gross weight was 8,850 lbs and empty 5,275 lbs.

Mark III With the Bristol Jupiter VIII engine

Top speed:	140 mph at 10,000 ft
Landing speed:	54 mph
Weight:	10,200 lbs (gross)
	6,010 lbs (empty)
Wing loading:	10.6 lbs per sq. ft
Ceiling:	24,000 ft
Climb:	19 mins to 15,000 ft

Mark IIIA   With the Jupiter XFB engines

Top speed: 167 mph at 11,000 ft at a weight of 10,200 lbs
Climb: 8 mins 30 secs to 11,000 ft
Ceiling: 30,000 ft was accredited

PARTRIDGE   The aircraft incorporated advanced design innovations, many of which represented the transition from wood to metal manufacturing techniques devised by Boulton and Paul. The fuselage comprised two major assemblies, the forward portion constructed from high tensile steel tubing, bolted together and locked into light alloy sockets and magnesium pads at the tube ends. Oversize top longerons in the cockpit section gave great strength and rigidity. They provided solid mounts for the two Vickers machine guns, which were suspended from them and fired alongside the fuselage, the bullets passing forward through hollow steel troughs.

The section aft of the cockpit was of typical Boulton and Paul construction comprising thin gauge steel strip rolled into tubes with the edge joint locked by internal crimping - the 'closed joint method'. Truss bracing was by tie rods, except in the cockpit area, where they were substituted by diagonal tubes to absorb landing loads from the undercarriage struts. Lower wing spars were attached to the fuselage by high tensile steel discs which allowed the spar roots and the wing bracing wires and their associated fittings to be secured by pin joints. All the mainplane ribs, spars and the tailplane structural members were fabricated from tubular sections or metal pressings. Instead of the usual separate centre section for attachment of the upper mainplane to the fuselage, the main wing spars were butt-jointed, which resulted in a much stronger and simplified arrangement.

Wing spars were of standard Boulton and Paul design comprising a box section with flat side plates, riveted and locked by corrugated top and bottom flanges with root and strut attachment stiffener plates. This gave a spar of light weight, highly resistant to twisting and bending loads. Ribs were made up of 'U' and 'T' light alloy sections which were attached to the V-section trailing edge by small die castings riveted to the web flanges. Interplane struts were fairly substantial, high tensile steel tubing, streamlined with wooden fairings and fitted to the wing spars by a single bolt. An orthodox V-type landing gear was attached at its lower apex by a single spreader bar, and oleo-pneumatic units at the upper end of the main struts absorbed landing loads. No brakes were fitted, but the tailskid was steerable, enabling a measure of directional control when taxiing.

The 440 hp nine cylinder Bristol Jupiter Series VII super-charged air-cooled radial engine had an extended propeller shaft which enabled the forward fuselage to terminate in a gently tapered nose around the cylinders. The specification had originally called for the Bristol Mercury radial engine to be fitted, but this was not yet available. Contouring the line of the front fuselage, the hub of the large two-bladed propeller blended into the frontal profile. Formers over the basic fuselage gave an unbroken, streamlined effect which curved into an unusual bulge where the guns were housed.

The fuel tank consisted of two separate tanks, one within the other and supported by an internal arrangement of plates which constituted a load-bearing section of the fuselage. When being refuelled the inner tank, which acted as a baffle to prevent fuel slosh and resultant shift of weight, was filled automatically through a re-entrant filler from the outer tank. Fuel could flow from either tank through a three-way selector valve controlled from the cockpit.

Simplicity was the keynote of the lubrication system for the oil tank was ingeniously positioned in the forward fuselage. One side was ribbed with fins and ducted to act as an oil-cooler, thus no intercooler was necessary. Oil temperature and pressure were regulated by an automatic by-pass valve.

Span: 35 ft
Wing area: 311 sq. ft
Wing loading: 9.9 lbs per sq. ft
Weight: (empty) 2,021 lbs
Climb: 6 mins 30 secs to 10,000 ft was good
                    15 mins to 20,000 ft

PHOENIX The fuselage was notable for its square box-like section which continued from the engine mount to the stern-post, completely unfaired in any respect. An undercarriage structure of wide-track layout was attached to the top and bottom longerons, the main strut incorporating a shock absorber unit. The aircraft sat very close to the ground. A mainplane of constant chord, with a small cut-out on the trailing edge over the rear cockpit, was mounted on a cabane of steel struts above the fuselage to which it was braced by struts. Square tips terminated the mainplane at the outer ends and there was no dihedral. A curved fin, rudder and tailplane brought up the rear end, with the fin forward of the tailplane. The wing-span was 30 ft and the weight 1,000 lbs.

P.32 Of all metal construction throughout, covering was in the main fabric, except for cowling panels and some plywood and metal sheeting at the nose and stern. Handley-Page slats were fitted to the leading edge of the outer upper mainplanes to delay stall effect over the fairly deep aerofoil section of the wing. Twin fins were spaced out on the broad tailplane which was mounted atop the rear fuselage. To assist the pilot in moving the quite large rudders, they were fitted with Flettner servo rudders.

   Two pairs of widely spaced mainwheels were mounted on an elaborate array of struts beneath the lower mainplanes, and twin tailskids coupled to operate with the twin rudders were contemplated, but were replaced by a central tailwheel. The slab sided fuselage with its curved fore section housed the main fuel tanks, but there was no bomb bay within the fuselage, the armament being slung beneath it. Although the parallel chord mainplanes spanned 100 ft, they could be folded to give an overall width of 47 ft 6 in. With a fuselage length of 64 ft and a height of 21 ft, the P.32 grossed at around 20,500 lbs.

P.64 Of relatively short span, 54 ft, the constant chord mainplanes with square tips were rigged single bay with the minimum of flying and landing wires. Fabric covered overall, except for various metal panels, the new creation was doped aluminium, the silver only being broken by the large black registration letters on the mainplanes and fuselage sides, G-ABYK. Fuel was carried in four main tanks of 74 gallons each in the wings and a collector tank of 29 gallons in the centre section.

   Other details of the P.64:

Length: 42 ft 6 in.
Height: 13 ft
Wing chord: 7 ft
Wing area: 756 sq. ft
Wing loading: 13.9 lbs per sq. ft
Weight: (gross) 10,500 lbs
                    (empty) 6,125 lbs
Disposable load: 4,375 lbs
Speed: Maximum 190 mph at 5,000 ft
                    Cruising 172 mph
                    Landing 60 mph

Rate of climb: 1,400 ft per min.
Ceiling: 22,500 ft
Range: 1,250 miles

P.71A   The difference between the P.71A and the P.64 was most apparent at the tailend; the large fin and rudder was now replaced by a fixed central fin and two balanced rudders which were spaced along the square tailplane, which was in turn braced to the fuselage. Slight sweepback was built into the mainplanes and the tip had become rounded. The tailwheel sported a streamlined cover. Gross weight had risen slightly to 11,300 lbs, but surprisingly the top speed had also risen by 5 mph, in spite of the lower powered engines.

SIDESTRAND V   From earlier models changes had appeared in the mainplanes, for the outer panels were now rigged with sweepback to improve longitudinal control. Frise ailerons were fitted and large Handley-Page slats operated on the outer panels of the upper mainplanes. Stagger was also slightly increased, and a large Flettner servo rudder was rigged aft of the main surface.

OVERSTRAND   Longitudinal control problems were investigated and the aerofoil section of the fin, as well as the horn-balance on the elevators, was modified. The aileron cables from the automatic pilot were re-routed through larger fairleads. On the armament side, provision was made for a larger type of universal bomb carrier to be fitted.

Span: 71 ft 11.5 in.
Length: 46 ft 1.75 in.
Height: 15 ft 9 in.
Weight: (take-off) 12,000 lbs
Speed: Maximum 153 mph at 6,500 ft
Ceiling: 22,500 ft
Range: 545 miles
Armament: Three 0.303 in. Lewis machine guns and bomb load 1,600 lbs

DEFIANT   It was a low wing monoplane of all metal construction, with the exception of the fabric covering of the control surfaces and the wood and plywood turret fairings. The wing was made in five sections: large centre section, two outer planes and detachable wing tips. Frise-type ailerons were fitted. The centre section extended right across and the fuselage rested upon it, so much so that the top of the wing was the pilot's cockpit floor. Two main spars which stretched the full length of the centre section comprised an upper and lower boom, jointed by vertical corrugated webs and formed into a box with built up ribs and spacers. An angled forging carried the upper undercarriage mountings. Machined fittings at the spar ends provided the outer wing attachments.

The Defiant was constructed by attaching preformed stringers and ribs to the light alloy skin before assembly onto the wing spars and fuselage frames. This method required only very little surface preforming, each panel being jig-drilled before any assembly took place, thus ensuring a surface finish of high standard, but using only the minimum number of skilled technicians to achieve it. The top skin was flush-rivetted and had 'Z' section stiffeners, but the underside skin had cut-outs for the undercarriage stowage. Outboard of the undercarriage wells were the main fuel tanks, the bullet resistant covering of these forming the lower wing surface. Most of the undercarriage legs were enclosed by fairings when retracted, two small doors, hinged on the lower fuselage centre line, completed the closure. A conventional nose section was bolted ahead of the main spar whilst aft of the rear spar, another built up assembly made up the trailing edge. Under this section were the large landing flaps.

Outer wing panels were of similar construction, except that there were no fuel tanks. The ailerons were mounted outboard, whilst a small landing flap was fitted underside, from the inboard end of the aileron to the wing joint. Landing lights were fitted in the leading edge of each outer panel. Detachable wing tips completed the wing assembly. The gap between the centre section and outer wing panels was sealed by a specially shaped rubber strip with a fitting at each end. This strip circumposed the wing from the trailing edge and back again and was screw-tensioned to ensure a secure fit.

The front fuselage was a box shape with two 'L' section light alloy extrusions at the top and bottom, the lower ones shaped to fit the wing contour. Heavy bulkheads at front, centre and rear were interposed with stiffening ribs. Sides were covered with light alloy sheet stiffened with 'Z' section stringers and in parts with corrugated sheet. Front and rear of the assembly were covered also with corrugated sheet.

A large oil tank occupied the front fuselage, and aft of this was the windscreen casting. The pilot's seat was bolted to the centre bulkhead and a corrugated decking behind this carried the radio equipment. Aft of this was the mounting for the gun turret. The rear fuselage was constructed in two halves with longerons top and bottom, the whole covered with light alloy skin. The top longerons were joined by corrugated sheet and an aperture under the turret gave access to this assembly. A tubular structure supported the tail unit and the tailwheel strut was attached to the rear bulkhead. The front and rear fuselage units were bolted together. On the top decking, retractable wooden fairings actuated by pneumatic jacks allowed the guns to traverse, but provided streamlining when the guns were positioned aft. Similar fairings also located between the pilot's cockpit canopy and the leading edge of the turret performed the same task. The tailplane was in two sections, bolted in the centre and of conventional construction, as was the vertical fin. Elevators which were interchangeable, side for side, and the rudder, were fabric covered.

The engine compartment was constructed as a whole and consisted of an oval shaped fireproof bulkhead to which was attached the steel engine mountings. The Merlin III, with its constant speed, three-bladed propeller of 11 ft 6 in. diameter, sat in this mounting with the glycol cooling tank fitted over the engine reduction gearing at the front. Underneath this were the oil cooler and air intakes. The engine cooling radiator was mounted beneath the centre section and the connecting pipes provided heating for the cockpit. Wireless aerial masts were located beneath the fuselage, the front one fixed, but the aft one linked to the undercarriage so that it was extended when the undercarriage was retracted. An innovation was a small brush located to bear on the mainwheel tyres to keep them clean when operating from muddy or grass airfields, as mud on the tyres could impair undercarriage retraction, or jam the wheels in the retracted position. Undercarriage and flap operation was hydraulically actuated, whilst the brakes and turret fairing were pneumatic.

BARRACUDA Spanning 49 ft 2 in., and 39 ft 9 in. long, the Barracuda stood 15 ft high and had a wing area of 367 sq. ft. The Mark IIs and Mark IIIs both used the Rolls-Royce Merlin 32 of 1,640 hp which gave them a top speed of 228 mph and 239 mph respectively.

BALLIOL The use of large wing flaps was required which in turn demanded a wing of considerable span on which to hang these flaps. To add to the problem, a large span wing was out of the question as a 90 degrees per second rate of roll was also called for, only obtainable with a wing of fairly short span. Because the trailing edge of the wing needed both the flaps inboard and the ailerons outboard, a compromise was made in the design. A creditable rate of roll was achieved by employing large span ailerons and the incorporation of a low drag wing with maximum ordinate at around 40 per cent of the wing chord. This combination, coupled with the NACA.65 wing section, resulted in a wing with excellent characteristics. The main structure was designed in built up sections and to simplify the replacement of the main components, the tailplane, ailerons, elevators, undercarriage units and wing tanks were interchangeable side for side. There was an absence of removeable wing and tailplane fillets which were always difficult to maintain in their correct profile. The wing centre section in aircraft of this type was generally carried straight through the lower fuselage, but in the P.108 it was divided into two separate units. This greatly assisted replacement as well as transportation, for in the case of the straight-through centre section some dismantling was usually required for movement by road.

Construction in the main was of light alloy stressed skin construction with the exception of the front section of the fuselage which was built up of light alloy and steel tubing. Side and under fairing panels were all detachable in order that full access could be gained to the interior of the fuselage. Hydraulic services were dispensed with as the undercarriage, flaps, dive brakes, windscreen filters and wheel brakes were all pneumatically operated. All the joints on the wings, engine mountings, tailplane and fin were fitted with replaceable bushes which made maintenance a simple matter.

The undercarriage could be replaced as a complete unit. Boulton and Paul had been pioneers of the oleo-pneumatic shock absorber undercarriage leg, and the Design Office once again commenced the design and manufacture of these units. The tailwheel was steerable, fully castoring and self-aligning to help eliminate 'shimmy' when running at speed. It could be locked in the fore and aft position for take-off, but engaged or disengaged at will from the rudder control. Selective controls in the cockpit regulated heating and ventilation, and the sliding cockpit hood and the windscreen wipers were electrically operated. Fuel was carried in three tanks, one in the fuselage and one in each wing, and all were crashproof.

A later modification resulted in ailerons of 'hollow-ground section' – slightly cambered on the underside – which in practice were very effective, but also were very heavy to operate. These were replaced by flat-sided ailerons which gave the right combination of control action and ease of movement.

The leading particulars of the Balliol with the Rolls-Royce Merlin 35 were:

Span:	39 ft 4 in.
Load:	(disposable) 1,696 lbs (gross) 8,175 lbs
Speed:	288 mph maximum cruising at 10,000 ft
	305 mph maximum at 11,500 ft
Climb:	10.64 mins to 15,000 ft
Service ceiling:	32,500 ft
Take-off distance to clear 50 feet:	450 yards
Landing distance:	650 yards
Power Unit:	Rolls-Royce Merlin 35 twelve cylinder Vee liquid cooled rated at 1,240 hp at 9,000 ft and with 1,280 hp available for take-off at 3,000 rpm and 12 lbs per sq. in. boost
Pneumatic system:	1,000 lbs per sq. in.
Electric system:	24 volt DC single phase
Radio:	Very High Frequency (VHF) Transmitter/Receiver Beam approach equipment

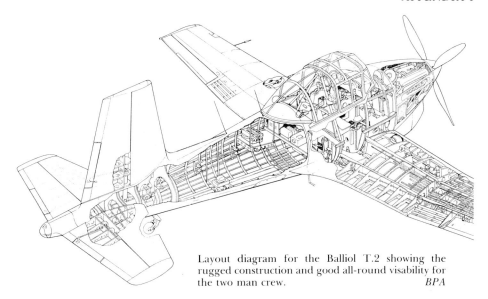

Layout diagram for the Balliol T.2 showing the rugged construction and good all-round visability for the two man crew. *BPA*

P.111 A single seat, single jet, midwing monoplane, it was powered by a Rolls-Royce Nene jet engine of 5,100 lbs static thrust. Of the all-metal, stressed skin fuselage, the front portion was of 'egg-box construction' with an inner skin covering, the rear portion was conventional monocoque. Forward of the wing leading edge was the cockpit, which was fitted with a Martin-Baker ejector seat, the detachable cockpit canopy could be jettisoned in flight. Mounted midway along the fuselage was the power plant and its broad, oval air intake in the nose, divided around the cockpit. The mainplane leading edge terminated in four separate ducts on entering the plenum chamber. The jet pipe was mounted in the rear portion of the fuselage. An all-metal triangular fin and rudder were mounted on the rear fuselage and a manually operated trim tab was provided for the rudder. There was no tailplane or elevators.

The delta type wing, with an extremely low thickness/chord ratio and 45 degrees sweepback, was of stressed skin construction and incorporated three main and one auxilliary spars, meeting on the centre line of the fuselage, thus giving a continuous wing. Provision was made for the three flexible fuel tanks on each side, one aft of the rear spar at the inboard end, and the other two forward of the front spar, also at the inboard end. The wing tips were detachable and three alternative types were provided – there were also alternative fin tips. Two pressure heads were fitted, one on the leading edge of the port wing and the other to the front of the air intake in the nose. Provision was also made for the fitting of a wind vane to the leading edge of the starboard wing, whilst the port wing was fitted for pressure plotting. Sealed, balanced type elevons were fitted to each wing and one incorporated a trim tab which could be electrically or manually operated.

The main undercarriage units retracted inboard into a recess in the underside of the wing and a nose unit folded aft into the fuselage. The units were of Dowty 'liquid-spring' type. Undercarriage recesses in the wing and fuselage were covered by doors and fairings. Normal operation was by hydraulic power and air power was used for emergency operation. A braking parachute was carried in a fairing on the port side of the rear fuselage.

The controls were fitted with a simple spring feel system, but this could be over-ridden to operate the elevons manually – the rudder being manual only. Power operation of the control surfaces used self-contained electro-hydraulic pumps operating hydraulic rams. Later designated 'packaged units', this distinguished them from conventional valve/ram systems which were also being developed at the same time. The 'packaged unit' was a development of the electro-hydraulic pump unit used by Boulton-Paul for their gun turrets and these were later used in the Avro Vulcan and Vickers VC.10 aircraft.

Two units were used each consisting of an electric motor and a pump unit known as a 'three-bank generator'. The motor drove three radial piston pumps, each of which was of the variable delivery type. Two of the pumps were used to operate rams, whilst the third, known as the servo-pump, operated the small servo which controlled the two main pumps. This system required only small operating forces from the pilot. One three-bank unit controlled the elevons, whilst the second was split to operate the rudder and undercarriage, as the P.111 had no engine-driven hydraulic system. A fuel flow proportioner ensured that fuel was used equally from either side tank and so alleviated harsh trim problems. Two electric generators charged two series-connected 12 volt 40 ampere batteries. Radio equipment consisted of an ARI.5454 installation with the TR.1920 unit mounted above the automatic observer behind the pilot's head. A suppressed VHF aerial was built into the top of the fin.

Details of the P.111A are (estimated performance):

Maximum speed at:	Sea level – 650 mph
	20,000 ft – 638 mph
	30,000 ft – 633 mph
	35,000 ft – 622 mph
Climb:	9,400 feet per minute
Weight:	Loaded – 11,400 lbs
	Empty – 9,380 lbs
Span:	33 ft 6 in.
Length:	26 ft 1 in.

P.119 Details are:

Maximum speed:	Derwent 475 mph at 22,500 ft
	Nene 555 mph at 10,000 ft
Climb to 30,000 ft:	Derwent took 8 mins
	Nene took 14 mins
Service ceiling:	Derwent 41,000 ft
	Nene 50,000 ft
Span:	38 ft 9 in.
Length:	42 ft 5 in.
Height:	12 ft 3 in.
Wing area:	298.5 sq. ft
Weight:	9,650 lbs

Aircraft Manufactured at Norwich and Wolverhampton

'N' denotes Norwich. 'W' denotes Wolverhampton

Aircraft Type		Quantity	Serial Nos.	Remarks
N.	FE.2b	50	5201–5250	Contract.
N.	FE.2b	100	6928–7027	Contract.
N.	FE.2b	50	7666–7715	Contract.
N.	FE.2b	50	A.5438–A.5487	Contract.
N.	FE.2d	250	A.6351–A.6600	Contract.
N.	FE.2d	50	B.1851–B.1900	Contract.
N.	Sopwith 1.F.1 Camel	100	B.5151–B.5250	Contract.
N.	Sopwith 1.F.1 Camel	200	B.9131–B.9330	Contract.
N.	Sopwith 1.F.1 Camel	100	C.1601–C.1700	Contract.
N.	Sopwith 1.F.1 Camel	100	C.3281–C.3380	Contract.
N.	B&P P.3 Boblink	3(1)	C.8655–C.8657	Later named Bobolink. Only C.8655 delivered.
N.	B&P P.5 Hawk	3	C.8652–C.8654	Not delivered. Cancelled.
N.	B&P P.6 Un-named	1	X.25	Research biplane.
N.	Sopwith 1.F.1 Camel	300	D.6401–D.6700	Contract.
N.	Sopwith 1.F.1 Camel	150	D.9381–D.9530	Contract.
N.	Sopwith 7.F.1 Snipe	400	E.6137–E.6536	Contract.
N.	Sopwith 1.F.1 Camel	250	F.1301–F.1550	Contract.
N.	Sopwith 1.F.1 Camel	75	F.1883–F.1957	Contract.
N.	B&P P.7 Bourges Mk I/IA/II	3	F.2903–F.2905	Mk I F.2903 became K.129 G-EACE. Mk IA F.2904 became P.8 Atlantic. Mk II F.2905 became G-EAWS.
N.	B&P P.8 Atlantic	1	Ex. F.2904	Atlantic contender. Crashed.
N.	Sopwith 1.F.1 Camel	200	F.6301–F.6500	Contract.
N.	Sopwith 1.F.1 Camel	50	F.8646–F.8695	Contract. Deliveries up to F.8673.
N.	Sopwith 1.F.1 Camel	100	H.2646–H.2745	Contract.
N.	Vickers FB.27A Vimy	150	H.4046–H.4195	Ordered 30/8/18 then cancelled.
N.	Martinsyde F.4 Buzzard	350	H.8763–H.9112	Ordered and later cancelled.
N.	Sopwith 7.F.1 Snipe	100	J.451–J.550	Up to J.465 delivered. Balance cancelled.
N.	Martinsyde F.4 Buzzard	150	J.1992–J.2141	Ordered but later cancelled.
N.	B&P P.9	20	Civil Register	2-seat civil sporting biplane.
N.	B&P P.9-1	1	G-EAPD	Used by B&P as company aircraft.
N.	B&P P.9-2	1	G-EASI	Delivered to South Africa.
N.	B&P P.9-6	1	G-EAWS	B&P aircraft. Crashed 12.6.29.
N.	B&P P.9-7	1	G-EBEQ	To Switzerland. Written off 1/32.
N.	B&P P.10	1	Not registered	All metal P.9. Not completed.
N.	B&P P.12 Bodmin	2	J.6910–J.6911	Postal biplane to A.M. Spec. 11/20.
N.	B&P P.15 Bolton	1	J.6584	Metal development of Bourges.

N.	B&P P.25 Bugle I	2	J.6984–J.6985	Bomber to A.M. Spec. 30/22.
N.	B&P P.25 Bugle I	1	J.7235	Trials aircraft Jupiter IV radial engines.
N.	B&P P.25 Bugle I	2	J.7259–J.7260	Ordered for RAF.
N.	B&P P.25.A Bugle II	2	J.7266–J.7267	Modified aircraft Napier Lion engines.
N.	B&P P.29 Sidestrand	2	J.7938–J.7939	Medium bomber to A.M. Spec. 9/24.
N.	B&P P.29 Sidestrand II	6	J.9176–J.9181	RAF machines. Converted to Mk III.
N.	B&P P.29 Sidestrand III	5	J.9185–J.9189	RAF J.9185–6 to Overstrands.
N.	B&P P.29 Sidestrand III	4	J.9767–J.9770	J.9770 converted to Sidestrand V.
N.	B&P P.29 Sidestrand II	3	K.1992–K.1994	Replacement aircraft for No. 101 Squadron.
N.	B&P P.31 Bittern	2	J.7936–J.7937	Twin engined fighter to Spec. 27/24.
N.	B&P P.32 Un-named	1	J.9950	Heavy bomber to Spec. B.22/27
N.	B&P P.33 Partridge	1	J.8459	Single seat fighter to Spec. F.9/26.
N.	Airship Hull Structure	1	R.101. G-FAAW	Government contract.
N.	B&P P.41 Phoenix	1	G-AAIT	2 seat sporting lightplane.
N.	B&P P.64 Mailplane	1	G-ABYK	To A.M. Spec. Crashed M/H.
N.	B&P P.71A Un-named	2	G-ACOY "Brito-mat" G-ACOX "Boadi-cea"	Twin engined feeder airliners for Imperial Airways.
N.	B&P P.75 Overstrand	19	K.4546–4564	Medium bombers to A.M. Spec. 23/34.
N.	B&P P.75 Overstrand	5	K.8173–K.8177	Last Norwich built aircraft.
W.	Hawker Demon	50	K.5683–K.5741	Contract for 2 seat fighter biplanes.
W.	Hawker Demon	10	K.5898–K.5907	Contract for 2 seat fighter biplanes.
W.	Hawker Demon	37	K.8181–K.8217	Contract for 2 seat fighter biplanes.
W.	B&P P.82 Defiant I	1	K.8310	Turret fighter to Spec. F.9/35. Prototype.
W.	B-P P.82 Defiant I	1	K.8620	Second prototype of above.
W.	Blackburn Roc	136	L.3057–L.3192	Contract. Only 105 delivered.
W.	B-P P.82 Defiant I	87	L.6950–L.7036	First production batch.
W.	B-P P.82 Defiant I	202	N.1535–N.1812	Production aircraft.
W.	B-P P.82. Defiant I	150	T.3911–T.4121	Fighters converted to Target Tugs.
W.	B-P P.82 Defiant I	50	V.1106–V.1141 V.1170–V.1183	Conversion to Target Tug T.T.III.
W.	B-P P.82 Defiant I/II	300	AA.281–AA.713	AA.281–330, 350–362 Mk I; AA.282–286, 288–292, 294–296, 298, 300–301, 306, 308, 310–311, 313–314, 316, 317, 320–324, 326–330, 354, 358, 361 to T.T.III, AA.363–369 Mk I to Mk II; AA.370–384, 398–447, 469–513, 531–550, 566–595, 614–633, 651–679 Mk II; AA.671–673, 687–713 cancelled.
W.	B-P P.82 Defiant II	298	AV.508–AV.944	Cancelled. AV.508–557, 571–605, 633–682, 698–742, 768–787, 805–839, 910–944

184

W.	B-P P.82 Defiant TT.I	150	DR.863–DS.169	DR.863–896, 914–949, 961–991, DS.121–159. Only 140 built, balance cancelled.
W.	B-P P.92/2 Un-named	1	V.3142	Half-scale turret fighter to F.11/37
W.	Fairey Barracuda II	300	DP.855–DR.335	Contract.
W.	Fairey Barracuda III	300	MD.811–ME.293	Contract
W.	Fairey Barracuda III	300	RJ.759–RK.328	Contract. Only 92 built.
W.	Fairey Barracuda III	50	TW.806–TW.857	Contract received but later cancelled.
W.	Fairey Barracuda III	50	VH.901–VH.934 VH.962–VH.977	Order received but later cancelled.
W.	Vickers Wellington Mk X XIII XIV XVIII	164	Various serials in ME, NA, NC, PF and PP blocks.	Bomber aircraft completely rebuilt at T.10 heavy aircrew trainers.
W.	B-P P.108 Balliol T.I	4	VL.892, VL.917 VL.925, VL.935	Prototypes to Spec. T.7/45.
W.	B-P P.108 Balliol T.2	17	VR.590–VR.606	Production aircraft.
W.	B-P P.108 Balliol T.2	4	VW.897–VW.900	Prototypes to Spec. T.14/47.
W.	B-P P.108 Balliol T.2	100	WF.989–WG.230	Built in non-consecutive batches.
W.	B-P P.108 Balliol T.2	(4)	WG.224, WG.226–7, WG.230	Converted for Royal Ceylon AF, CA.310, CA.301, CA.302, CA.311.
W.	B-P P.108 Balliol T.2		Withdrawn RAF aircraft for transfer to Civil Register and The Royal Ceylon Air Force	WN.164 to G-ANYL to CA.306. WN.166 to G-ANYM to CA.307. WN.147 to G-ANZV to CA.308. WN.148 to G-ANZW to CA.309. WG.224 to G-APCN to CA.310. WG.230 to G-APCO to CA.311. WN.132 to G-APCP to CA.312.
W.	B-P P.108 Sea Balliol T.21	20	WL.715–WL.734	Royal Navy aircraft.
W.	B-P P.108 Sea Balliol T.21	138	WN.132–WN.303	Only WN.132–171 (40 built), balance cancelled.
W.	B-P P.108 Balliol T.2	120	WN.506–WN.674	Built under contract by Blackburn Aircraft. Only 40 delivered. Balance cancelled.
W.	B-P P.108 Sea Balliol T.21	10	WP.324–WP.333	Production aircraft for Royal Navy.
W.	B-P P.108 Balliol T.2	2	XF.672–XF.673	Replacement aircraft for Royal Ceylon AF.
W.	B-P P.108 Balliol T.2	3	XF.929–XF.931	Replacement aircraft for Royal Ceylon AF.
W.	B-P P.111/111A	1	VT.935	Research delta winged jet aircraft to E.27/48.
W.	B-P P.119 Un-named	1	Not serialled	Mock-up only of 2 seat jet trainer.
W.	B-P P.120	1	VT.951.	Research delta winged aircraft to E.27/49. Crashed.

Boulton-Paul Aircraft and
Dowty Boulton Paul Directors

1934   When the separate Boulton-Paul Aircraft was formed, Mr North and Mr S. Hiscock were Joint Managing Directors.

1937   Mr H. Strickland, Managing Director. Mr North, Director and Chief Engineer. Mr Hiscock had resigned.

1941   Mr Adshead replaced Mr Strickland and Mr North made Managing Director. Mr Strickland resigned due to ill health.

1942   Mr Kissane and Mr Simpson appointed Directors. Mr Simpson appointed Chairman. Mr North and Mr Adshead appointed Joint Managing Directors.

1944   Mr Beasley appointed Director. He was also Production Manager.

1945   Mr Haynes appointed Secretary.

1948   Mr Adshead left and Mr North appointed Managing Director.

1949   Dr Redshaw and Mr Haynes appointed Directors. Dr Redshaw was Chief Engineer and Mr Haynes continued as Secretary.

1951   Dr Redshaw left to go to Birmingham University, but remained a Consultant. Later a Professor. Mr F.F. Crocombe appointed Director. He was also Chief Engineer.

1958   Mr Haynes appointed Joint Managing Director. Mr Woolsey appointed Secretary. Mr Haynes relinquished this post. Mr Kissane left company. Mr Roxby Cox appointed Director.

1960   Mr Beasley retired.

1962   Sir George Dowty appointed Director after take-over in 1961 by Dowty Group.

1965   Mr Millard, Lord Kings Norton and Mr R.F. Hunt appointed Directors.

1968   Mr North died. Mr A.W. Turner appointed as Managing Director.

1969   Mr Hunt appointed Chairman.

1978   Mr R. Squire appointed Chairman.

        In later years Mr Turner left and Mr Millard was appointed Managing Director. When he retired Mr Goodier was appointed Managing Director, and when he left Mr Frank Nugent became the Managing Director.

Details of Work on Canberra Aircraft under Contract

Date	Original	Serial	Modification State
1953–54	Canberra B.2	WH.671	Trials with methanol and hot air de-icing system.
1954	Canberra B.2	WJ.730	Trial installation of 2 × F.97 cameras and photoflash discharger crate for 400 photoflashes for night photography. Not accepted for service but used on Indian AF B.58.
1955	Canberra B.2	WK.128	Trial installation of 'Window' dispenser crates in bomb bay. One further aircraft (serial unknown) modified. Production installation accepted for T.11 fit.
1954–55	Canberra B.2	WJ.565	Trial fit of Boulton Paul gun pack with 4 × 20 mm Hispano cannon and 16 photoflashes. Standard fit of pack later for B (I) and B (I) 8.
1955	Canberra B.1	VN.828	B.1 aircraft fitted with B.8 front fuselage to frame 12. Nose radome carrying independently developed scanner for GEC AI.18 radar.
1955	Canberra B.2	WJ.646	B.2 aircraft modified as VN.828 for RRE trials.
1955	Canberra PR.3	VX.181	Trial installation of 2 × F.97 camera fit accepted for production PR.3 & 7.
1956	Canberra B.8	WT.327	Nose modified to carry A.I.23 radar and associated equipment for system trials by Ferranti (A.I.23 Lightning fit). See also 1963.
	Canberra B.2	WJ.643	As WT.327.
1956–57	Canberra B.6	XH.567	ATDU Culdrose trials modification to carry 4 × 1,000 lb and 2 × 2,000 lb mines on special beam. No doors to bomb bay in modified state.
1957	Canberra P.R.7	WH.780	Trials installation of 2 × F.89 high altitude night cameras for production P.R.7 fit.
1957–63	Canberra B.2	WK.161	Trials in covering portions of airframe with radar absorbent material and reducing reflective surfaces.
1957	Canberra B.2	WG.789	Similar fit to WJ.646 for GEC trials.
1957	Canberra B.8	XH.232 WT.338	Prototypes for Canberra B.58 (India)
1958	Canberra B.2	WJ.734	Prototype for conversion of T.11 to AI.17 trainer. Radar nose fitted forward of frame 1.
1958	Canberra P.R.7	WT.541	Prototype for P.R.57 (India).
1958–59	Canberra B.8	WT.329	Prototype for B.12 (RNZAF)
1959	Canberra T.4	WE.190	Prototype for T.13 (RNZAF)

1959	Canberra B.2	WV.787	Nose radome fitted for Ferranti radar trials (Buccaneer Radar).
1959–62	Canberra B.6	WT.305 WT.301 WJ.775	Nose fuselages modified with radomes for trial installations by C.S.E. Watton.
1963	Canberra B.8	WT.327	Further modifications for Ferranti trials on T.S.R.2 radar system.

Before 1953 work was carried out on improved cabin conditioning systems for Canberra B.2 aircraft but their serials are not recorded.

APPENDIX FIVE

Modern Aircraft With Dowty Boulton Paul Fittings

Maker and Aircraft	*Country of Origin*
Aeritalia G.222	Italy
Aeritalia/Aermacchi/Embraer AMX	Italy
Aérospatial. Caravelle	France
Aérospatial/B.Ae Concorde	France/United Kingdom
Airbus Industrie A.300	France
Airbus Industrie A.300-600	France
Airbus Industrie A.310	France
Augusta A.129 Manjusta	Italy
British Aerospace ACT Jaguar Fly-by-Wire	UK
British Aerospace Advanced Turboprop.	UK
British Aerospace Bassett	UK
British Aerospace Buccaneer	UK
British Aerospace Canberra	UK
British Aerospace Harrier	UK
British Aerospace Hawk	UK
British Aerospace Hunter Mk 12	UK
British Aerospace/MBB/AIT EAP	UK
British Aerospace Nimrod AEW.3	UK
British Aerospace Nimrod MR	UK
British Aerospace One-Eleven	UK
British Aerospace Rapier	UK
British Aerospace Sea Harrier	UK
British Aerospace Sea Vixen	UK
British Aerospace VC.10	UK

British Aerospace Vulcan Mk 1 & Mk 2	UK
British Aerospace 146	UK
British Aerospace/McDonnell Douglas AV-8A Harrier	UK/USA
British Aerospace/McDonnell Douglas GR.5	UK/USA
British Aerospace/McDonnell Douglas Hawk T.45	UK/USA
Boeing 727	USA
Boeing 737	USA
Boeing 747	USA
Boulton-Paul P.111	UK
Boulton-Paul P.120	UK
Bristol T.188 Research Aircraft	UK
Casa C.101 Aviojet	Spain
Dassault Breguet Falcon 10	France
Dassault Breguet Falcon 50	France
Dassault Breguet Mystère 20	France
De Havilland Canada Dash Eight	Canada
Fokker 100	Holland
Hindustan HF.24 Mk I	India
Lockheed L.1011 Tristar	USA
Mikoyan MIG.21	USSR/Egypt
Mil M.8	USSR/Egypt
Panavia Tornado ADV	UK/France/Germany
Panavia Tornado IDS	UK/France/Germany
Rombac One-Eleven	Rumania/UK
Saab Viggen	Sweden
Short Belfast	UK
Short 360	UK
Soko G.2 Gabeb	Rumania
Soko G.4 Super Gabeb	Rumania
Soko J.22 Orao (Juram)	Yugoslavia/Rumania
Sukhoi Su.7	USSR/Egypt
Sukhoi Su.9	USSR/Egypt
V.F.W. SG-1262	Germany
Vickers Valiant	UK
Vickers Viscount—Tay powered	UK
Westland Sea King	UK
Westland WG.34	UK

General Index

A

Admiralty, 9
Adshead, Mr N.R., 138, 186
Aeronautical Inspection Directorate (AID), 114
Aeroplane Acceptance Park No. 3, 18
Aeroplane & Armament Experimental Establishment (A&AEE), 46, 49, 52, 57, 60, 63, 65, 68, 75, 79, 82, 85–88, 132, 142, 144, 146, 148, 150
Aircraft construction, 10
Aircraft Division, 28
Aircraft Expansion Scheme, 71
Aircraft Technical Services Ltd, 64
Aircraft Parks, 27
Air Gunnery Schools, 107
Air launching experiments, 18
Air Ministry, 27, 28, 31, 37, 38, 41, 44, 48, 49, 56, 57, 59–61, 68, 69, 82, 83, 87, 89, 90, 112, 114, 116, 142, 152
Air Observers, 107
Air raids, 110, 167
Air Sea Rescue, 80, 94, 106, 127
Airships, 52, 55
Allied Expeditionary Force, 9
American Army Air Corps, 29
Armstrong Siddeley Aircraft Engine Co., 141
Annual Air Exercises, 48
Anti-Bomber Formation Fighter, 52, 81, 91
Anti-Surface Vessel Radar (ASV), 121
Argentina, 5
Armament Design Office, 84
Armament Squadron (A&AEE), 68, 69, 73, 86
Armistice, 20, 27
Armstrong Whitworth Aircraft Co., 83, 114
Artillery, 19
Atlantic Ocean, 31, 129
Austin Motor Co., 26
Australia, 5, 34
Automatic pilot, 67
Avro Aircraft Co., 61, 77, 118, 146

B

Babettes, 52, 132
Bakelite Dilecto, 37
Barbers Aeronautical Syndicate, 24
Barker, Major W.G., 20
Barnard, Mr J.H., 1, 2
Barnards Flying Circus, 60
Barnhurst, 71
Barthropp, S/Ldr P.P.C., DFC, 146
Batchelor, Mr J.W., 116, 159

Battle of Britain, 91, 93, 102
Beagle Aircraft Co., 165
Beasley, Mr R., 114, 186
Beaverbrook, Lord, 99
Belgium, 18, 19, 65, 98
Bicester, 48
Biggin Hill, 103
Bilbrook, 73
Bircham Newton, 49
Blackburn Aircraft Co., 61, 65, 78, 120, 127, 147
'Boadicea', 64, 65
Boer War, 5
Bomber Command, 93, 106, 128
Boscombe Down, 87, 142, 144–146, 152, 153, 156
Bosworth, Mr, 19
Boulton, Mr W.S., 2–4
Bristol, 60
Bristol Aeroplane Co., 81, 83
British Aerospace, 163
'Britomart', 65
Brooklands, 25
Browning machine gun, 81, 83, 123, 125, 128, 129, 131, 147
Bushbury, 117

C

Camm, Sir Sidney, 168
Camouflage, 9, 78, 79, 96, 97, 106, 113
Campbell, Col., 11
Campbell, Sir Malcolm, 55
Canada, 18
Cancellations, 7, 27, 33, 90
Cannons, 90, 93, 123, 133, 151
Cardington, 52, 53, 54
Carfoss Ranges, 48
Carr, Major R.H., 26
Centimetre Wavelength Radar, 104
Central Flying School, 87, 147
Central Gunnery School, 147
Certificate of Airworthiness (C of A), 58, 65
Chambers, Mr John, 85, 109, 112, 136, 159, 171
Chapel Field Works, 11, 12
Charlton, Mr Alfred, 54–55
Chenery, Mr David, vii
Chief Designer, 24, 26, 46, 72, 118
Clarke, Mr B.F., 136, 159
Clarke, Mr H.V., 72, 116
Clarke, S/Ldr D.H., 80, 95
Clouston, F/O A.E., 77

Coastal Command, 127, 129
Coastal patrols, 97, 102
Cobham, Sir Alan, 60, 76
Codsall, 139
College of Aeronautics, 154, 168
Colman Limited, 20
Committee of Management, 23
Construction Engineering, 6
Contracts, 12, 13, 15, 18, 20, 21–23, 26, 38, 44,
    52, 56, 61, 65, 69, 74, 78, 81, 84, 89, 94,
    114, 116, 119, 146, 161
Controller of Supplies, 21
Cooke, F/Lt Nicholas Gresham, DFC, 109
Co-operative Wholesale Society, 8
Cosford, 93, 115, 134, 148
Court of Inquiry, 54
Coven, 110, 143
Courtnet, Cap. Frank, 23, 28–30, 32, 35, 40
Coventry, 71, 155
Cowlings, engine, 50, 66
Crashes, 32, 34, 38, 41, 49, 52, 54, 61, 62, 65,
    81, 84, 88, 100, 104, 106, 108, 117, 141,
    143, 148, 153, 156, 165
Crilly Airways, 60
Crocombe, Mr F.F., 136, 137, 152, 186
Croydon, 65

D

Deanesley, Wing Cmdr C., DFC, 104
Debden, 100, 103
de Boysson, Antoine, 84, 122, 123, 126, 130
Deck landing, 150
Decoy factory, 110
Deed of Partnership, 3, 4
Design Office, 31, 36–38, 45, 54, 57, 66, 70, 78,
    93, 112, 134, 139
Disasters, 4, 20, 54, 55, 74, 143, 156
Dive bombing, 96, 100, 119
Dobson, Sir Roy, 146
Dollydo, 7
Dope Shop, 12, 75
Dowding, Lord, 102
Dowty, Sir George, 169, 186
Dowty Aerospace, 154, 162, 163, 166, 169, 170
Draw benches, 37
Drogues, 94
Duchess of Bedford, 60
Dunkirk, 98–100, 103, 105, 109
Dunstall Park, 76
Dunworth, Mr G., 160, 161, 164
Duxford, 97, 98, 99, 139

E

Eastern Group Command, 15
Ejection, 90, 95, 156
Electric Lighting, 7, 9

Electronics Department, 138, 162
Emerson Armament Company USA, 130
Empire Test Pilot's School (ETPS), 144, 146
Employment, 71, 72, 112, 136
Engineering Department, 7, 11
English Channel, 64, 65, 104
English Electric Co., 161, 163
Evaluation Trials, 46, 48, 50, 53, 68, 79, 147
Experimental Shop, 83, 123, 145, 152

F

Fabric Shop, 12, 36, 45, 75, 137
Factory erection, 71
Factory extension, 73
Factory Inspection Department, 114
Fairey Aircraft Co., 119
Farnborough, 9, 10, 12, 14, 70, 89, 145, 148–
    150, 152–154
Farran, Mr Rex, 139
Farran, Capt. Roy, 139
Feather, F/Lt Cecil, 73, 75, 85, 90, 138
Felixstowe, 21, 22, 44, 46, 80
ffiske, Mr G., 6, 8, 23, 55
ffiske, Mr Guy, 61
ffiske, Mr H., 23, 55
ffiske, Mr W., 11, 12, 14, 20, 21, 22, 55
Fighter Command, 94, 100, 106
Filton, 83
Fire watching, 112
First flights, 13, 14, 23, 29, 39, 40, 54, 60, 61,
    68, 75, 79, 83, 85, 87, 93, 120, 121, 140,
    141, 153, 154, 155
First World War, 7, 19, 35, 36, 81
Fiske, Mr H., 4
Fitters' Shop, 11
Fleet Air Arm (FAA), 65, 78, 79, 81
Flettner, 46, 177
Flight Refuelling Limited, 70
Flight Shed, 29, 58, 77, 84, 85, 112, 137, 152
Flight testing, 12, 18, 27–29, 31, 32, 34, 41, 46,
    51, 56, 68, 84
Flight No 1692, Drem, 107
Flow System, 112
'Fly by Wire', 160, 162, 163, 170
Flying Schools, 117
Focke-Wulf (VFW), 162
Fokker Aircraft Co., 162
Foundry, 6
Foundry Bridge Mills, 20
Four Mile Square (Mousehold Heath), 12
France, 7, 9, 14, 54, 70, 84, 98, 122, 123, 126,
    130, 135, 166
Frazer-Nash turret, 75, 76, 81, 131, 135, 137
Freeman, Mr J., 11
Freya CTR Early Warning Radar, 108
Frise, Mr Leslie, 46

Fuji Yama, 7
Fuses, 20

G

Garretts of Leiston, 19
Gatwick, 103
Goodier, Mr, 186
Gorell, Right Hon. Lord, CBE, MC, MA, 64, 115
Gosport, 80
Gould, Mr H.P., 20
Grahame White, Mr Claude, 24, 25, 26, 76
Gray, Mr C.G., 24
Great Yarmouth, 6
Greece, 18
Greenstead, Mr Brian, 95
Ground attack, 93
Groups, RAF
 No 11, 99, 101
 No 12, 99, 103
 No 13, 101, 103
 No 51, 117
Guinness, Mr Kenelm Lee (KLG), 55
Gunn, Mr A.E. 'Ben', 144, 145, 151, 153, 155, 156, 161, 165
Gunners, 14, 15, 28, 30, 42, 44, 45, 59, 66–68, 75, 81, 83, 85, 87, 88, 92, 98, 100, 102, 104, 122, 131
Gurney, Sir E., 19
Gust alleviation, 139, 158, 160

H

Handley-Page Aircraft Co., 44, 46, 140
Hardy, S/Ldr Stephen, 96
Harland & Wolff Ltd, 24
Hart, Mr Jack, 75
Hattrell, Mr Stanley, 71
Hawker Aircraft Co., 57, 74, 83, 168
Hawkinge, 101
Haynes, Mr G.C., 138, 168, 186
Helensburgh, 80
Hendon, 24–26, 44, 46, 68, 109, 134, 137
Heston Aircraft Co., 89
Hiscocks, Mr S.W., 64, 72, 186
Hispano-Suiza Cannon, 123, 131
HMS *Exeter*, 170
HMS *Fearless*, 170
HMS *Illustrious*, 150
HMS *Intrepid*, 170
HMS *Triumph*, 150
Hoare, Sir Samuel John Gurney, 45
Holland, 75, 129
Hope, Lt/Cmdr Linton, 21
Hornchurch, 102
Horsham St Faith's, 97
Hounslow, 30

Howden Airship Station, 52
Howes and Son Ltd, 9, 11, 12, 14, 22, 55
HRH Duke of Kent, 117
HRH King George VI, 114, 115
HRH Queen Elizabeth, 115
HRH Queen Elizabeth II, 148, 169
HRH The Duke of Edinburgh, 148
Hughes, Mr H.A., 73, 126, 130
Hull Shop, 21
Humber, River, 52
Humphrey, Mr J.H., 7
Hunt, Mr R.F., 186
Hunter, S/Ldr Phillip, DSO, 96, 98–100, 102
Hydrogen, 52

I

Immelmann, Max, 14
Imperial Airways, 65, 70, 126
Imperial War Museum, 139
India, 54, 55
Institute of Aviation Medicine, 148
Intruders, 103
Ipswich, 18, 46, 53
Ireland, 19
Ironwork, 1, 5, 6
Italian Air Force, 161

J

Jackson, Mr F.A., 138, 160
James, Mr Ian, 56, 63, 79, 136, 158
Japan, 7
Jewitt, Mr F.A., 166
Jewson, Mr Richard, JP, 61
Johnson, Miss Amy, 60, 77
Johnston, Mr V.J., 53, 136, 159
Jones, Mr L.R., 112
Jones, Mr R.O., 121

K

Kenmer, Mr Charles, 118, 170
King Street, 6
King's Cup Air Race, 34
King's Norton, Lord, 167, 186
Kirton in Lindsey, 100
Kissane, Mr, 186

L

Lanning, F/Lt F.C.A., DFC, 30, 105
Law, Mr J., 13
Lee, Professor Peter, 138
Leicester, 60
Leigh Mallory, Air Vice Marshal, 97
Leiston, 19
Leslie, Mr Stuart, 15, 18
Lewis, Miss, 11

Lewis, machine gun, 14, 28, 42, 45, 52, 59, 67, 75, 81, 112, 122
Leyland, 9
Lichtenstein Air Interception Radar FuG 202/213, 107
Liebher Aerotechnik, 162
Limited Company, 5
Lindsey Neale, Robert 'Robin', 112, 113, 138, 139, 141, 143
Liverpool, 60
Lloyd George, Mr David, 9
'Lobster Back' Turret, 75, 76, 81
Lockheed Aircraft & Hydraulics, 86, 96, 116, 128, 129
London, 9, 12, 24, 30, 61, 103, 112
Lowestoft, 167
Lucas, Joseph, Limited, 130, 131
Luftwaffe, 91, 98, 100, 102, 103, 107, 108, 110, 116

M
MacDonald, Mr Ramsey, 52
Machine gun, 14, 16
MacInnis, General, 21
Mailplanes, 61, 65
Mancus, Mr R.R. 'Dickie', MBE, 145, 151, 160, 161, 163, 164
Mann Egerton Limited, 19
Manning, Mr Colin, 22, 128
Manston, 98, 99, 102, 103
Marine Aircraft Experimental Establishment, 44, 80
Martin Baker, 95, 180
Martlesham Heath, 18, 31, 41, 43, 44, 46, 49, 50, 52, 56, 57, 58, 60, 61, 68, 69, 73, 75, 79, 82, 85, 87, 96, 97, 101, 167
Mason, Mr, 19
McRae, S/Ldr D.M.T., DFC, 146
Metal Workshops, 11
Middleton, Mrs Rosemary, vi
Midland Aero Club, 76
Midland Woodworking Co., 167
Millard, Mr D.J., 159, 163, 186
Ministry of Aircraft Production, 99, 146
Ministry of Aviation, 154
Ministry of Defence, 116, 134
Ministry of Munitions, 8–11, 19
Ministry of War Production, 130
Ministry of Supply, 139, 152
'Moonshine', 100
Moore, Mr W., 1, 2
Motor boats, 1, 6, 7, 9
Motor Department, 9
Mousehold Heath, 12, 13, 15, 18–20, 22, 27, 29, 32, 33, 39, 41, 45, 46, 47, 49, 50, 52, 58, 60, 61, 68, 73, 166

Mousehold Light Railway, 20

N
National Factory, 19
National Motor Museum, 55
Noble, Major, 73
Norfolk & Norwich Aero Club, 60, 61, 166
North, Mr John Dudley, CBE, 24–26, 30, 36, 37, 50, 51, 53, 55, 62, 64, 71, 72, 81, 90, 114, 114, 117, 130, 134, 136, 137, 138, 152, 167, 169, 170, 186
Northampton, 60
Northolt, 87, 108
North Weald, 103
Norwich, 1–3, 5, 6, 8, 9, 11–14, 16, 18, 21, 24, 26, 27–30, 31, 32, 34, 35, 37, 40, 41, 45, 50, 51, 55–57, 61, 64–66, 69–71, 73, 82, 83, 122, 123, 126, 134, 159, 166, 167
Norwich Airport, 60
Norwich City Council, 60
Norwich Components Limited, 19
Norwich Union, 4, 61
Nottingham, 60
Nugent, Mr Frank, 186

O
Observer Corps, 102
Odbert, F/Lt A.V.M., 68
Odgers, Doctor, 73
Odiham, 148
Oleo Pneumatic, 49, 66
Olympia, 48, 58
Operational Research Club, 168
Operational Research Society, 168
Orfordness, 86, 96, 172
Oxygen, 12, 125

P
Parachute, 26, 58, 77, 92, 99, 105, 126, 132
Parnell Aircraft Co., 38, 134
Paul, Capt., 54, 55, 61
Paul, Mr Dawson Jnr, 8, 22, 55
Paul, Mr J.J. Dawson, 2–6, 13, 14
Pendeford, 71, 75–77, 85, 97, 110, 113, 115, 116, 118, 119, 120, 121, 128, 133, 138, 139, 141, 143, 155, 161, 166, 169
Penkridge, 107
Percival, Mr Edgar, 34
Performance Testing Squadron (A&AEE), 63, 69, 86
Philips Radio Works, 129
Photographic, 26, 60
Pickthorn, Mr W.J., 73, 116
Piecework bonus, 73
Pixton, Capt. H., 13, 14
Porte, Cmdr. John, 21

Power controls, 152, 155
Power, Mr John, 161, 168
Price-Owen, S/Ldr Waldo, 142
Postal Aircraft, 38, 40, 41, 63
Private Venture (PV), 56
Production, 12, 20, 21, 34, 37, 50, 69, 74, 78, 81, 87, 91, 94, 112, 120, 131–133
Propellers, 21, 23, 25, 31, 33, 39–41, 43, 58, 61, 65, 68, 83, 86, 141
Pulham Airship Station, 18, 52
Pumps, 7, 9, 86, 134, 181
Purefoy, Mr J.B., 73

Q

Quick Action/High Cover, 106

R

Radar, A.I. Mk IV, 91, 92, 103, 104
Radio counter-measures, 93, 107
Radio-location, 82, 103
Ransomes, Sims & Jefferies Ltd, 19
Rea, S/Ldr C.A., 44, 46, 58, 73
Reid & Sigrist Limited, 95
Records, 25, 26, 34, 48, 55, 60, 77
Redshaw, Prof, S.C., 116, 138, 156, 186
Research & Experimental Section, 26
Resettlement, 72, 75
Returned colours, 11, 16
Richmond, Col., 54
Richmond, F/Lt G.L.G., 63
Richthofen, Baron Manfred von, 16
Riverside Works, 8, 11, 16, 20, 21, 23, 38, 39, 55, 166, 167
Roberts, Mr George, MP, 9
Rochford, 102
Rocket projectile, 134, 147
Rose Lane, 3–6, 8, 11, 12, 21, 38
Rotol, 93, 95, 162
Royal Aeronautical Society (RAe.S), 167
Royal Aircraft Establishment (RAE), 70, 84, 89, 145, 150, 152, 184
Royal Aircraft Factory (RAF), 9, 12, 26
Royal Air Force (RAF), 20, 27, 28, 38, 41, 44, 46, 51, 55, 56, 66, 68–70, 73–75, 81, 90, 95, 107, 109, 113, 117, 134, 145, 147, 148
Royal Airship Works (RAW), 52, 53
Royal Ceylonese Air Force, 145
Royal Flying Corps (RFC), 10, 14, 18
Royal Mail, 61
Royal Naval Air Service (RNAS), 18, 21
Royal Navy (RN), 1, 106, 119, 145, 150, 151, 180
Roxbee-Cox, Mr, 186

S

Sadd, Messrs John & Sons, 167

Salhouse, 13, 19
Sanders, Wing/Cmdr A.T.D., DFC, 104
Sanders, S/Ldr P.J., DFC, 104
Sandon, Rt Hon. Viscount, DL, JP, 64, 115
SAT, 122
Saunders-Roe Aircraft Co. (Saro), 74
Scarff gun mounting ring, 28, 42, 45, 59
Schefer, Karl, 14
Schneider Trophy, 13
School of Fighter Control, 149
Second World War, 45, 46, 73, 101, 131, 127, 130, 131, 161, 167
Secretary of State for Air, 45
Secrets List, 69
Seighford, 161, 164
'Serrate', 107
Service Trials, 44, 46, 49, 57
Shares, 7
Shute, Mr Neville Norway, 53
Simpson, Mr, 186
Sitka spruce, 35
Skelton, Mr George, 75
Smith's shop, 5
Société d'Application des Machines Motrices (SAMM), 122, 123
Society of British Aircraft Constructors (SBAC), 140, 147, 153, 167
South Africa, 6, 75
Spot welding, 57
Squadrons & units, RAF & RFC; FAA
  No 1 Air Navigation School, 137
  No 2 Squadron, 96
  No 2 Anti-Aircraft Co-op Unit, 78
  No 2 Flying Training School, 147
  No 5 Operational Training Unit, 88
  No 7 Flying Training School, 147, 148
  No 9 Maintenance Unit, 147
  No 12 Squadron, RFC, 10, 14
  No 15 Squadron, 73
  No 22 Maintenance Unit, 149
  No 25 Squadron, RFC, 14
  No 25 Squadron, 137, 157
  No 25 Reserve Flying School, 137
  No 29 Squadron, 68
  No 30 Squadron, 75
  No 32 Squadron, 75
  No 46 Squadron, 77
  No 58 Squadron, 44
  No 66 Squadron, 97
  No 85 Squadron, 104
  No 96 Squadron, 104
  No 101 Squadron, 48, 49, 69
  No 111 Squadron, 87
  No 141 Squadron, 30, 101–103, 105, 132
  No 151 Squadron, 104
  No 201 Advanced Flying School, 137

No 209 Squadron, RFC, 17
No 255 Squadron, 104
No 256 Squadron, 104
No 164 Squadron, 75, 91, 95, 96, 98, 99, 101–103, 109
No 275 (ASR) Squadron, 106
No 276 (ASR) Squadron, 106
No 277 (ASR) Squadron, 106
No 278 (ASR) Squadron, 106
No 281 (ASR) Squadron, 106
No 307 (Polish) Squadron, 104
No 501 Squadron, 144
No 515 Squadron, 108
No 702 (FAA) Squadron, 150
No 750 (FAA) Squadron, 150
No 781 (FAA) Squadron, 150
No 801 (FAA) Squadron, 79
No 806 (FAA) Squadron, 79
No 1566 Met. Flight, 109
Squire, Mr R., 186
Steel buildings, 1, 6, 7, 61, 77, 167
Stephens & Carter Limited, 167
Stewart, Mr Jack, OBE, 61
Strickland, Mr Herbert, 99, 115, 116, 186
Strike, 73
Sub-contracting, 7, 65, 73, 165
Summerfield Airfield runway, 167
Sunbeam racing car, 55
Sweden, 751

T

Target Tug, 94, 107, 109, 147
Technical Department, 27
Technical Training Schools, 108
Tenders, 9
Tensile steel, 37–39, 45, 54, 61, 65, 73
Test pilots, 23, 28, 29, 44, 63, 68, 73, 73, 82, 85, 95, 113, 138, 139, 141, 143, 144
Test Reports, 43
Thetford, 12
Thomas, Capt. A.C., 65
Thomas, F/Lt, Acting S/Ldr, S.R., 103, 105
Thorpe, 6
Tisshaw, Mr Kingsley Peter Henry, 138, 143, 144
Top Escort Fighter, 94
Townend ring cowlings, 69, 74
Training, 73, 77, 95, 106, 147
Transport, 73, 74, 83, 113, 117
Trials, 12, 49, 50, 52, 57, 58, 61, 65, 69, 70, 75, 79, 81, 84, 85, 86, 90, 91, 95, 123
Tropical Experimental Unit, 145, 146
Turner, Mr A.W., 166, 186
Turrets, 66–68, 78, 79, 82, 83, 85, 89, 90, 93, 94, 115, 116, 123, 124, 127, 131, 133, 135

U

United States Air Corps (USAC), 15, 18
United States Army Air Force (USAAF), 107, 130
United States of America, 15, 73, 129
University Air Squadrons, 148
University of Birmingham, 168

V

VHF radio, 104, 180
Vickers Aircraft Co., 44, 52
Vickers machine guns, 52, 75, 120
Victoria Cross, 20, 129
Vicuna, 7
Viscount Templewood, 45

W

Wales, HRH Prince of, 60
Wallis, Dr Barnes, 52
War Office, 10, 11, 13, 13, 15
War work, 112, 113
Wensum, River, 6
Westland Aircraft Co., 38, 74, 121
West Malling, 101, 103
Wharf, 6, 9
Whitehall, 47
Whitehouse, Mr R., 138
Wilson Lovett & Sons, 71
Wilson, Mr Peter, 18
Winch, 94
'Window', 161
Wind tunnel, 21, 55, 62, 73, 89
Winter Experimental Establishment, 148
Wire netting, 1, 6, 9, 11, 61
Wittering, 95, 97
Wolseley Motor Co., 56
Wolverhampton, 1, 11, 24, 64, 71, 72, 73, 76, 78, 83, 85, 86, 89, 93, 104, 110, 112, 117, 118, 120, 122, 126, 130, 133, 134, 137, 139, 143, 150, 152, 154, 161, 162, 163, 166, 171
Wolverhampton Aero Club, 165
Wolverhampton Airport, 76, 77, 116, 117, 137, 165
Wolverhampton Express & Star, 77, 143
Women, 8, 11, 20, 75
Women's Land Army, 114
Wooden flying boat hulls, 21
Woodman, S/Ldr R.G., DSO, AFC, 146
Woodwork, 1, 5, 6, 7, 9, 11, 21, 61, 167
Woolsey, Mr, 186
World Wars, *see* First World War, Second World War
Wortley, Mr Percy S., 71

Index of Aircraft and Engines

A

ABC Dragonfly engine, 28, 29, 31, 173
ABC Scorpion engine, 58
Aeritalia G.222, 162, 188
Aeritalia/Aermacchi/Embraer AMX, 188
Aérospatial Caravelle, 188
Aérospatial/B.Ae. Concorde, 162, 166, 188
Airbus Industrie
    A.300, 188
    A.300–600, 188
    A.310, 188
Airspeed
    Horsa, 167
    Oxford, 139, 167
Armstrong-Siddeley engines
    Jaguar, 56, 65
    Lynx, 51
    Mamba, 139, 141, 142
    Puma, 31
    Terrier, 83
Armstrong-Whitworth
    Albemarle, 129, 131
    Argosy, 65
    Starling, 57
    Whitley, 77, 78, 134
Augusta A.129, Manjusta, 170, 188
Auster Alpha J/1, 164
Austro-Daimler engine 120 hp, 25
Avro
    Anson, 106, 137
    Athena
        T.1, 142, 146
        T.2, 142
    Lancaster, 129, 131, 134, 158, 160
    Lincoln, 129–132, 134
    Shackleton, 129
    Type 504, 61
    Type 627, 61

B

Beardmore
    engine, 13, 15
    Inflexible, 60
Bentley Motors
    BR.1, 20, 27
    BR.2, 28
Blackburn
    B.2, 65
    Beverley, 136
    Roc, 78–81, 124, 147, 184
    Shark, 65, 80, 147
    Skua, 77–79

Boeing
    727, 189
    737, 189
    747, 189
    P.6, 33, 34, 173, 183
    P.7, 183
    P.8, 183
    P.9, 34, 35, 37, 61, 173
    P.9-1, 183
    P.9-2, 183
    P.9-6, 183
    P.9-7, 183
    P.10, 36, 37, 38, 183
    P.12, 39, 40, 174, 173
    P.15, 41, 43, 183, 184
    P.25, 41, 42, 175, 184
    P.25.A, 44, 175, 184
    P.29.A, 45, 47, 184
    P.31, 51
    P.32, 59, 60, 177, 184
    P.33, 56, 57, 184
    P.41, 57, 58, 184
    P.64, 61, 62, 63, 65
    P.71.A, 64, 65, 175, 184
    P.75, 66, 67, 79, 82, 112, 177, 184
    Atlantic, 31–33, 173
    Bittern, 51, 52, 184
    Bobolink, 26, 27, 28, 172, 183
    Bodmin, 38, 40, 41
    Bolton, 41–43, 174
    Bourges
        Mk 1A, 27–31, 66, 69, 173
        Mk 1B, 31
        Mk IIA, 28–30
        Mk IIIA, 31, 41
    Bugle, 41, 43, 44
        Mk I (Modified), 44
        MK II, 44, 61
    Hawk, 26, 183
    Overstrand, 1, 67, 68–70, 73, 77, 81, 84, 123
    Partridge, 35, 56, 57, 176, 184
    Phoenix
        I, 57, 58, 177, 184
        II, 58
    Sidestrand
        Mk I, 45–47, 50, 66, 175, 184
        Mk II, 47–49, 70, 184
        Mk III, 48–50, 60, 66–69, 73, 175, 184
        Mk III.A, 176–178
        Mk V, 66–68
    Superstrand, 70

Boulton-Paul Aircraft Ltd
P.81, 82
P.82, 78, 81–83, 93, 123
P.92/2, 89, 90, 184
P.94, 93
P.105, 136
P.108, 139–142
P.111, 152–154, 185, 188
P.111.A, 154, 155, 180, 182, 185
P.119, 157, 158, 182, 188
P.120, 155, 185, 188
Balliol
T.1, 140–146, 184
T.2, 141, 145, 148, 151, 152, 184
Defiant 1, 1–30, 75, 82, 85, 87, 89–91, 93–95,
96, 97, 99, 100, 102, 106, 109, 119, 131,
132, 140, 151, 171
Mk II, 93, 94, 104, 106, 184
Mk III, 94
NF.
Mk I, 91, 94, 184
Mk I.A, 91, 103
Mk II, 91, 94
Special features, 95
TT
Mk I, 94, 184
Mk III, 95, 107
Sea Balliol T.21, 145, 150–152, 184
Bristol
Beaufighter, 93, 103, 104, 106, 108, 119
Blenheim, 69, 70, 74, 77, 78, 91
Centaurus engine, 95, 136
Freighter, 165
Hercules engine, 83
Jupiter engine
II, 43
IV, 44
VI, 48
VII, 175, 176
VII.F, 48
VIII, 175
VIII.F, 48, 49
XFD, 50, 176
XF, 60
XFBM, 60
Lucifer, 37
Mercury
V, 60
30, 140, 142, 176
Pegasus
IM2, 61
IM3, 50, 66
IIM3, 68
IV, 70
Perseus XII, 79, 83

Type
105 Bulldog, 57, 68, 75
120, 81
147, 83
188, 189
British Aerospace/English Electric
ACT Jaguar Fly-by-Wire, 163, 188
/Avro, A.T.P, 188
/Beagle Bassett, 188
/Blackburn Buccaneer, 188
/De Havilland
Nimrod AEW.3, 188
Nimrod MR, 188
/English Electric
B.2, 161, 187
B.6/7, 161, 187
B.15, 161, 187
Canberra, 134, 161, 187, 188
PR.3, 161, 187
PR.7, 161, 187
T4/11, 161, 187
/Hawker
Harrier, 188
Hunter Mk 12, 188
/MBB/AIT/EAP, 188
Vickers One Eleven, 188
Rapier, 188
Sea Harrier, 188
Sea Vixen, 188
/Vickers VC.10, 188
/Vulcan Mk I & 2, 134, 182, 189
146, 189
McDonnell Douglas
AV-8A, 189
GR.5, 189
Hawk, 189

C
Casa C.101 Aviojet, 189
Clerget Motor 110 hp Long Stroke, 18
Consolidated
Catalina, 74
Liberator B.24, 129, 130
Curtiss H.12 Large America, 21

D
Dassault Breguet
Falcon 10, 189
Falcon 50, 189
Mystère 20, 189
De Havilland
6, 18
10, Amiens, 48
72, Canberra, 59, 60
Dove, 166

Dragon, 60
Giant Moth, 60
Gipsy Major engine, 89, 90
Moth, 35, 60, 61, 65, 77, 117
Mosquito, NF.93, 104, 134
Tiger Moth, 137
Vampire, 159
Canada Dash Eight, 189
Dornier 17, 102
Douglas
  Boston, 118
  Dakota, 113
  Havoc, 118

E
English Electric
  Lightning, 161
  TSR.2, 163

F
Fairey
  Albacore, 119
  Barracuda, 119, 120, 177
    Mk II, 119, 120, 184
    Mk III, 120, 121, 184
  Battle, 77, 78, 96
  Long range monoplane, 60
  Swordfish, 119
Farman Biplane, 76
  No 2, 12
F.E.2.b, 9, 12, 15, 26, 183
F.E.2.d, 15, 19, 183
F.E.2.h, 15
Felixstowe
  F.3, 21
  F.5, 21
Fighting Scout Mk 1, 12
Fokker
  100, 189
  D.VII, 20
  F.VII, 60
  F.27, 162
  Monoplane, 14

G
General Aircraft Hamilcar, 136
Gloster
  Gauntlett, 57, 77
  Meteor, 161
  SS.18, 57
Gnome Monosoupape engine 150 hp, 18, 29
Grahame White
  Charabanc, 25, 26
  Scout Pusher Type II, 26

H
Handley-Page
  Halifax, 128, 131, 134
  Hampden, 78
  Victor, 134
Hawker
  Demon, 66, 74, 75, 76, 78, 81, 82, 184
  Hart, 74, 75
  Hawfinch, 57
  Henley, 83
  Hotspur, 83, 84
  Hurricane, 78, 81, 83, 84, 87, 93, 98, 99, 104
  Tempest 5, 144
Heinkel
  He.59, 80
  He.111, 102–106, 132
Hindustan HF.24, Mk I, 189

J
Junkers
  Ju.52, 98
  Ju.87.B, 98–100
  Ju.88, 98–102, 104, 116

K
Kirby Kite, 77

L
Le Rhône engine
  80 hp, 16
  110 hp, 18
Lockheed
  Hudson, 114–116, 128, 129, 131
  Tristar, 189
  Ventura, 129

M
Martin Baltimore, 129
Martinsyde F.4 Buzzard, 27, 183
Messerschmitt
  Bf.109E, 98, 99, 101, 102
  Bf.109E, 102
  110, 99
  210, 51
Mikoyan MIG 21, 189
Mil M.8, 189
Miles
  Gemini, 165
  Magister, 96, 165

N
Napier engine
  Lion, 31, 32, 40, 44
  Sabre, 89
North American Aviation Harvard, 147

P

Panavia Tornado
  ADV, 162, 189
  IDS, 189
Percival Prentice, 142

R

R.38 airship, 52, 53
R.100 airship, 53, 55
R.101 airship, 53, 54, 55, 189
Rolls-Royce engines & turbo jets
  Dart, 140, 141
  Derwent, 157
  Exe, 119
  Kestrel, 75
  Merlin
    F, 82
    I, 86, 87
    II, 87
    III, 87, 93, 177
    XX, 93
    24, 93
    32, 179
    35, 142, 143, 145, 180
  Nene, 155, 180
  Vulture, 89, 90
Rombac One-Eleven, 189
Royal Aircraft Factory engine 1A, 33

S

Saab Viggen, 189
Salmson engine 40 hp, 58
Saunders-Roe London, 65, 73, 74
Short
  360, 189
  Belfast, 189

'C' Class, 126
'G' Class, 126
Empire Class, 127
Sunderland, 126
Soko
  G.2 Gabeb, 189
  G.4 Super Gabeb, 189
  J.22 Orao (Juram), 189
Sopwith
  Camel 1F1, 16–20, 29, 183
  Snipe 7F1, 18–20, 27, 183
Sukhoi
  Su.7, 189
  Su.9, 189
Supermarine Spitfire, 78, 97, 104, 144

V

VFW SG-1262, 189
Vickers
  B.19/27, 70
  Valiant, 134, 189
  Vanguard, 159
  Vannock II, 70
  Vimy, 27, 33, 183
  Virginia, 44
  Viscount–Tay powered, 160, 189
  Walrus, 94, 106
  Wellesley, 78
  Wellington, 131, 134, 137
    T.10, 137, 138, 184

W

Westland Lysander, 78, 94, 106, 107
  Sea King, 189
  WG.34, 189

WOLVERHAMPTON FACTORY 1940

A.   Claregate and Wolverhampton Road
B.   Shropshire Union Canal
C.   To Bilbrook and Codsall
D.   To Stafford Road
E.   Main Entrance
F.   New Entrance for Staff Car Park
G.   Gate House
H.   Underground Air Raid Shelters
I.   Extra Canteen
J.   Bridge (widened 1937/8)
K.   Road (widened 1938)
L.   Salvage Area
M.   Garage
N.   Canteen
O.   Drawbench
P.   Wind Tunnel
Q.   Coal Store
R.   Boiler House
S.   Foundry
T.   Personnel
U.   Electronics
V.   Gun Store
W.   Dope and Cover Shop
X.   Wood Shop
Y.   New Flight Shed
Z.   Entrance
AA.   New Works Entrance
AB.   Offices
AC.   Factory Layout Changed Many Times
AD.   First Factory Extension 1938
AE.   Covered Roadway
AF.   Area originally for Gun Turret Production
AG.   Aircraft Assembly Bay
AH.   Rigging Shed
AI.   Paint Shop
AJ.   Bellman Hangars
AK.   Boiler House and Stores
AL.   Pilot's Office
AM.   Apron.
AN.   Runway to Airfield
AO.   Decontamination Room
AP.   Sprinkler Water House
AQ.   Sewerage Beds, later used as Water Supply for Hydraulic Test Shop
AR.   High Ground used for Air Raid Shelters
AS.   Stream
AT.   Gun Firing Butts
AU.   Underground Shelters
AV.   1984 Boundary Fence
AW.   These Areas Demolished 1983/4